T0306034

"Shahana's book is a revelation in child-centric education, blending personal insights with actionable strategies, offering a compassionate roadmap for educators and mental health professionals alike. As someone who has long-admired her work, I am thrilled to see Shahana's invaluable insights reaching the widest possible audience."

—**Pooky Knightsmith**, *Child Mental Health Expert*

"This book is a remarkable story of Shahana's personal and professional journey. Documenting all aspects of her work; from the people themselves (considering stress, trauma, mental health and well-being, to name but a few) to the environments in which these people work (the therapeutic classroom, connection and regulation and whole-school/setting approaches). The book is a real treasure trove of useful information, elements that challenge your thinking, actual examples and practical advice. Throughout the book the real-life examples and scenarios to frame the discussions along with opportunities to reflect upon your own practice. This book will be useful for anyone working with young people, families and professionals alike, but also stands up as a great read whatever your profession or role in life. A real triumph in practical, evidence-based story telling that has a direct impact on those involved. Very much recommend reading."

—**Gareth D Morewood**, *Education Advisor, Studio III, previously a Secondary SENCo*

"This is a crucial book for everyone involved in education. Shahana Knight shares her expertise, centring mental health and wellbeing at the heart of the teaching profession and supports the reader, through taking a critical stance, to evaluate their own practice. This is a powerful read which brings new knowledge and understanding to trauma informed education and will certainly impact on the lives of many children in our schools."

—**Roger McDonald**, *Associate Professor, University of Greenwich*

"This book is essential for any school leader or educator looking to create a truly nurturing and supportive learning environment for their pupils. It goes beyond academics, delving deep into the importance of a child's mental health and wellbeing. Shahana paints a compelling picture of a 'therapeutic school' where children's emotional needs are acknowledged and addressed.

This involves understanding how trauma, stress, and attachment styles can impact behaviour and learning. The book highlights the importance of staff development, equipping them with the tools to respond to pupils in a therapeutic and emotionally safe way, fostering a culture of self-reflection and continuous improvement, and ensuring that every child feels supported to thrive. I highly recommend this book to anyone dedicated to creating a school that truly reflects the needs of today's children."

—**John Magee**, *Founder of Kindness Matters and Author of The Happy Tank*

The Therapeutic School Approach

The Therapeutic School Approach offers teachers and school leaders a step-by-step guide to embedding a trauma-informed approach that is tangible, practical, and brings the underpinning science to life in a way that is relatable and relevant. Placing a keen focus on moving towards a more inclusive way of working, it advocates for a culture that puts wellbeing and mental health at the core of teaching and school life.

This whole school approach gives readers the tools needed to support children when they are dysregulated by reframing 'difficult' behaviour and focusing on emotional intelligence and self-regulation strategies to help children flourish in school and beyond. The book evidences the 'why' behind the approach, exploring childhood trauma, attachment theory and stress, and explaining how these factors are impacting children today. It then introduces the 'how', looking in detail at trauma-informed responses, behaviour policies, relationships, and the power of the environment. Chapters leave the reader with a wealth of practical strategies, as well a full understanding of key theory so they can champion trauma-informed approaches in their work.

With real life case studies and scenarios woven throughout, this empowering book challenges perspectives, raises awareness, and inspires the reader to re-evaluate the norm to make a true difference to the children in their care. It will be essential reading for primary school teachers, head teachers, SENCOs, and support staff who want to put children's wellbeing at the core of their practice.

Shahana Knight is a childhood trauma and behaviour specialist, and the Founder and Managing Director of TPC Therapy, a mental health service which supports schools, care agencies, and national charities through whole organisation courses, therapeutic interventions, and bespoke wrap around support. Shahana's expertise is in helping people to embed trauma-informed, attachment-aware approaches in a practical, tangible way that make an evident significant difference to children's lives. She has a background in child therapy, psychology and education and grew up experiencing adversity and trauma herself. This lived multifaceted experience underpins her work. She is not afraid to question the norm and is dedicated to raising children's emotional intelligence, self-belief, and mental health.

The Therapeutic School Approach

How to Embed Trauma-Informed,
Attachment-Aware Practices to
Improve Outcomes for All Children

Shahana Knight

Routledge
Taylor & Francis Group

LONDON AND NEW YORK

Designed cover image: © Sarah Hoyle / © shutterstock / orchidar / pikisuperstar - Freepik.com

First published 2025
by Routledge
4 Park Square, Milton Park, Abingdon, Oxon OX14 4RN

and by Routledge
605 Third Avenue, New York, NY 10158

Routledge is an imprint of the Taylor & Francis Group, an informa business

© 2025 Shahana Knight

British Library Cataloguing-in-Publication Data
A catalogue record for this book is available from the British Library

ISBN: 978-1-032-53160-1 (hbk)
ISBN: 978-1-032-53155-7 (pbk)
ISBN: 978-1-003-41065-2 (ebk)

DOI: 10.4324/9781003410652

Typeset in Optima
by Apex CoVantage, LLC

To my dad

Contents

Acknowledgements and Thanks

They say you become the adult you needed as a child. I certainly did. This book is my legacy, and my life work so far. It is dedicated to my wonderful, beautiful dad who was the most magical human I have ever come across and who taught me so much. Without him showing up as the fun, caring, authentic, broken, darkest and true representation of himself, I would never have become the person I am. And for that I am truly thankful.

To my beautiful children, Aariya and Amari and my husband Duwayne, who taught me what unconditional love feels like. Duwayne, you came into my life at 17 and became my best friend and partner in everything. With you by my side, I can do anything! Your support and belief in me have never faltered! I love you with all my heart. Aariya and Amari, you are more than I could have ever dreamt of. You make me so proud every single day and fill my heart with sunshine and happiness. You are my greatest gift and my biggest teachers – I just love you! Thank you all of you, for supporting me in my career and always cheering me on like you do.

To my brother Matthew for always being by my side throughout every season of our lives together. We always had each other! I love you!

And to my mum, for inspiring me at an early age with your work ethic and modelling how to keep going despite adversity. For helping me realise the importance of working with children, care for others and go after a career whilst also raising children. You did everything you could to be the best mum you could be. I miss our karaoke sessions in the car together.

This book and approach might not have existed without some key people, so I want to say a huge thank you to Kyrstie Stubbs for being the first Head Teacher to roll out my therapeutic teaching course, initial therapeutic classroom vision and for being the first school to embrace my whole school approach. Our work together made it on to the BBC and Newsround! Thank you for helping me believe I can make a difference! You are an inspiration, and I am so grateful for your role in my journey.

A big heartfelt thank you to Andy Houghton who was the first Head Teacher to believe in and embrace my therapeutic classroom approach, allowing me to transform his Year 3 class into the first ever therapeutic classroom, all based on a vision that lived in my head. What we did together was a pivotal part of my career! You are a legend, and I am thankful for your belief in my approach and for your bravery! What you do for the children at Shevington Vale is outstanding!

And, finally, to Helen Smart for being one of the first Head Teachers to believe in my therapeutic classrooms right from the start and being brave enough to pioneer the approach in your school. I miss you and your inspirational light.

Introduction

Who is this book for?

It is for you!

It's for Head Teachers, Executive Head teachers, Deputy head teachers, teachers, TA's, NQT's, SENCO's, learning support staff, lunchtime organisers, the office admin team and anyone else who supports children in an educational setting and beyond.

You might be an educator learning this information for the first time, or be familiar with the theory and want to embed it further. Whatever your reason for picking up this book, there will be things within these pages you haven't considered, that will help redefine ways of thinking, simplify the theory and give you a road map to follow. This book is aimed to help you make a real, practical, tangible difference to the lives of the children in your care.

What is a therapeutic school?

A therapeutic school is a term I use to describe a school who embeds a whole school approach, ethos and culture that puts children's mental health and wellbeing at the heart of everything they do. It is a school that considers the whole child, specifically with regard to their internal processing, mindset, belief system and ability to regulate their emotions. A therapeutic school acknowledges child development, how trauma and stress can impact the brain, how insecure attachment can affect relationships and how neuroscience informs children's behaviour. It is a school that takes responsibility as caring, nurturing adults to help guide their children through their formative years, helping develop emotionally intelligent children who can understand their own feelings, how those feelings impact their behaviour and then what they can do to manage that for themselves. A therapeutic school acknowledges that they are a key part in moulding children socially and emotionally and this is a foundation for success. Its offer to children evidences this throughout its practice and runs throughout the whole school. It is a school who considers what is going on behind behaviour and helps guide and teach children, rather than punish and reject them. It is a school that is brave enough to question the norm and to say, 'This isn't working' and to change the status quo by doing things differently, using the children as their moral compass at all times. A therapeutic school is a school that considers the world we live in today, and prepares the children to be able to access that world and flourish in it, regardless of their experiences. It is trauma-informed, attachment-aware and therapeutic in its approaches and it is forward thinking enough to break the mould. A therapeutic school invests in its staff's skillset so that everyone feels empowered and confident to make a difference in the children's lives, every single day. A culture is created where staff feel supported enough to embrace change and practice self-reflection, without fear of judgement, helping them to shred old 'teaching responses' that have been handed down to them by previous generations and no longer work, and develop new 'therapeutic responses' that make a tangible difference. In a therapeutic school, teachers become attuned to the children's emotional needs and respond in a way that meets those needs, helping children feel emotionally safe in their care, recognising that this is the only way in which children will be able to learn. A therapeutic school is a school that reflects the needs of our children today and meets them. It is a school that makes a positive, tangible difference in the lives of their students every day.

So how do you become a therapeutic school? Well, it starts here . . .

PART 1

The 'Why': What We Really Need to Know

1

My Story

When we talk about children's mental health and wellbeing, we can often use buzz words like 'adversity,' 'childhood trauma' and 'insecure attachment.' These words then become part of our everyday language but, unfortunately, they can lose their true meaning. When we talk about mental health and wellbeing, we are talking about real people, real lives, real brains, and real stories. We all have a story, and it is those stories that inform who we become, what we believe, how we think and how we behave. So, before we delve into the teaching elements of this book, I think it is important to revisit the reality behind these buzz words by telling you a story. My story.

When people ask me who I am, I usually start with something like . . . my name is Shahana Knight and I am a childhood trauma specialist. I am also the Director of a mental health service named TPC (which stands for Teaching Positive Connections). I tell them I have a history in education, psychology, therapy and trauma. That I am a writer for *Head Teachers Update Magazine*. That I speak at conferences, chair events, teach both teachers and foster care agencies. I talk about how I have been a governor of two primary schools, leading on wellbeing. How I sat on a foster care panel for three years helping approve new foster carers. How I have appeared on the BBC and Newsround and won Business Entrepreneur 2021 at the Inspirational Women's Awards with the Katie Piper Foundation. I might tell them that I married my first serious boyfriend, who I met at 17 and we have now been together for 18 years. That I am also a mum of two amazing children who are nine and eight (at the time of writing this book) and who are the most wonderful humans I could ever wish for. I talk about TPC and how I started it at 23 and built it from the ground up. How we now have over 40 therapists working across the UK and how we roll out our Therapeutic Teaching Course to help schools become more trauma informed and support children's behaviour in a connective way. I talk about being the first

DOI: 10.4324/9781003410652-2

person to transform UK classrooms into therapeutic classrooms and how we have appeared on many local news channels as a result. I share the parts of me people can see, the parts of me that demonstrate my capabilities and credibility as a specialist in my field. But . . . that is not me. It is the outcome of who I have become, it is the product of a story that is rooted deep inside me, informing every decision, belief, how I think, how I behave . . .

This is who I am . . .

I grew up in a family of four, there was mum, dad me and my brother who was 12 months younger than me. I come from a family of people who really care about others. My parents both worked with children in some capacity and were pretty inspirational. My mum went from nursery nurse, to childminder (whilst we were in primary school), to nursery manager, assessor and then lecturer. Her CV was so impressive by the time I was in high school that she got every job she ever applied for and was highly sought after. Watching her build her career whilst raising us was such an inspiration to me and influenced my own work ethic. My Dad was the Head Teacher of our primary school (yes, the one my brother and I went to!) Dad was a caring, open human who always did his best for the people around him. He was focused on children's wellbeing before it was even a 'thing.' He opened the first hearing impaired unit at his school and taught every child to sign so that the school was inclusive. His was the first school in the country to do this! He supported the families who were struggling, went out on to the community, and did his best to make a difference. He was fun, playful and charismatic and he loved the limelight! He would put on daft assemblies for the children where he was dunked in baked beans or water, he would dress up and put on silly shows, create bubbles in the playground on sports day with large bits of string and genuinely try to make school a friendly, fun place to be. Making people feel good was one of my Dad's natural talents and one I have adopted myself! Because of how successfully my Dad ran his school, I grew up a mini celebrity in the local area, where people asked me, 'Are you Mr Mathieson's daughter?' on a daily basis – and I loved that!

While Dad was at school, mum was a childminder, caring for local children whilst their parents were at work. It meant she could take care of us and earn money for the family at the same time. She was highly regarded in the community and was registered to take children from the Local Authority who needed good quality care. She was caring, nurturing and attentive to every single child who came through our doors. We had a lovely big house that was dedicated to the children mum cared for. Our front room was a playroom where the children would spend their days. Mum hung colourful nursery rhymes on the wall and had two huge floor to ceiling shelves full of toys and resources. When you opened the playroom door, Mum would be fully engaged with the children, sat inside a pretend train made of chairs, wearing a silly hat with children as they went on an adventure to an imaginative zoo. If not inside, she would be out and about with her assistant, both pushing double trollies with children walking either side, off on a trip out. Our garden was full of play equipment, slides, swings, playhouses and bikes, and children ran up and down it, digging up worms and picking apples off the trees. My mum was really creative and would set up activities for the children where they learnt to make bird feeders, paint with potatoes and make pasta art. There was always something going on and every child was special when they were with mum. I remember clearly how she would throw tea parties whenever it was somebodies' birthday, complete with banners and small sandwiches to make them feel special. The house was constantly full of laughter, play and fun and everyone felt loved.

We lived in a semi-detached house with a large extension that meant we had loads of space to grow up. The house was always warm and welcoming, and we never wanted for anything. In her spare time, mum could be found in her 'little room' (which was a box room packed to the brim with shelves of art resources, paints, pens, paper of every kind, stamps and ribbon that surrounded a desk!) doing crafts, making cards and studying, whilst raising us at the same time. She published a series of children's books and a card making book and she later went on to do her masters whilst we were in school. Dad loved music and he played the guitar and the drums. If the Beatles were not echoing through the house, then it would be the sound of Dad strumming on the guitar, or the cricket on the TV.

Because Mum and Dad worked in education, we had every holiday off together. Dad loved France, and so each summer we would hitch up our caravan and spend four weeks out of the year sunning in the south of France, exploring castles and history, having bike rides and reading books on loungers (we all loved reading). Summers are some of my favourite memories of my childhood, along with Christmas. Christmas was a big event for us. We would buy a huge Christmas tree that touched the ceiling and would take pride of place in the middle of the living room. We would decorate it together with brightly coloured tinsel and baubles whilst blasting Wizard's 'I wish it could be Christmas.' Mum would hang balloons from every light fitting and streamers from every corner of the room. The fire was always lit and glowing in the corner making everything feel cosy and Christmassy. The house would be full of excitement and anticipation as we watched the tree fill up with presents which would flow out from beneath it, not to be opened until Christmas day. But the most exciting thing was putting out treats for Father Christmas and waiting for him to visit our house – which he always did, filling two huge stockings (which later become sacks) for us by the fire.

The whole thing was magical. The whole thing sounds idyllic. We were set up for the perfect family life. It all had so much potential. But it wasn't perfect, it was far from it and around the age of eight my rose-coloured glasses came off and I realised the reality of our family was much darker. Soon, instead of bright warmth and light pouring through the house, there was a dark, grey cloud that didn't ever leave.

Although my Dad was the most wonderful, charismatic person you would ever meet, he had a history of trauma which shadowed his whole life. As a result, he became an alcoholic and suffered with manic depression. The details I have of dad's life are pieced together by fragments of conversations with different people over the years. I am not sure I have the full facts, but what I do know is that he was born in Manchester in 1949, into a family of five sisters and single mum, he was the youngest and only boy. I don't think he ever met his dad, although he was named after him. When he was young, his family moved to Barrow – I recall him often talking about living with very little money, sharing a bed with his mum and drinking out of jam jars. Throughout his childhood and teenage years, he was moved about a lot, living with various sisters and their husbands and slotting into their lives.

Dad was married before meeting my mum, and he had a young son. Their relationship didn't work, and they split up. Dad loved his son and saw him regularly after the breakup. Both my parents would care for him together, taking him on adventures and getting out in nature. Dad had every intention to be a constant figure in his son's life, however, when he announced he was going to marry my mum, his ex-wife said she would stop dad from seeing him. This was a devastating blow for my Dad and although he tried every-thing to get parental rights, his ex-wife managed to stop all contact. The last time he saw him, his son was five. He never saw him again.

These events were mixed in with many different traumatic experiences for my Dad, including some of his sisters dying and his beloved dog run-ning away on a beach with a pack of dogs on holiday, and never coming back. Each event often following the same pattern of abandonment and loss. When I was in Year 5 at school, Dad's was amongst the first school to have an Ofsted inspection, but around the same time his mum died. The pressure and the grief were too much, and he had to take time off work due to his mental health and depression. Unfortunately, although he desperately wanted to get better, he had been out of work too long and the school was taken over by another Head, so my Dad was unable to return. He saw this as a huge betrayal, and was again, a form of abandonment and rejection. He began to struggle more obviously with his drinking and depression. I must have been about eight around this time and that is where my own childhood trauma began.

Because of my family's status in the community, our experiences were always kept behind closed doors. Mum referred to Dad's behaviour as his 'illness' and would explain everything away with the phrase, 'It is his illness.' Our lives became chaotic and unpredictable and our relationship with our parents became strained and often scary. Dad would spend a lot of his time in deep depression, initially struggling to get out of bed, spending full days in his room, asleep. Mum said it was the depression medication that caused him to sleep so much, and I recall Dad trying to wean himself off the tablets several times. I more recently learnt that he would spend all night awake drinking during this period, mulling over his adverse experiences and blaming himself. Although he was struggling, he still tried to be the dad he imagined himself to be and would promise us trips to the swimming baths followed by a MacDonalds on Sunday (which was tradition for a while). He would tell us to knock on his bedroom door and wake him up, but when the morning came and we knocked, he couldn't get out of bed. He would tell us to come back later and we did, lots of times, but he couldn't get up. Soon we stopped knocking and dad would spend long lonely days upstairs whilst we spent our days trying to be quiet downstairs. If we were too loud, he would use a walking stick to bang on the floor to tell us to be quiet. The laugher and the music stopped. Other times, Dad would sit for hours in his armchair in the living room, drinking and surrounded by clouds of cigarette smoke. The stereo was beside his chair, and he would play Eva Cassidy for hours and cry whilst staring through the patio doors in front of him. He would be unable to get dressed and spent every day I can remember in a grey tracksuit, with bare feet and unkempt hair. He had beautiful long hair.

Every day was unpredictable with Dad, sometimes he would wake up and be the charismatic, happy, magical dad we knew so well. He would play with us in the garden, lie in his hammock outside, potter by the pond and take us swimming. He would let us brush his hair with water spray bottles and bobbles, and play games like hide the teddy in the dark around the house. On Dad's good days, he was the best dad. Better than every dad we knew. On those days our lives were filled with magic and wonder. He would blast his favourite songs and strum on his guitar. He brought magic to the house. But then the very next day, he would be drunk, dark and scary. He would be unmotivated, emotionally abusive, or completely disconnected. His mannerisms would change, he would pursue his lips and cross his legs. He would stare through you and smirk at you. He would say unkind hurtful things and he would lie. Those bad days became more and more frequent as we grew up and we started to experience a lot of emotional abuse.

Dad had so many experiences of rejection, loss, and abandonment in his life. As a result, he had an ingrained belief that he was unlovable, unwanted, and unworthy. So, on those dark days, he would self-sabotage and push us away, believing he couldn't be loved unless he was the fun version of himself. Believing his whole true self wasn't worthy of unconditional love. This became a pattern we endured right into our early twenties, as dad found different creative ways to break down his relationships with us, rejecting us before we could reject him, because he believed in his heart we eventually would.

Everything that happened to us, happened behind closed doors. I have so many stories to tell but this isn't the book for that! I will share however, some examples in this book of the things we endured in our childhood, so you can understand what life was like. I hope that by sharing some of my own experiences, it will help highlight the science behind my therapeutic school approach and bring to life the experiences of the children in your care.

Now, my dad was a pretty cool guy and had long hair to his shoulders, he would wear ripped jeans in winter and hot pants in summer. He was really good looking and somehow pulled off anything he wore! As I have mentioned a few times, we loved his hair (and so did he!).

One night, when I was around nine, my dad, in a drunken state, shaved off that beautiful head of hair. He left two bits at the back, two round tufts he couldn't reach, or maybe he left on purpose. He came to my brother and I in the night, waking us up and asked my brother to shave off the rest. I don't remember him shaving it, but I do remember the fear I had. Dad then went to bed, to lay by my mum, putting her hand on his head to shock her awake. It doesn't sound like much now, but at the time it was traumatising for us all. We had many disturbed nights with Dad's drunken antics but that may have been one of the earliest memories I have. He knew it would hurt us deeply to see him like that, he knew it would hurt him too, I think that fuelled his motive to do it. That and the alcohol. He needed to be noticed and seen, he needed to self-sabotage and so he demanded that attention in those moments. These shock tactics became a regular occurrence and left us in a constant state of overwhelmed and fear.

Dad's hair took ages to grow back, and to this day I can't watch my husband shave his head or help him with bits he has missed. The details of that night are sketchy, but seeing an electric razor on a bald man's head makes me feel that fear all over again, right to my core.

Dad was only physically aggressive once, outside of that one time, our lives were filled with constant emotional abuse. Emotional abuse is a hard one. You often don't know it is happening, and it leaves no visible trace. But it is painful and damaging and it began to tear us all apart. As children, we couldn't turn to our parents for support, we couldn't tell anyone outside of our home. Our life was our own private hell. In my mum's effort to protect my dad, and maybe herself, she wouldn't discuss what happened with us. We were left to try to make sense of things alone, unsure of what that meant about us, our family, and the world. She didn't help us understand it or process anything and soon she even began to deny events even occurred. We were living in a dark cloud of lies, we didn't know what was true and what wasn't.

As time went on and we became teenagers, my brother and I learnt to stay in our bedrooms. We had large front door locks on our bedroom doors which came with a set of keys. After school we would lock ourselves inside, knowing we were safe, if only in our rooms. Mum would shut the door in her 'little room' and keep busy with work, constantly in a state of avoidance. Dad would sit downstairs on his armchair, drinking and smoking, watching TV or listening to music. The downstairs was his domain, and we didn't enter it unless we had to. We no longer ate dinner together as a family, the house was no longer full of people. Our summer holidays abroad became strained and although we continued them until we were about 13 and although they were better than our lives at home, they would often result in dad drinking in the caravan before bed. They then stopped altogether, and our caravan sat on the drive unused for years. Dad tried his best at Christmas and most Christmases, he held it together, but he increasingly smelt of drink and cigarettes and his hair was never washed. The last Christmas I remember having as a teenager, consisted of my brother, Mum and I opening presents on my brothers' bedroom floor, with the door locked and Dad downstairs, on his chair, on his own, with a present he kept trying to give my mum but she refused to open. It was a beautiful silver necklace in the shape of a heart with a pearl inside. The whole thing was devastatingly sad.

Unfortunately, unlike most fairy tales, the ending of this story wasn't a good one. Things went from bad to worse, with Dad sabotaging every good event we had coming up. I vividly remember that he would have an outburst of some sort before every exam I ever took. I was constantly juggling my family's emotional states whilst trying to maintain a 'normal' life on the outside. I learnt to look after everyone but myself and to read peoples body language and facial expressions so I could be one step ahead of what they would do, think, or what they needed. It left me acutely aware of people's feelings and emotional states and I managed my own behaviour based on that. I learnt to be 'a good girl' and to not to need anything from anyone because I was more lovable that way. I learnt not to tell people when I was struggling and to manage my own emotions because relying on others meant being let down or hurt. I learnt to take care of myself and keep control of whatever I could, in a world where everything else was out of control and un-predictable. I still have these beliefs and coping strategies even now!

When I was in college, Dad threw himself down the stairs and nearly died – he was in hospital for a long time, and came home with a head brace and promises of changing. He tried. He really did, but his coping mechanisms were too strong, and he ended up drinking again. Finally, when I was in university, my dad's drinking had gotten so bad that my brother and Mum were no longer speaking to him, and my mum was filing for divorce. We had finally abandoned him, and his self-sabotaging finally pushed us all away, just as he predicted. He was drinking full bottles of whisky by this point and had stopped eating. One night I had a bad feeling, my radar for the emotional states around me was going off and I knew something wasn't right. I had a feeling Dad was going to die. I spent that evening painting a picture of him, with his lovely long hair and bright blue eyes, surrounded by music notes, a guitar, and his favourite lyrics. I wanted him to see that I hadn't given up on him and that he was loved. I took it downstairs to him that evening and he put his arm around me and said, 'If I look like that, I must be a handsome man indeed,' that was the last time I saw him alive. He died the next night. My final university exams were the week after.

Dad dying wasn't the end of my story – the trauma continued as I supported my mum through the aftermath of those years. Not long after his death, she began to struggle with dementia. I think the trauma she endured caught up with her, and her avoidance strategy manifested into a distorted reality. It progressively got worse and over the last six years, I have been her carer. Very recently, on my daughter's ninth birthday, she was sectioned and later moved into a dementia home, with psychosis as a symptom. She is only 58.

Writing this is painful – as I read it back I can hear how tragic it is. There was so much potential and yet the potential was overshadowed by pain and trauma. Much like the children in our schools. My dad's trauma impacted his whole life, making it impossible for him to be able to move past. Nobody ever acknowledged his pain, his frame of reference and the emotional impact his experiences had on him. My mum couldn't guide him through his feelings and emotions, she wasn't able to give him validation and insight to help him heal. She was drowning in her own experiences and couldn't meet her own emotional needs, never mind anyone else's, including her children's. Dad was a slave to his trauma responses, with no healthy coping mechanisms to fall back on. His fear of rejection fuelled his self-sabotaging behaviours which then produced the exact rejection he feared. It was a tragic cycle that tore him apart.

. . .

Sometimes I find myself minimising the validity of my trauma, I tell myself that we didn't have to live through domestic violence, experience life in care or suffer through physical abuse or sexual abuse. I recognise that we were truly loved, even if it didn't feel like it. Sometimes, I wonder if my story is even worth telling, but I remind myself that it is. Any experience that is emotionally challenging, tests your sense of self-worth, makes you feel unsafe and forces you to constantly be in a place of survival is worth telling. We all have different experiences at different degrees but the very fact that it has impacted you makes it valid.

For the first seven years of developing my business, I didn't even reference my own experiences, but I recognise now that for you to understand my therapeutic school approach, you have to understand me. This is me. This is where I came from, this mixed-up world of pure love and magic and intense fear and pain. When I move into the next chapters of my book, I hope you can recognise how much my history informs my work. I feel the feelings of the children I support; I have lived them in some capacity, I battle triggers they battle, I have coping mechanisms they have, I have intrusive thoughts just like they do. I had to navigate school and adversity at the same time.

I am that child in the back of your class.

I developed my approach with them in mind, from a place of deep understanding. That paired with my training in psychology, therapy and education makes this (I hope) a unique approach and one I know makes a real, impactful, tangible difference to the lives of the children who benefit from it.

Learning from history

Dad's story impacted his whole life, it then impacted *my* whole life and resulted in me also having my own childhood trauma. That is the thing with trauma, the impact can be passed down from generation to generation. My family's story is not unlike so many of the children's stories today, right now in your school. That ending, didn't need to be the outcome for dad, and didn't need to be the outcome for me. It doesn't have to be the outcome for the children you know either.

When Dad was growing up, nobody acknowledged his emotional wellbeing and mental health, nobody had insight in to how his experiences were affecting his beliefs and thoughts, nobody explored how these thoughts and beliefs were then affecting his behaviour. I kind of get it, it was the 50s. But when I was growing up in the 90s, nobody acknowledged mine either. I was a well-behaved, happy, bright girl who did everything I was told, and I brought happiness to the rooms I was in, but I was at the very school my dad had to leave due to his health. There must have been red flags for the adults around me. There must have been signs in my behaviours somewhere. Not once, in all my life as a child, teenager and adolescent did anyone offer me some insight into how my experiences might be affecting me. Not once did someone help me unpick my beliefs, thoughts and behaviours. Nobody acknowledged it.

There are countless families out there like mine, where trauma is repeated from generation to generation and where the parents and children have very little self-awareness and insight into what is going on. For things to change, and for us to truly support children's mental health and wellbeing, we must realise our own power as adults in beginning to change the narrative of these stories. We must start helping children to make sense of their feelings, emotions and behaviours and cultivating emotionally intelligent, self-aware people who have the sense of self and self-belief to break the cycles of trauma in their lives.

Trauma can be all consuming, but if you work with children, there is so much more you can do to help, and this book is dedicated to how you can do that.

My mission

I write this book at 35 years of age, after 11 years running my business and 19 years of working with children. I have worked with children in various roles and capacities, and I have a vast amount of experience in different settings and there is one thing I have learnt through it all and that is: every single child needs support with their emotional and mental health. Although my own story is rooted in trauma, the focus on children's mental health and wellbeing is relevant for *every* child, regardless of their experiences.

They all need help from the adults around them to learn to recognise what their feelings are, how those feelings impact their behaviour, thoughts, beliefs, perceptions and ultimately the health of their minds. Every child needs to be taught to not only be aware of these things but know how to manage them. Every single child. They need to learn how to be emotionally intelligent and have the real life, tangible coping strategies to take care of their own wellbeing and mental health. It is a basic developmental right and if we fail to do this, we are failing them.

My mission is to teach every adult what they can do to contribute to that learning. We all have a part to play. We *can* all make a difference in the lives of the children we spend time with, but we need to know how. In this book I will be guiding you through my step-by-step approach. An approach that is underpinned by neuroscience, childhood trauma theory, attachment theory, life experience and more. I promise it will be easy to understand, relatable, inspiring, and practical and that you will be able to implement actual actions, strategies and responses as a result of reading it. We will start with the 'why' and then move in to the 'how.' This approach has helped thousands of children across the UK and works with every age, from two years old to adults. Alongside those I have taught to implement this approach, I have also tried and tested it throughout my life, even with my own children.

What I need from you, is to read this book with an open mind and an open heart. We are going to be putting the children at the core of all we do from now on. I will be asking you to be brave enough to question what you know so far, to challenge the status quo and to think about teaching in a whole new way. I hope this book can transcend the current teaching model and take us on to a new wave of teaching that puts mental health and well-being at the core.

So, if you are ready, let's get started!

2

Understanding the Buzz Words 'Mental Health' and 'Wellbeing'

The education system has moved on since my time at school and we are beginning to acknowledge the importance of children's mental health and wellbeing more now. However, before we can understand how to help children with their mental health and wellbeing, we must understand what these words actually mean.

Mental health is

> The state of health of somebody's mind.
>
> Oxford Learner's Dictionary

Our mental health is how healthy our minds are, and that is relevant for us all. Our mental health relates to the quality of our inner thoughts, perceptions, outlook, and assumptions about the word. And just like our wellbeing, our mental health can be affected by external factors and experiences in our lives like trauma, stress, demands and life circumstances.

Wellbeing is

> With reference to a person or community: the state of being healthy, happy or prosperous.
>
> Oxford English Dictionary

Wellbeing in its simplest form, refers to how 'well' we feel within ourselves and our state of happiness. It is internally something we feel in our bodies. Our sense of wellbeing can be impacted by several factors in our lives such as stress, sleep, food, friendship, work, finances, physical health, trauma and more. If we stop for a moment and listen to our bodies, we can often tell whether we have a positive feeling of wellbeing or not. Sometimes life

DOI: 10.4324/9781003410652-3

is so full of external stresses, pressures and demands our sense of wellbeing is compromised. This however can leave us feeling unhappy, tired, over-worked, emotionally drained and can impact or sense of wellbeing.

> **Note: Our wellbeing and our mental health are linked**. You cannot have a positive, sense of internal wellness (wellbeing) if you struggle with intrusive thoughts (mental health). So, the two things come hand in hand. We will explore what this means for our children later.

Taking care of our wellbeing

We can take care of our wellbeing in small ways every day. These things help us manage our sense of wellness and happiness day by day, week by week. Small ways to improve your wellbeing might include walking in nature, having a long hot bath, reading a book, going to bed early, seeing friends or gardening. We all have different things that feed our souls and make us feel happier, and so it's important to find what works for you. Life is full of stressors and is fast paced and demanding and we can often struggle to find time for ourselves. If we are honest, so many of us put our ourselves on the back burner and prioritise everything and everyone else. We tell ourselves we are too busy to go out with friends, that working in the evening is more important than that bath we want, that our walk will need to wait, because the kids need us at home. The more we do this, the more we begin to feel the impact of neglecting our own needs and thus our wellbeing. If we stop for a moment and evaluate our behaviour, we can start to see signs in that we no longer feel 'well' or happy within ourselves. You can also identify it in your feelings, thoughts, or behaviour. You might be more negative and find yourself blaming others or outside circumstances for how you feel. You might become more irritable and snappier with friends or loved ones. You might notice you have reoccurring headaches, struggle to sleep, feel anx-ious, eat more, or eat less. We are all different, but we all have indicators that help us alert us to the fact that we don't feel very happy!

Regularly doing small things that help you relax or make you feel good, is a key part of maintaining your wellbeing and sense of happiness. It helps you feel more productive and helps you manage your emotions better too. When we take care of our wellbeing, we can manage those life stressors so much better with a clearer outlook and sense of control.

Taking care of our mental health

We also have more control over our mental health than we might think. Let's look at the example of physical health. When we want to take care of our physical health, we might exercise more or eat better. We are more mindful about the activities we do to promote our physical health and might put routines in place to help us maintain our physical goals, for example going to the gym every Friday, or going for a walk on the weekend. We know we can improve our physical health ourselves by making these changes. The same strategies can be used for our mental health. However, this isn't something we are every really taught how to do! Taking care of our mental health means firstly paying attention to what is going on in our minds and realising that we decide what we think. If we catch ourselves thinking things that are not in our best interest, we can choose to reject those thoughts. However, that can be really hard to do and takes practice.

Mindfulness

Taking care of our mental health includes becoming aware of our thoughts, perceptions, mindset and behaviours and looking inward to reflect on these, adjusting them where we can. This is where mindful practice can help.

Mindfulness is

The quality or state of being conscious or aware of something.

Oxford English Dictionary

This is the definition of mindfulness, but in a busy world with constant demands and everything bidding for your attention, it can be extremely difficult to be 'still' enough to even notice any of these things are even happening in the first place! The practice of mindfulness is to create circumstances within your day-to-day routine where you can give yourself moments to focus on your mind. Helping you become present in the moment and still or quiet enough to hear your thoughts and check in with your body. This creates the right circumstance to be able to feel and be aware of, what is going on internally for you. Ways to achieve this state might be through calm breathing, sitting in a quiet space for ten minutes, meditation or just having a quiet cup of tea without your phone or distractions. The idea is that you focus your attention on what is happening internally in the present moment and paying attention to how you feel, what you are thinking and your current surroundings. Try it now, close your eyes for a moment and take three calm breaths in and out, focus on the sounds you can hear around you and notice how your body feels in this moment. Are you comfortable? What thoughts pop into your head? Give it a go now . . .

Sometimes all it takes is a few moments to just stop and focus on yourself for a moment, to bring you clarity and a sense of calm. When we carve this time out for ourselves daily, it can have a huge impact on our sense of wellbeing, helping us feel more in control and more peaceful. It reduces our heart rate, steadies our breathing and even lowers blood pressure. Studies have found that practicing mindfulness regularly can also improve sleep and help you cope with pain and stress (Rusch, 2019; Creswell, 2017). Being more mindful also allows you to be more aware of your thoughts, which means you can begin to be more in control of what you choose to allow into your mind and therefore helps you have more control over your mental health.

Wellbeing and mental health in the classroom

If we take this information into consideration, there are two key areas we should be focusing on with children:

1. To help children feel happy within themselves (their sense of wellbeing)

This means giving them the skills to manage their own sense of wellness, happiness and to develop a positive outlook. Helping them to have those self-care strategies, to be present, calm and mindful.

There are so many ways to help improve children's awareness of their mental health and wellbeing in the school setting and this is something I see school doing well. Some put on wellbeing lessons, PHSE sessions, mindfulness, yoga or meditation. Some talk about wellbeing and mental health with the class in circle times. This is a great start to helping raise awareness and give the children some important self-care tools.

However, it is important to recognise that these things help with only a small part of the puzzle and you are not likely to see huge changes in dysregulation, anger or challenging behaviour just because you introduce these things. You will of course see some impact, but tackling the growing problem of children's mental health and wellbeing is a much bigger and more deep-rooted issue than can be solved by a meditation and PHSE lesson.

2. To help children to take care of their minds (their mental health)

Guiding them to become aware of their own feelings, thoughts and behaviours and teaching them how to feel in control and have the emotional intelligence they need to navigate them and manage them.

We can help children achieve these skills through our own interactions, responses, and approaches to them, as adults. To really make a difference to a child's wellbeing and mental health – the change needs to start with you. This is so important in today's world where children's mental health and wellbeing are at risk more than ever before.

References

Creswell J.D. (2017) 'Mindfulness interventions.' *Annual Review of Psychology*, 68, 491–516.

Rusch, H.L., Rosario, M., Levison, L.M., Olivera, A., Livingston, W.S., Wu, T., and Gill, J.M. (2019) 'The effect of mindfulness meditation on sleep quality: A systematic review and meta-analysis of randomized controlled trials.' *Annals of the New York Academy of Sciences*, 1445(1), 5–16. https://pubmed.ncbi.nlm.nih.gov/30575050/

3

Why Things Need to Change

Before we can look at your own practice and skillset, we must be clear on the 'why.' Changing and adapting responses and approaches takes commitment and time, and being brave enough to question the norm takes conviction. I want you to believe in this approach to your core, to live and breathe it so that you can be an agent for change and truly impact children's lives. So, our first step is to understand what is going on for the children of today so that the 'why' becomes your drive to do this.

We are living in an age where children's mental health and wellbeing is a real concern. The truth is, it has always been an important factor to consider and has always been something children have struggled with. It's significance in a child's development has not changed, but our awareness has, and so have the factors that negatively affect children's mental health too. I write this book after we have all collectively been through the Covid-19 pandemic, the impact of which is yet to be fully known, however, we can already see a direct correlation between those events and our children's mental health, in both their behaviour and recent studies.

In 2021–2022, the number of referrals to the NHS for mental health treatment for under 18s increased to more than 1.1 million In the UK (NHS, 2023). These figures include children who were suicidal, self-harming, suffering from depression, anxiety or eating disorders.

The Children's Society (2023) has found that in the last three years, the likelihood of young people having a mental health problem has increased by 50%. They also found children's happiness is declining, with five children out of 30 children in a classroom likely to have a mental health problem (The Children's Society, 2022).

These concerns are reflected in official figures for education, with the 2022/2023 academic financial year reflecting that there were 403,090 children in need of mental health support, which was an increase on

DOI: 10.4324/9781003410652-4

figures in 2020/21. This includes 50,780 children on protection plans (DFE, 2023).

These are official figures, most of which are based on studies or data gathered on those who accessed help and support or took part in surveys. It is important to remember that there are so many more children who are not included in these statistics that are also struggling. We can see that these numbers are probably much higher just by considering the children in our own classrooms. Children struggling with their mental health doesn't just mean those children who are self-harming, have an eating disorder or have a diagnosable condition. It also includes those children who are lacking in confidence and have intrusive thoughts or who are struggling with their anger and flip tables. It is the child in your school who refuses to go into the dinner hall and so lies on the floor in the corridor, and the child who feels as though they have no friends so sits on the wall at breaktime. Mental health is much more than a diagnosable condition, it is our day-to-day state of our mind and this is relevant to every child.

Since starting this work, I have seen firsthand an increase in the level of need year on year. Ten years ago, there were around two to three children in every class that were struggling, but now, it is more like half the class. 2021–2023 has seen a significant rise in 'difficult' behaviour in school with increasing numbers of Head Teachers talking about spending most of their day dealing with behaviour incidents or helping children who are struggling to calm down. Similarly, increasing numbers of teachers are reporting that their class is often disrupted by children who are finding it hard to engage.

Why?

Aside from covid, the state of children's mental health is declining, and I would argue that is true for most of our children, even those who do not stand out as obviously as others, but why? What is going on?

There are two key factors at play that we must consider:

1. The increase of adversity and childhood trauma
2. The way we live our lives

These are important when we are evaluating our support in schools to meet children's mental health and wellbeing needs.

The increase of adversity and childhood trauma

The numbers of children struggling with childhood adverse experiences and trauma in their lives are rising. Studies have found that almost 50% of adults in England and Wales experienced one adverse experience and one in ten suffered four or more (Public Health Network Cymru, 2016; Bellis et al., 2014).

Adverse childhood experiences (ACES) refer to highly stressful, potentially traumatic events or experiences that occur during childhood. Some common things might include (this list is not exhaustive):

Abuse:
   Physical, emotional and sexual
Neglect:
   Physical or emotional neglect
Family circumstances:
   Domestic violence
   A parent with depression or mental health needs
   Living with an alcoholic
   Being taken in to foster care
   Loss through death/divorce/separation/a parent going to jail/abandonment
   A parent/carer with depression or mental health needs
   Living with a parent who uses drugs
Events:
   Death
   National disasters (floods/earthquakes)
   Global issues (Covid/war)

Adverse experiences can be single events that were traumatic, such as a car crash or death and ongoing prolonged events such as abuse or living with a parent struggling with depression. Although not listed on official categories under ACES, it is important to also recognise the impact of things like living in a household with low income, living with a large family, moving house a lot and someone being unwell or in hospital. These experiences can also be considered an adverse experience, but because they are less complex, their impact can sometimes be forgotten.

A note on Covid-19: It is important to recognise that Covid-19 was a collective traumatic experience for everyone. It affected every household, every family and every child. It disrupted routine, social contact, connection and safety. It contributed to experiences of loss and increased a fear, anxiety and a sense of unpredictability in even the most stable family. As a result we must acknowledge that every child has at least this one ACE to consider which is significant contributing factor to the increase in mental health needs across the board and is one we cannot ignore.

Adversity and trauma can be emotionally distressing for a child both when it is happening and afterwards. Extensive research shows that adversity and trauma can significantly affect a child's quality of life and future outcomes, putting them at higher risk of developing mental, social and physical health issues in adulthood (Webster, 2022) in fact they are statistically more likely to struggle with things like:

- Drug misuse
- Alcoholism
- Dropping out of school
- Getting involved in crime
- Financial problems
- Disease and health issues
- Poor academic achievement
- Difficulty forming healthy, long-lasting relationships
- Poor mental health
- Difficulty controlling behaviour and emotions

These children are coming into our schools every day and are battling with high levels of stress and adversity at a young age. Many have a combination of the ACES listed above which puts them at greater risk of having long term social, emotional and health problems. It isn't uncommon for me to hear stories about children like Jack who lived through early domestic violence and abuse, has seen dad sent to prison and mum having a new baby with someone else. Or Stephen who was taken into care after living with abusive parents, but has been moved from care home to care home. Or Sarah who lives in a large family of siblings and mum is pregnant again but there is very little money in the household so the children are often seen out on the streets in the evenings stealing from the shops. These examples can be found in schools up and down the UK and are happening every day.

If you have been in the education sector long enough, you will also probably have seen these higher risk factors unfold over time with the children you have taught. I remember working with a Year 1 child who was living with domestic violence and abuse, his behaviour at school was aggressive and volatile and he didn't respond to the consequences put in place. The staff didn't know how to support him and often felt overwhelmed with his behaviour. I remember the Head Teacher telling me he wouldn't last long in high school – years later he had been permanently excluded from high school and was in the newspaper for a local crime. This is a pattern we see time and time again, but regardless of what popular narratives will lead you to believe, the problem is not with the child, it is with the adults around the child, and our norms and approaches (which we will look at more in later chapters of this book).

It is vital we consider adversity and childhood trauma in school because these experiences impact their developing brains, behaviour, thoughts, perceptions, belief systems and outcomes. The experiences the children are living through have the potential to affect so much of their lives and so we must use the research and theory to develop our whole school approaches and our core offer. If we fail to do that, we are failing our children.

Trauma-informed practice

We often hear schools refer to themselves as being trauma-informed and ACE aware, and that means that the school understands the impact these experiences have on children, physically, socially, and emotionally. They acknowledge trauma will affect children's behaviour, their relationships, and their ability to meet some expectations at school. Trauma-informed approaches embed the science and research into school life to ensure they are meeting the child's emotional and mental health needs and not re-traumatising or triggering them. Their goal is to help children understand their feelings, emotions, and behaviour and to teach them the skills, strategies, and insight they need to be able to manage them long term. A trauma-informed approach embeds this ethos into every aspect of their approach. As we move through this book, we will explore how trauma affects children in more detail and then what you can do to help.

Being a trauma-informed practitioner means:

- You understand and recognise how trauma can impact children's thoughts, beliefs, feelings and behaviour in school
- You are skilled at recognising trauma responses and have the training and skills to support them
- You are able to meet children's emotional and wellbeing needs using your understanding of trauma theory
- You avoid re-traumatising and triggering children which can cause distress by re-thinking approaches, culture and policies
- You put children's emotional and mental health at the core of teaching/ your school
- Everyone understands their contribution is key
- Building safe, trusting relationships is a fundamental part of your approach
- You recognise your own trauma responses and acknowledge when they impact your responses and reactions

These contribute to the foundations that form my approach.

Be kind to yourself

As we move through this book, I will be talking a lot about trauma and its impact on children. Like me, you might have experienced trauma in your life too and as you read, you might find that you are learning new things about yourself and getting insight into some of your own behaviours. It might feel a little overwhelming at times as you have 'ah ha' moments and realisations so remember to be kind to yourself. Take your time, process your feelings and allow yourself to feel them. Life can be tricky and can leave you with difficult memories and relationships, it is okay for you to feel a bit triggered and to feel a bit emotional as you unpick them. Please don't let this be a reason not to continue reading though, you are more powerful with this information and you can use it to harness your trauma into something that will fuel your work. Trauma happened to you, it doesn't need to become you and it doesn't have to define you, only you get to do that.

The way we live our lives

Alongside ACES and childhood trauma, there is a second factor to consider when looking at the rise in children's mental health and wellbeing needs, and that is the way in which we live our lives.

For both adults and children, life can be busy, fast-pace and often overwhelming. There is so much to do in such a short space of time, and it can often leave us feeling stressed and burnt out. For us adults, trying to juggle the many responsibilities and roles we have, has led to us developing unhealthy coping mechanisms we now consider normal. We are juggling parenting, working, looking after loved ones, maintaining a home, marriage and all the micro bits in between, like deadlines, the food shop, appointments and so on. We are on a treadmill of 'doing' that keeps us in a constant state of stress. Unfortunately, a culture has emerged where we have glorified that stress and there is now an unspoken norm, where we place value on being busy, tired and even burnt out. We might say things to each other like, 'I am so tired, I didn't go to bed until past midnight trying to get my work done!' or 'I was so busy yesterday I didn't even eat dinner!' We wear our tiredness like a badge and share it with others to reflect our worthiness, dedication and hard work. Somehow, we have been led to believe that being stressed equals success, without realising that we are actually developing unhealthy coping mechanisms that are affecting our own mental health and wellbeing.

Our children are also experiencing a similar, fast-pace, high-stress culture. Many spend most of their day in a state of 'doing' and have very little time to rest or just be. An average week could include breakfast club, school, after school club and weekend clubs. When not in clubs, children are spending increasing amounts of time on social media and technology. Choosing to play on games consoles, phones or tablets instead of going outdoors, socialising, playing make belief games, or playing with toys. They are always being stimulated by something, whether it is television, gaming, tablets or clubs and this often paired with factors such as late nights and lack of boundaries which can have a negative impact on their mental health.

Social media and technology

Social media and technology are now an entrenched cultural norm in society, with most of us relying on different tools to help us navigate our daily lives. The majority of us have a mobile phone, a computer, a television, games consoles and tablets. We also use apps and social media such as Facebook, Ticktock, Instagram and YouTube. Using technology has opened up the world for us, helped us stay connected and allowed us to learn and work in innovative ways. However, it is also highly addictive and can significantly impact our mental health and wellbeing. This is particularly important when we consider that children's access to both social media and technology are increasing.

Almost all primary aged children between 5-10 years old have some sort of access to technology, the most common devices being phones, tablets and games consoles, and many of them also have access to social media.

What we need to know:

Although it has become a cultural norm for children to use technology, there is little guidance around the safety of using it. When a parent buys a bike, they know that that it comes with risk and they know what those risks are, so they might buy a helmet to go with it. They will also teach their child about managing that risk. Similarly, if they buy scissors for the art box, they are aware of the dangers and can teach their child how to safety use those scissors. The same is not true for phones, tablets, computers and games con-soles nor for the apps they might be using. This information can be found of course but is not part of people's basic knowledge, yet the risks are just as dangerous, if not more so!

So, what do we need to know and how does it relate to wellbeing and mental health?

Gaming

A report published by Ofcom (2023) found that nine in ten children (89%) ages 3–17 play games online. Whether on an app or on a device, online gaming has become a big part of a child's play and we can see the evidence of that in school. Popular games such as Roadblocks and Minecraft are topics in children's discussions or the theme of their play. It is easy to see the influence these games have on children when they come into school, and so since they have such a prominent role in their lives, it is important to consider their impact on children's mental health and even behaviour.

Many of the online game's children are playing have clever design features to keep their attention, they are quick paced, colourful and stimulating and this can mean children struggle to turn them off. Their core objective is usually anchored around 'killing,' 'defeating' or 'winning' which releases stress hormone and puts the child's brain into a heightened state of stress. This can be overwhelming to the brain, especially if used for long periods of time.

When a child is playing an online game and the purpose of that game is to survive or win then this has a direct impact on the way the brain responds. Our brains are designed with clever mechanisms that keep us safe when we are in danger. They do not know the difference between reality and fantasy and so, when presented with a situation which feels threatening, the brain will respond with survival mechanisms. Have you ever watched a scary movie where your body has reacted with fear? Maybe your hands went clammy, or your heart was beating really fast. Maybe you hid behind a pillow or needed to leave the room. Even though you knew on a practical level that it wasn't real, your body responded as though it was. That was your brain trying to protect you. As you were watching the movie, you began to feel emotions linked to it, you might have felt scared or worried, or maybe you were anticipating what was coming next. Your body processed these feelings as signs that you were unsafe or under threat. As a result, it responded by making you hide behind a pillow to keep you safe. It shifted into a survival response to help you. The same happens when a child is playing on a game that is anchored in death, defeating, or winning. The child is sucked into a world where they are at risk in some way, they might be trying to win a car race or running away from a zombie, or even trying not to 'die' by letting the balloons hit the ground – and so their brain responds accordingly. These games switch a child's survival responses on, and their bodies and minds will respond as though they are really under attack. The longer a child plays, the more threat the brain perceives. The more this is repeated, the more the body begins to believe that the threat is constant. This increases stress levels in the body and makes it very hard for the child's brain to 'calm down.' In some children (often those who game a lot) the stress levels will stay high so that the body is ready to jump into action next time there is an attack. Playing games like this is having a direct impact on children's brains and is shifting them into a state of survival. This can then have an impact on their behaviour and we see more intense melt downs, struggles to regulate and calm down and what seems to be irrational responses like crying and demanding more. Although this looks like challenging behaviour, it is often the result of high levels of stress hormone and is a survival response. We will explore the impact of hight stress levels, the brain and survival modes in chapter four.

Social media

There is also the impact of social media to consider here too. A study by Ofcom (Cited by Barnardo's 2019) that found that in 2019 children aged 5–15 were spending an average of 5 hours a day on social media, despite being in school for seven hours five days a week (Barnardo's, 2019). In a later study, Ofcom also reported that 48% of 8–11-year-olds use messaging apps or sites and 64% use social media (Ofcom, 2022). Although there are many positive factors associated with social media, like children being able to contact friends and family, share photos or the potential for reducing feelings of social isolation, there are also many concerning factors to consider too. There are, of course, all the obvious factors like cyberbullying, harmful content and exploitation but the impact of using social media I would like us to consider in this book, is more specific to the actual apps themselves, how they are designed and the impact on our children's brains.

In 2020, a documentary called 'The Social Dilemma' was released on Netflix which explored the rise of social media and the damage is it doing to society. What was interesting, was that the film interviewed many of the former employees and professionals who created the technology on the most popular social media platforms, like Google, YouTube, Twitter, Instagram and Facebook. These early creators were concerned about the impact of the social media platforms they contributed to creating, and wanted to speak out about the dangers. The creators discuss how specific functions are designed to ensure the user becomes addicted to the platform. They explain that the information on our 'feeds' are competing for our attention and that their business model is to keep people engaged on screen. This is how they make money, and it explains why we feel children are addicted to their devices!

In the program, Edward Tufte says, 'There are only two industries that call their customers "users": Illegal drugs and software.' And Dr Anna Lembke, an America psychiatrist and chief of addiction medicine at Standford University explains how we are biologically programmed to feel good when we connect with other people. In fact, it releases a hormone called dopamine, that sends signals to the brain reinforcing feelings of pleasure and reward.

We need human connection, and we thrive off it, but social media has fabricated an online world that plays on this need, making it addictive. It creates an opportunity to get that dopamine hit but removes the human quality we get from face-to-face interactions and real physical connection, making it fleeting and empty, which triggers us to need more. She goes on to say that the smartphone itself is also addictive, saying 'Smartphone screens light up the same area of the brain as opioids and cannabis. The rewards pathways mediated by dopamine respond to screens in a very similar way to opioids.' So, using smart phones and devices is just as damaging and addictive as using drugs, but we give them to children freely because this is not common knowledge.

If we are honest with ourselves, devices and social media are addictive for everyone, regardless of age! Our lives are constantly interrupted by our phones, leaving us feeling distracted and anxious because of the relentless intrusion. We have all experienced that phenomenon of checking our phone quickly and then being sucked into mindless scrolling, only to look up and realise that we have just lost 40 minutes of our life doing something which has absolutely no value at all. This level of engagement and constant interaction is draining and can leave us feeling tired and overwhelmed, especially if we are sucked into the same cycle multiple times a day.

This is a concern when thinking about children, especially those without boundaries and limited usage at home. Being in this state constantly is not healthy and has a direct affect on mental health. It might also explain why devices have replaced traditional forms of play and why less children are playing out in their gardens during the school holidays. In fact, the number of children and young people who played outside, read books and get enough sleep has dropped sharply in comparison with teenagers from previous decades (Barnardo's, 2019).

Tristen Harris, former Google design ethicist, says,

"These technology products were not designed by child psychologists who are trying to protect and nurture children. They were just designing to make these algorithms that were really good at recommending the next video to you, or really good at getting you to take a photo with a filter on it. It's not just that it's controlling where they spend their attention, social media starts to dig deeper and deeper down into the brain stem and take over kids' sense of self-worth and identity."

Technology and learning

In a world where social media and technology has such an influence on our children, the impact must be considered by professionals in schools. Why? Because the effects are filtering in, creating barriers to learning and contributing to the emotional and mental health needs of the children. Think about it like this, if children are being programmed by social media, to consume information quickly, without really taking their time to read or appreciate it, then their ability to sit and reflect on a piece of writing or literature in school will be more difficult. Their brain is literally being taught to process information instantly and then move on, and it is being rewarded for that through the dopamine hits. The skills needed to process, reflect, and critically think about things are being lost as the brain develops to meet the needs of the ever moving, fast paced society we live in. Think now about a child who posts a photo of themselves on social media and receives no likes, they then later see a photo of all their friends together at the park without them. This child is left feeling rejected, devalued, unseen and unwanted which can cross over and contribute to issue at school on the playground.

Just like trauma, technology and social media are triggering our children and young people to live in a constant state of stress and is activating the survival responses of the brain. We cannot separate what happens to our children outside of school from the school experience. It is all one.

The way we live our lives in such a fast-paced way, allows no time for space, rest and reflection. Children are no longer able to be alone with their thoughts, to be present in the moment and still. If they do get that space, some find it uncomfortable because it isn't the norm and so they find ways to fill it. This is affecting their ability to process their own emotions, problem solve, reflect and ultimately have control over their mental health.

Meeting mental health needs

In this chapter we have discussed two important factors that are impacting mental health:

1. ACES and childhood trauma and
2. The world we live in today

Every child will experience some of the issues we have discussed here, many will experience more than one, and we can now also assume that almost every child in the UK has had at least one ACE since covid, experiencing the feeling of fear, inconsistency and overwhelm it bought over a prolonged period of time.

This book is written to support every single child's mental health, because every single child needs to have the insight and skills to navigate themselves through challenges. The fact that we are seeing a rise in mental health issues, tells us that we are not doing a good enough job in helping with that. So, from now on, we must acknowledge that we cannot write a behaviour policy without considering how Jack's experience of domestic violence is impacting his levels of aggression and his internal sense of safety. We cannot expect Sarah to play nicely at dinner time, if we don't consider her self-belief, confidence and ability to socialise. We can't expect Abdul to come in and get on with maths, without considering his concentration levels and whether he is tired from gaming and going to bed too late.

We must begin to create a culture, environment and approach which takes all these things into consideration if we are to truly support the development and learning of our children and prepare them for the real world.

The impact we see in school

The increase of childhood trauma and the arrival of technology is having a direct impact on children at school, and this can be seen in their behaviour. Year on year I hear reports of children struggling, children who are finding it difficult to listen, concentrate, manage friendships, and follow school rules. There are more children refusing to engage, running away and pulling down displays and more children struggling to calm down and manage their emotions. Since the pandemic, even children who seemed engaged and settled before are now displaying higher levels of anxiety and stress and lower confidence.

Some common things include:

- Low level disruption: Fidgeting, shouting out, distracting others
- Behaviour incidents: Hurting others, stealing, biting, scratching, throwing, pulling down displays, refusing to go into the classroom

- Relationship struggles: Falling out, struggling to share, difficulties seeing other perspectives, lack of empathy
- Lack of self-awareness: Unable to explain why they did something, unable to identify their feelings, how their actions contribute to a situation
- Anger: Arguments, swearing, shouting, lashing out, destroying things
- Lack of self-regulation: Not being able to recognise their emotions and have the tools to calm down in a healthy way
- Refusals and absences: Refusing to come into school, refusals to participate, refusals to follow instructions
- Withdrawal: Not getting involved, not sharing ideas/thoughts/feelings, quiet, retreating from situations, lack of contribution
- Low mood: Irritable, unhappy, negative mindset, unenthusiastic about things
- Low confidence/self-esteem: Not feeling good enough, struggling to join in, struggling to be centre of attention, not believing in themselves, struggling to see their worth
- Lack of concentration: Fidgeting, daydreaming, distracting themselves and others, difficulty paying attention
- Hyperactivity: High energy, short attention span, flitting from one thing to another, easily distracted

In many schools, teachers are finding it hard to manage the needs of their children in the classroom, and Head Teachers are spending much more time responding to behaviour incidents.

Interestingly, in my conversations with school leaders, I am finding that these changes in children's behaviour and emotional states are not exclusive to just schools in areas of high need and deprivation, although of numbers might be higher in these areas. Instead, I am hearing accounts from Head Teachers who lead schools of all different set ups. Inner city primary schools, suburban schools, large and small schools, mainstream schools, SEMH schools, SEN schools and even prep schools! I have spoken to schools across the country from London and Northumberland to Wigan and they all say the same! It is evident that children across the UK are collectively struggling with their emotional wellbeing and mental health and although on a case-by-case basis, it might seem like the problem is the child, maybe the problem lies with the adult's and the system. Maybe we are getting it wrong. Maybe we should step back, reassess and be brave enough to challenge ourselves and our perception of how we can meet the children's needs.

Self-reflection

As you read this, you can probably think of several children in your school who are displaying these behaviours on a daily basis, just stop and make a note of them for a moment. Jot down what they do and what they say. Then come back to them as we move through the book.

What is important to remember, is that these are the outward signs that a child is struggling. This is what we *see*. There is so much more going on than just what we see. In fact, these behaviours are only the symptoms. Think of it like a cold, when you have a cold, inside you are fighting off a virus that is attacking your system and is causing you to feel poorly. Nobody can see the virus, but you have symptoms that are evident on the outside which are signs that you are not well. You might have a runny nose or a cough, you might be more sleepy, irritable and tired. Nobody tells you off for struggling with these symptoms, because they understand they are signs of the virus and it is not in your control. The same is often true for children's behaviour, their behaviour is a sign that they are struggling. However, there is no common, collective understanding that these symptoms could be the cause of an internal difficult experience, feeling or thought. Instead, we focus on the behaviour itself rather than the underlying cause and we tell them off! We must remember though, that we wouldn't expect to treat a cold by trying to stop the outward symptoms, and so we cannot expect to help a child if we are only focused on trying to stop their behaviour!

As professionals, Head Teachers, teachers, support staff, parents, carers, aunties and uncles, it is so important we begin to see past the external behaviour and instead, focus on what is going on for the child. Focusing on how we can help support them.

With that said, let's now look beyond that external behaviour so we can understand what is going inside the minds and bodies of the children.

References

Barnardo's (2019) *Left to Their Own Devices: Young People, Social Media and Mental Health.* Available at: www.barnardos.org.uk/sites/default/files/uploads/

B51140%2020886_Social%20media_Report_Final_Lo%20Res.pdf (accessed 13 March 2023).

Bellis, M.A., Hughs, K., Leckenby, N., Perkins, C., and Lowey, H. (2014) 'National household survey of adverse childhood experiences and their relationship with resilience to heath-harming behaviours in England.' *BMC Medicine*, 1. Available at: https://bmcmedicine.biomedcentral.com/counter/pdf/10.1186/1741-7015-12-72.pdf (accessed 13 March 2023).

DFE (2023) *Children in Need.* Available at: https://explore-education-statistics.service.gov.uk/find-statistics/characteristics-of-children-in-need (accessed 13 March 2023).

NHS (2023) 'Monitor 2021/2022 Annual Report.' Available at: www.england.nhs.uk/wp-content/uploads/2023/01/monitor-ara-21-22.pdf (accessed 13 March 2023).

Ofcom (2023) *Children and Parents: Media Use and Attitudes.* Available at: www.ofcom.org.uk/__data/assets/pdf_file/0027/255852/childrens-media-use-and-attitudes-report-2023.pdf (accessed 13 March 2023).

Public Health Wales (2016) *The Welsh Adverse Childhood Experiences (ACE) Study.* Available at: https://phw.nhs.wales/topics/adverse-childhood-experiences/ (accessed 13 March 2023).

The Children's Society (2022) *The Good Childhood Report 2022.* Available at: www.childrenssociety.org.uk/information/professionals/resources/good-childhood-report-2022 (accessed 13 March 2023).

The Children's Society (2024) *Children's Mental Health Statistics.* Available at: www.childrenssociety.org.uk/what-we-do/our-work/well-being/mental-health-statistics#:~:text=In%20the%20last%20three%20years,have%20a%20mental%20health%20problem (accessed 13 March 2023).

Webster, E.M. (2022) 'The impact of adverse childhood experiences on health and development in young children.' *Global Paediatric Health*, 9. Available at: www.ncbi.nlm.nih.gov/pmc/articles/PMC8882933/ (accessed 13 March 2023).

4

Stress, Trauma and the Brain

Stress, trauma and the brain

If we truly want to understand how we can help children with their mental health, wellbeing and therefore their behaviour, we now need to look at what is going on inside! Why are children ripping down displays, running out of the classroom, refusing to follow instructions, and struggling with their friends on the playground? What is going on?

We are going to spend some time looking at how stress, trauma and adversity can impact a child's developing brain, processes and responses. This is relevant for every child and is not exclusive only to those who have been through trauma. Every child will experience stress or difficult feelings and emotions – so bear that in mind as we move through the chapter.

I teach this fundamental neuroscience (science of the brain) to everyone I come across and anyone who will listen! Whether it is a teacher, parent or carer or just a friend asking for advice. I think it is the most underused, undervalued science in society when it comes to understanding our children, and it should be informing our roles as parents and professionals. I honestly believe, if everyone understood how this science relates to the children they support, in whatever role or capacity, it would change their responses, relationships, perception and understanding and have a much bigger, significant impact on positive outcomes for children across the board.

Now it is important to note that I have no intention of delving too far into anatomical diagrams of the brain or to use lots of jargon here. This topic could be a whole book in itself but my job is not to teach you all to be neuroscientists. My job is to teach you to be therapeutic teachers who lead with connection and to use this neuroscience and research to inform your practice. You don't need to put down this book knowing all the technical

DOI: 10.4324/9781003410652-5

terms and studies for it to have a profound impact on your work. In fact, that can often be a barrier. This information should be accessible to everyone, so we can all make a difference, every day. I have spoken to countless educators who tell me that they have been on courses detailing the many mental health needs out there, or who have done extensive trauma and attachment training but that is hard to translate to practice. They have certificates and badges to show for it, yet when I observe them or hear them talking about their children, I cannot see evidence of how any of that knowledge is applied to their work. The truth is, you can go on as many courses about neuroscience, attachment and trauma as you like, but if you don't know how that relates to Jack on a Monday morning when he comes in angry and pulls down a display, then unfortunately you are not trauma-informed or attachment-aware in your practice, and that was the whole point of doing the learning!

My intention is to help you to truly understand how this science relates to the children in your care but most importantly, to help *you* to guide, teach, respond and create the environment the children need on a day-to-day basis. For me the difference is in those small, daily interactions and the culture you create. I would much rather you put down this book armed with a real understanding, that you can weave into your school on every level, paired with practical strategies and tools to help you support every child, than being able to recall the different parts of the brain.

That said, this is a fascinating area of learning, and I would encourage those of you with a keen interest in the science to source more books, do more research to further inform the approach here if you'd like to.

The impact on the brain

Our brains are very powerful things, yet we don't often consider their significance in our day to day lives. They work silently in the background, helping us breathe, talk, and move. Processing and storing information, and operating our thoughts, decisions, and emotions. Our brains use the information around us to adapt and learn, to ensure we can function and survive. When focusing on our mental health, wellbeing, emotions and behaviour, we must look inward and consider how our brains are contributing silently in the background to what we see on the outside.

For us to truly understand what is going on, we must recognise that our brain (and that of our children) is in part, responsible for our behavioural and emotional responses. Our brains are made up of many areas which help with many different things, but we are going to focus on the amygdala and the prefrontal cortex.

The amygdala triggers what we are going to call the emotional/survival response (survival brain), and the prefrontal cortex unlocks what we will refer to as the rational/thinking response (or rational brain). These are not separate brains of course, but they are separate areas and respond in different ways, both playing a huge role in the responses and behaviours of children and of you too!

The amygdala: survival/emotional response (survival brain)

The amygdala is small area of the brain that detects and processes threats or dangers in our environment, especially those that trigger an emotional response such as fear or anxiety. It is part of a larger network called the limbic system which processes and regulates emotion and memory.

Whenever we feel stressed, threatened, overwhelmed or attacked in some way, the amygdala switches on, processing our fear and activating our survival/fear responses to help protect us. The amygdala is in charge of keeping us safe, helping us survive by protecting us from danger or threat, whether real or perceived. This is often automatic and out of our control. It is our built-in mechanism to ensure our survival. Think for a moment of a lion in the wild, let's say the lion is with its baby cubs and suddenly another lion comes over to attack. The first lion will jump into action and attack back. They will fight and protect themselves and their babies until the danger is gone. They won't stop to think rationally about the situation, instead their reaction is instinctive. That is very similar to what we do as humans. Our brain will process anything we find threatening or unsafe and it will respond in a similar way, usually through survival responses called fight, flight, or freeze.

> **Important note:** Feeling 'threatened,' 'attacked' or 'unsafe' applies to lots of situations and doesn't just refer to times when a child or

person is in obvious danger. It could be when you are faced with a drunk parent who is aggressive, but it could also be when you feel challenged in an argument and feel like you have to prove your point or when you feel overwhelmed with work and everyone is demanding attention from you. It could also be when a child feels like they can't do their work, or when they don't feel like anyone is listening to them. We go into a state of survival over anything that makes us feel unsafe, overwhelmed, stressed, scared, anxious or attacked in any way shape or form. Think about what we learnt in the previous chapters about children living in a constant state of stress, technology and trauma. The amygdala is what is being activated and responding in all of those scenarios.

Depending on the circumstances, our brains will determine which one of these survival mechanisms are more likely to keep us safe and help us cope with the threatening situation we are in.

Fight mode

Sometimes we might go in to fight mode, this is where we fight back. We might be physically aggressive and wrestle, kick or hurt someone. We might use our words to fight back, by swearing, shouting, arguing or being unkind. We might bang doors or break things. In school, you are seeing a child in fight mode when they hurt others, flip over tables, swear, and shout and when they argue with you. These are the most common things that come to mind when people talk about fight mode, however there is more subtle ways of going in to fight mode too. For example, I go into fight mode whenever I have a lot of work, and tight deadlines, I feel overwhelmed and my brain perceives this as threatening, so my coping mechanism is to go in to fight mode and I work all hours of the day until I feel like I have it under control. This is not necessarily the healthiest way to respond, especially if I am tired and need to listen to my body and rest. However, I need to do something where I feel I am in control of the overwhelming situation I am in. Someone else might go into flight mode and avoid the work they have to do because it is too overwhelming! If you look carefully at the situations around you, you can see fight mode at the root of many behaviours.

Real life

Remember in Covid where everyone went out and bought toilet paper and there was a big uproar about how people were selfishly buying all the supplies? Well, the people buying the toilet roll were in a state of fight mode, they felt threatened and unsafe because they didn't know when they could get to the shops next. Everything was overwhelming and unpredictable, and so their brains were in a state of survival. Stocking up on toilet roll was their way of fighting back and taking some control in a situation where they felt they had none. It was a survival mechanism. Interestingly, the people angry with the people buying toilet roll were also responding through fight mode! They felt threatened by the perceived selfishness of other people – if *they* had all the toilet roll, there would be non-left for anyone else! This made them feel unsafe and threatened and so they responded with anger!

We can see fight mode in action when children are arguing, aggressive, swearing or spitting. We can also see it when they need to have control in a situation or are overpowering.

Flight mode

Another survival mechanism is flight mode, this is where you need to get away from the thing that is threatening. Obvious signs of flight mode in our children are running away, trying to climb school gates and hiding in toilets. Other more subtle signs are things like avoiding their work by fidgeting or distracting others, going to the toilet numerous times in lessons or asking for a drink of water. It might be avoiding a conversation, refusing to look at you, turning away from you or walking away. It might even be to refuse to come to school or to take part in an activity. These lower-level forms of flight mode are common in school, and it is important to identify them as means to cope – rather than a form of bad behaviour.

Freeze mode

Finally, freeze mode is where we, or the children, shut down. The threat is so overwhelming we don't know what do to or how to respond. Freeze mode could be exactly what it says on the tin, the person is rooted to the spot and can't move. In school, it can often look like staring in to space or standing and looking at you blankly. It might be not responding when a response is expected or being silent and not participating. They may seem confused or unsure about what is happening. Something inside has shut down as a mean to protect them and they can look as though they have completely 'blanked out.' This might be a sign of disassociation – which is where the person becomes disconnected from the situation/circumstance/person to protect themselves.

It is important to recognise that we *all* respond to difficult experiences, stress and threat with fight, flight or freeze responses. You may find you default most often in to one particular response, or that it depends on the situation, but there is power in realising that the children you work with, and you yourself will be pulled into these self-protection modes regularly.

 Self-reflection

Hopefully, as you read this you can recognise some of these responses in the children you know, but also in yourself. Think for a moment about yourself. Which one do you respond with? Maybe when you are having a disagreement with your partner, you find yourself in fight mode and you argue back, or maybe you go in to flight mode and need to leave the room and go for a drive! Maybe when you're over-whelmed and stressed, you overwork yourself in fight mode, or you avoid it and procrastinate in flight. Maybe you go in to panic mode and freeze when there is an emergency, or you jump into action and try to help.

When you think about the scenarios where you have responded with fight, flight or freeze, you realise that you usually have very little control over your responses in that moment. We have all been in the situation where we are angry and arguing with someone and we go on and on and say things we don't mean. Somewhere inside us we can hear ourselves saying 'Oh my god be quiet, stop talking this isn't helping. . . . Why did I say that? I don't mean that!' but we can't stop ourselves! This is a normal, natural way of responding when things are threatening because our survival responses take over. We will also find that our brain has an emotional response and a survival response before we can rationally process what is going on and that is true whenever we are faced with a difficult emotion, thought or situation.

Important note: Remember, the perceived 'threat' or 'attack' might be a situation or circumstance like missing the bus and being late or an argument with someone. But it might also be a feeling. The feeling of being unheard and misunderstood, the feeling of being 'not good enough' or judged or the feeling of fear or anxiety. These can all make us respond with our survival mechanisms and turn our amygdala (survival, emotional) part of the brain on. Sometimes it is easy to link these responses to outward behaviour but it's less easy to link it to a feeling. We will look more at the significance of feelings and how to make these links as we move through the book.

The pre-frontal cortex: rational/thinking response

The other important part of our brain to consider in this approach is the pre-frontal cortex. This area of our brain oversees our executive functioning – which means it helps us to rationally regulate our thoughts, actions and emotions. The rational thinking part of our brain helps us to reason and reflect, problem solve, have empathy for others and concern. It helps us to plan, make decisions and manage our social behaviour and helps us to have self-control, stay focused and remember things. In my approach I refer to these responses as our rational/thinking responses and may refer to this part of our brain as the rational or thinking brain.

Have a think about those skills for a moment. These are the skills we expect children to be using when they come in to school. We expect them to be able to think rationally and problem solve both in their learning and with their friendships. We expect them to stay focused and be able to remember things and to have empathy for others. Everything we do is hinged upon the fact that children are using this part of their brain. However, this is a flawed expectation and is one of the most significant explanations as to why our approaches with children are not working.

This is really important- what we don't realise is that when children's stress levels increase and they are overwhelmed or feel threatened or attacked in some way, when their amygdala is activated and they go into survival mode, their rational thinking brain **shuts down**. They cannot access any of those reflective, executive functioning skills we demand of them. So, when Jack is angry and pulling down a display in fight mode, he literally cannot access the part of his brain that helps him reason, reflect and manage his responses. When Sarah has kicked her friend on the playground for not including her in the game, she literally cannot access the part of her brain that makes her feel sorry and empathetic. Like a flip of a light switch, that area of the brain has turned off.

So why does the rational brain turn off when we are in survival mode? Well, this is an important mechanism to ensure our survival in a situation, because if our brain was able to think rationally, we might respond completely differently and that might not be the best way of ensuring our survival.

 Real life

Imagine it like this, imagine you were with a crowd of people but a car was coming toward you all, your brain would quickly process the danger and would activate your survival response. You might respond with flight mode to help you escape and your body would instinctively jump into action, you would not be thinking clearly or processing the situation rationally, instead you would run! That might mean pushing past people, or even hurting someone by accident. In that moment, it is not in your best interest to be able to think rationally and have empathy for others, to stop or think for too long about the situation, because that might result in you being harmed or worse, killed! So, your rational part of the brain shuts it off – to ensure your survival.

This same situation happens every day with children at school, it means that when Abdul is overwhelmed during a game of football, when he feels threatened because nobody is passing him the ball and feels angry and left out, he cannot access those rational thinking skills like problem solving, reflection, empathy for others. Instead, he responds with his survival brain and goes into fight mode. He kicks Adam and then goes into flight mode and runs off. He is unable to process or think rationally in the moment and so when you ask, 'How do you think Adam feels?' he won't look as though he cares. It also explains why when you asked him what happens, he can't recall it very clearly or accurately. This is because the rational thinking brain is turned off and he is unable to properly process the situation and store it in his memory.

The rational thinking part of the brain can only 'switch on' when we are calm and when the threat or danger has passed. The stress levels need to have decreased and the person or child needs to feel safer, both physically and emotionally. This is why some children show remorse after a behaviour incident when they didn't seem to care in the moment.

This is essential information for teachers and schools as a system because it informs so much of what we are seeing in our children and explains why our approaches are not working. We will unpick this in chapters to come.

To recap: When we feel stressed, threatened, unsafe, challenged or have big emotions, our survival part of the brain perceives this as danger and activates our survival responses, fight, flight and freeze

- This is often automatic and out of our control
- When we are in survival mode, our thinking, rational parts of the brain shut down and we are unable to problem solve, reflect, reason, have empathy, recall or remember and have very little self-control
- We can only access our rational, thinking part of the brain when we feel safer or are out of danger – children often need a safe adult to help them calm down
- The survival response can be activated by anything we perceive to be threatening or an intense feeling rooted in fear. It might be a real attack like an emergency to smaller things like feeling overwhelmed with work, a conflict or disagreement or even feeling unsure about a new routine

What about children who have experienced trauma/prolonged stress?

This process of our brain flipping into our survival responses is normal part of being a human, it ensures our survival and is designed to keep us safe. Every child in school will do this when they feel overwhelmed or stressed and so will every adult. But why do some children do it more than others? What about those children who have experienced long term adversity and prolonged stress. How does that impact those children and their behaviour?

When the stress hormone is activated, our brains send a signal to our bodies to respond and help us get out of danger. Alongside our fight, flight freeze response, we also have these physiological responses:

- Cortisol is released (stress hormone)
- Blood pressure increases
- The immune system shuts down
- Adrenaline is released – to increase strength
- Pain receptors are lessened
- Digestion slows down or stops
- We can lose bladder control
- Oxygen goes to our muscles
- We get tunnel vision
- We are in constantly surveillance of our surroundings
- Sweating
- Insomnia (struggle to sleep)
- ADHD type symptoms (due to increased stress hormones)

When we are in a state of stress, we might find our heart is beating quickly, our hands are clammy, and we feel hot. Internally, blood sugars are released into the body to help give us the energy we need, and blood is sent to the muscles so we can run or fight back. Our heart rate and blood pressure increase, and our breathing is often heavy and rapid. Extra oxygen is sent to the brain, helping us stay alert and our sight and smell become sharper. This is our bodies way of preparing us to survive and often happens so quickly we don't even realise it. These mechanisms cleverly help us when we need it most. That extra blood to your muscles is great if you need to lift something heavy, push past something or fight someone to protect yourself. The additional blood sugars released into the blood stream are useful when we need the energy to stay up all night to attend to a poorly loved one.

However, if our body is in a constant state of stress, and we are unable to reduce those stress hormones, it means we cannot get back to a state of calm. This can be toxic for our overall health and mental wellbeing. It can stop us sleeping and make us more susceptible to illness. It can also change the way the brain develops and responds long term. These physiological changes, that are designed to be a short-term coping mechanism, become a daily state of being. This explains why so many children who have experienced trauma struggle to sleep at night and go to the toilet frequently at school, struggle to concentrate and so much more. It is also important to note here that when a child experiences prolonged chronic stress, it means that stress hormones are constantly flooding their body with no release. This can leave children feeling hyperactive and unable to settle, they might find it hard to concentrate and flit from thing to thing. It can also cause them to fidget and be constantly on the move. These behaviours can be mistaken for ADHD when in fact it is high levels of stress hormone.

When a child is living with childhood trauma or adversity, they are often constantly exposed to high levels of stress hormone. Their lives are full of threat, and they repeatedly feel unsafe or overwhelmed. Maybe they are struggling with parents who fight a lot, so they are exposed to shouting, anger and aggression and the fear of somebody being hurt. They worry about the police coming again and about their little brother waking up during a fight. They try to manage the emotional states of their parents by not making a fuss or demanding too much attention for fear of making things worse. Their brains are constantly in a state of stress and survival, figuring out the best way to survive and to cope. Sometimes that might be through flight mode, where hiding upstairs is the safest thing to do. Other times it might be better to fight back and get in between them as they argue.

For children who live in continuous state of stress, the brain is consistently working from a place of survival. If the survival part of the brain is frequently on and their bodies are flooded with stress hormone then their amygdala is constantly scanning for danger. The child's life is full of danger, attacks and threats which all come in different shapes and forms. It might be in the form of their parents arguing, it might also be in the form of having to go to school hungry and being expected to do maths first thing. Because their brains are constantly in survival mode, their amygdala becomes hypersensitive to all possible threat, and the stress hormones are unable to leave the body just in case the child needs to respond with survival mode again. They then begin to respond to small things (that wouldn't otherwise be a problem) with fight flight, freeze responses. Like getting intensely angry over not being allowed the ball on the playground, or being told they can't do something. Although these things seem small to us, the brain perceives them as another attack. It is almost like the brain and body are waiting for someone to jump out from behind the door. They can't settle – because it could happen at any time, and they need to be ready.

Imagine that you are constantly swamped with stress and challenge and threat is all around you. You have listened to your parents shouting all night, tried to protect your brother whilst he slept, found your own breakfast and packed your own school bag, arrive to school late worrying whether mum will be okay on her own at home, and then you are told it isn't PE this morning and you will be doing maths. Your brain would process this as yet another stressful things (attack) and would respond accordingly. What you think you see is a child who refuses to do his maths work and becomes angry and aggressive. But in reality, you are seeing a child who is overwhelmed with stress hormone and responding from a place of survival in fight mode.

Remember we talked about adversity and trauma increasing poorer outcomes for children? When a child is in a constant cycle of stress and survival responses, it can significantly impact their ability to learn, regulate emotions, calm down, think, and reflect. This is because they are unable to access and develop their pre-frontal cortex (rational thinking part of the brain).

Important note: It isn't just trauma that increases stress. Remember when we talked about social media and technology? When children play stress inducing survival games like those focused on racing, fighting, or winning – their survival responses are activated. The brain doesn't know the difference between reality and fantasy, it just responds to the danger it perceives around it. The longer the child is exposed to these stress hormones and the longer they are using their survival responses, the harder it will be for them to access the rational thinking parts of the brain. So, if they play these games frequently for long periods of time, their brains will perceive there to be constant danger around them, and so will struggle to truly rest and release the stress hormone. Their brain is being taught to constantly scan for danger and will be waiting in the background, expecting the next threat and preparing to fight back. We then see an increase in survival responses such as fight flight freeze. Children become more irritable, angry, aggressive, and argumentative or might have more melt downs over seemingly small issues! They are not misbehaving though, they are still responding with fight mode and cannot calm down, regulate and access their rational thinking responses. This science can also explain why they seem hypervigilant and have high excess energy – it is the stress hormone running round their bodies! They are literally being programmed to go in to fight flight freeze and so are not developing those rational response skills, or able to release all the stress hormones and experience peace and calm.

Triggers

When you are exposed to prolonged stress, your brain can develop triggers. A trigger is something that activates your survival and emotional response, because it reminds you of a difficult feeling or experience where you were unsafe. Your brain then responds accordingly to try and protect you. Triggers are your brains way of helping you cope with a difficult situation and getting you in to fight flight freeze quickly to ensure your survival.

A trigger can be anything such as:

- The smell of alcohol
- A man with a beard
- A loud noise
- Being alone
- A certain song
- A certain word (like, 'sweetheart')
- Being challenged
- Being cared for
- Being alone
- Feelings (like, feeling scared, anxious or overwhelmed)

Triggers come in all shapes and sizes and can portal us back to the traumatic event in our lives. Our body says 'I remember the last time I felt like this/ experienced this . . . I was in danger . . . I was unsafe' and it quickly responds sending us in to survival mode in anticipation of the danger that came the last time. Our body and brains then respond as they would have done when we were in the traumatic situation itself. Triggers are internal 'memories' our bodies and brains store as a direct response to the experiences we have had. It doesn't matter when this experience was, in fact, we might not remember the event, but our bodies do!

This explains why when you can hear a piece of music that was your loved one's favourite, you are transported back to the moment you used to sing it together, or why a child who was removed from their parents at birth, but heard domestic violence in the womb, still struggles with conflict and loud noises. It is so important to consider triggers when thinking about the children in school and is something we must consider when approaching their behaviour.

Real life

My own history of childhood trauma means I have many triggers, some of which I don't even know about until they show up. I remember when my daughter was born, she was my first child and I was 25 years old. Duwayne (my husband) and I were renting a little house, the business was in its infancy, and we were navigating life as new parents. I loved being a mum, it was something I had always dreamed of, but I found myself struggling with the lack of sleep. The days were full of baby cuddles, trips out in the pram and seeing friends. The nights though, were so difficult for me. My daughter would wake almost every 15–30 minutes, throughout the night, every night. She would cry to be fed so frequently I was beside myself some nights, feeling as though I was being tortured by being woken up so much. The nurse told me it was called 'cluster feeding' and that it was normal. She said it would pass, but I remember feeling so overwhelmed, helpless and trapped, my feelings were intense, and they scared me. One night I rang my mum and told her I couldn't cope and felt like jumping out the window (I wouldn't have, but I was so distressed this was the only way I could describe how much I wanted to escape in that moment). Duwayne and I recognised that I was struggling beyond the scope of a normal tired parent, we put it down to lack of sleep so we made an agreement that we would work together and that each night, I would feed the baby and he would settle her back to sleep. The nurse was right, it did pass, and I didn't think of it much again.

Then, years later I was stood in front of a room full of school staff, delivering a twilight and talking about triggers and it dawned on me why I struggled so much. When I was a girl, probably about nine or ten years old. Dad would sit awake at night and drink, he would ruminate on his own traumas and become self-destructive. He would wait until we had all gone to bed and then set the alarm off, as though a burglar was in the house. This would shock us all awake and my mum would run downstairs to turn the alarm off. Dad would wait for us all to fall asleep again, and he would do it again and again, and again. He did this for hours on end until my mum was forced to sit at the bottom of the stairs to stop him. Those nights left me feeling overwhelmed and helpless, the frequent wakings and sound of my mum crying felt like torture. Every time I dropped off to sleep, the shock of the alarm would wake me, years later the same was happening with my baby and I recognised, stood in that hall delivering that twilight, that it wasn't the lack of sleep, it was the fact that I was being woken so suddenly, over and over again to the sound of crying and I was unable to do anything about it. The frequent waking, the sound of crying and those intense feelings of being helpless, trapped and overwhelmed were my triggers. It made me feel unsafe and my brain was reminded of a time those things meant danger. So, my body responded with fight flight freeze.

People refer to 'triggers' in school quite often and most commonly I hear, 'There was no trigger for it!' However it is important to recognise that triggers are not necessarily a tangible situation or a thing that happens. In fact, I would argue that instead, our triggers are often deep rooted in our feelings. It isn't the football game that is the trigger, it is the feeling of not being included, being rejected or not feeling good enough. It is not the maths work that is the trigger, it is the feeling of not knowing what to do and the fear of failure. You won't always be able to identify the trigger or reason for a child becoming unsettled or dysregulated, and it is impossible to know every trigger, that is not your job. Your job is instead to be skilled enough to assess the child's reaction, see behind the behaviour and reflect on whether they are displaying a fight flight or freeze response. It is then to explore what are the possible feelings are behind that reaction, given the circumstances and use that to inform your response. We will explore how to do this in chapters to come.

Here is how it all plays out in real life: Jack is 10 and he experienced domestic violence between his parents from birth to the age of five. When he was five, he was moved to live with a foster carer and has been happy there. When he was with his parents, the house was always chaotic, loud and unpredictable. Jack felt out of control and overwhelmed regularly. He often felt unsafe and unsettled and was constantly worried about the levels of violence in the house.

What you see at school: Jack struggles with break and lunchtime at school. He refuses to go into the hall and often runs off around the corridors when prompted to go to dinner by a teacher. If he goes out on to the playground, he will get involved in an argument and be sent back inside within 15 minutes.

What you don't see: Lunch and breaktimes are chaotic, loud and unpredictable. Jack feels like everything is out of his control and he is overwhelmed. He is left to navigate this on his own and he feels unsafe and unsettled. Jack's brain recognises that when he feels like this, he is usually in danger and so his survival responses are triggered and he goes in to flight mode. He refuses to go to the dinner hall. When the teacher comes over to prompt him to go inside, he feels trapped and attacked and feels as though he has no control. He feels like nobody understands and he needs to get away so he goes in to flight mode and he runs down the corridor to escape. Jack doesn't mean to respond like this, and afterward he feels badly about it, but in the moment, it feels like the only thing he can do. It is like he reacts without thinking. When Jack is outside on the playground, the noises and chaos trigger him to feel unsafe. He knows he has to be out there – it's the rules, but he feels overwhelmed and his body goes into survival mode, the blood is released to his muscles, he is hypervigilant and ready for an attack. Then his friend refuses to pass him the football on the pitch. Jack flips in to fight mode and gets into an argument. He later says he doesn't know why he did it, he just did! This is because he is unable to access his rational, thinking part of the brain.

Remember, all children have the potential to respond like this in some capacity, aside from those who have been through complex trauma. You might have a child who comes into school on a Monday after having very little sleep over the weekend. Maybe they were left to play fighting on their Xbox for hours on end, and then found themselves being told off by their parents frequently when they got into arguments with their siblings. This child is also more likely to struggle in school and you may see more fight flight freeze behaviours such as not listening, day dreaming or arguing with their friends.

Important note: A survival response can sometimes be confused with a conscious act made from choice, but it often isn't. I was recently in a school where one of the teachers asked what to do when a child chooses to run away and go up a tree. I unpicked this a bit, and it was evident the child was struggling with adversity at home. In school, he was being triggered into a state of stress and survival mode and was going into flight mode. His outward behaviour was to climb a tree to get away. The teacher commented that he was scared about being so high up and was shaking when in the tree, which is confirmation of this being a stress response where he had little control over his actions. Staff were confused though because after he came down, he became dysregulated again and threatened to climb the tree again. On the surface, this looks like it is a thought-out choice because the child is verbalising what he will do, however, it is important to recognise that this isn't something that he is saying in a calm, rational state whilst using the rational thinking part of the brain. Instead, it is coming from a place of stress and dysregulation. Him saying that is an indication that he is feeling overwhelmed and is trying to get some control. Although it can be confusing, remember that our survival responses hijack us not only in action but also in what we say. A child has just as little control over their words as they do their actions.

If a child is constantly responding from a place of survival, they will be unable to access their rational thinking responses to help them flourish at school. All of the parts of the brain we want and need them to be using to function in education have shut down. They won't be able to reflect on their behaviour, responses or learning. They won't be able to apply reasoning to their work or situations they are in. They won't be able to have empathy for others. They won't be able to concentrate or recall information. They won't be able to manage their social interactions. Now you can see why I started this chapter by saying this was the most underused, undervalued science in society when it comes to understanding our children, and it should be informing our roles as parents and professionals.

How can we help?

One of the biggest skills we can give to our children to help them learn how to access the rational thinking parts of their brains when they need it most. As we grow and develop, we can teach our amygdala and pre-frontal cortex to work together. Of course, we will all respond to danger or threat with our survival and emotional part of the brain first and we may go into our fight flight freeze responses. That is because the amygdala's job is to assess the danger for us and send signals to our brain and body to respond. However, we can learn to get more control over this as we grow, mainly through the input and support of adults around us. Developmentally, the connection between the emotional/survival parts of the brain and the rational thinking brain is still forming and they will only be able to move past the initial emotional, survival response and shift into that rational part of their brain with input and guidance from the adults around them.

Without that input, they will continue to respond with their survival coping mechanisms into adulthood. Adults around the child, have the power to help them to process and manage these challenging, difficult situations they perceive to be threatening. The key here is to:

1. Help reduce the sense of threat, fear or attack and increase their feelings of safety.
2. Help them understand the feelings they are having, because feelings are always rooted alongside the threat/situation.
3. Help calm their brain and to increase their self-awareness and emotional intelligence.

Our number one goal whenever a child is struggling is to help calm down that brain, because when the brain begins to feel safer, the rational thinking parts will accessible and will turn back on.

This is really important when we look at it in the context of school. It explains why children are running away, lashing out and struggling to engage. It also explains why they show no empathy to their peers, struggle to concentrate and lack self-awareness. One of the biggest keys here is to acknowledge that when a child is responding with their survival brain, they cannot learn. They cannot access their memory and therefore they are unable to process, reflect and learn from a situation. This might explain why children behave the same way again and again no matter how many times you tell them off and no matter how many conversations you have after a behaviour incident.

Children are often overwhelmed by their feelings and are unable to manage them without help. They lead with their feelings and so, we must focus on their feelings too! Helping to guide them through those tricky experiences and develop the insight and skillset they need to be able to manage their responses. This is essential for school and also later life!

. . .

I have talked a lot about stress and trauma up to now, but there is an added layer to the complexities of trauma I want us to look at before we can understand the 'why' behind the therapeutic school approach. So far, we have discussed how trauma can impact a child's developing brain and responses, but we must also consider how it can impact a child's relationships and perceptions of the world itself. To understand this, we must spend some time looking at attachment and how this, too, is relevant to schools.

5

Understanding Attachment in the Context of the Classroom

Attachment

'Attachment' is another word that is growing in popularity in the education sector and for good reason, but what does it mean, and more importantly, how does it impact children's responses, thoughts, feeling and behaviour? If we want our schools to be inclusive, trauma-informed and attachment-aware, then we must consider this theory in our approaches too! Acknowledging the existence and effect of attachment on children is vital, and it should inform your relationships with the children, responses and behaviour policies in school.

British psychologist John Bowlby developed the concept of attachment in 1958. He described it as a 'Lasting, psychological connectedness between human beings' (Bowlby, 1982). When we talk about a child's attachment, it refers to the type of connection they have/or had with their caregiver, particularly in their early years. However, like my own experience, struggles with attachment can come later in life too. When babies are born, they come with clever mechanisms to help their caregivers attach (connect) to them. They might grasp their fingers, mimic their expressions, gurgle, and smile for example, and this increases their chance of being taken care of. This is part of ensuring their survival because they must seek protection to avoid danger and it is their caregiver who helps them to do this. When a baby is small, they can't do much for themselves and so they are dependent on their caregiver to meet their needs both physically and emotionally. The quality of the attachment (connection) is important to help ensure their needs are met and they can survive. Caregivers meet their babies needs by feeding, changing and bathing them, they might play with them, cuddle them and help them settle when they are distressed. The caregiver is constantly on the lookout for cues from their baby that helps them to determine how to meet their needs best. The baby's

DOI: 10.4324/9781003410652-6

cry is one mechanism that helps them to do this, as it alerts the caregiver to a problem or need. The caregiver then spends time trying to figure out how best to meet that need. This isn't always easy and can be emotionally draining for the caregiver, but in most cases, they will eventually calm their baby.

 Real life

Have you ever been holding a crying baby but have no idea what is wrong? You have already changed and fed them so you know they can't be hungry or wet, so you try to figure out what else it could be! You might try talking to them, bouncing them on your knee or standing up with them, but your goal is to help sooth them. This is an example of a healthy attachment exchange, and we find this pattern is repeated as the child grows. As a baby, it might be soothing their cries, as a toddler it might be helping them figure out a jigsaw they are frustrated with, as a teenager it might be listening to their struggles with a friend!

A strong attachment between the child and their caregiver is essential for healthy development. As the child grows and the attachment develops, it forms the foundations of the child's external and internal world. They base so much of their perceptions and beliefs on those early connections with the people around them, especially their main caregivers. A strong attachment between caregiver and child helps the child learn how to love and trust and how to have empathy. It helps them understand themselves and their worth and gives them a sense of self. It also helps them to understand and regulate their emotions. However, early research into attachment theory found that not every child experiences a secure and healthy attachment. In the 1970's a psychologist named Mairy Ainsworth began to research the quality of relationships between caregivers and their children. She found that there were secure attachments and insecure attachment styles in relationships too. Her work formed the basis of our understanding of attachment styles today.

Secure attachment

A child who experiences a secure attachment with their caregiver is a child whose parent can meet their needs in an attuned, loving way – most of the

56

time (this does not mean their parent is perfect!) The caregiver provides a safe, trusting relationship where they are emotionally available and love the child unconditionally. The child is emotionally and physically safe. They know they can make mistakes, struggle with their behaviour, express themselves and their emotions freely, knowing that their caregiver will still love them and will try to help. This doesn't mean that the caregiver agrees with the child and their behaviours all the time, but they will still help the child through it as best as they can. When the child is dysregulated, upset or in distress the caregiver helps them through this by calming them down, talking to them and helping them make sense of it all. They are consistent in their approach to parenting and provide boundaries where needed. The parent is sensitive to the child's needs and is attuned to them, which means they understand the child as an individual and can appreciate their unique personality and needs.

When a child experiences a secure attachment with their caregiver, they learn some very important lessons that they can apply to the people and world around them. A securely attached child learns that even though there are times of difficulty and stress in life and in relationships, people will be there for them. They can learn what love is, through experiencing it and can use this in their own relationships as a foundation of connection. They might experience arguments or disagreements with their caregiver, but they learn that conflict can be resolved. They learn that although they will make mistakes in life and may have disagreements with people, that it doesn't mean they are unloved or a failure. They feel secure enough within themselves to take risks and feel safe enough to fail, knowing they won't be rejected and that it doesn't mean they are not good enough. They don't have to adapt their feelings to meet the needs of the people around them in order to be accepted and learn to believe in their own self-worth. They can be themselves and be open, honest and authentic.

These lessons are the result of day-to-day interactions with their caregiver throughout their childhood.

 Real life

When baby Rio cries because he is hungry and he is fed and cuddled by his dad, he learns that is he worthy, loved and safe.

When five-year-old Leo falls off his bike, and his caregiver helps him back up whilst soothing him with hugs before encouraging him to try again, he is being taught that he can make mistakes and still succeed. He is also being taught that when he feels upset or hurt, people care and will help him.

When two-year-old Georgia is crying and throwing herself on the floor, and her mum scoops her up with a soothing tone and settles her down for a nap. Georgia is learning that adults will help her learn how to manage and sooth her own internal states, that she is safe enough to struggle with her behaviour, and that her feelings matter.

When a child is securely attached, they:

- Learn what love is through experiencing it
- Develop emotional intelligence
- Feel valued, safe and secure
- Develop self-worth
- Develop a moral conscience
- Learn to regulate their emotions
- Learn to create secure attachments with others

A securely attached child is given the foundations of self-belief, confidence, love and connection they need in order to be able to flourish in life. A child's early attachment experiences wire the brain, forming pathways that inform their expectations, beliefs, relationships, perception, and behaviours for years to come. When a child has experienced a secure attachment to their caregivers, they are able to form secure attachments with other people in their lives too.

Insecure attachment

A child who experiences an insecure attachment (connection) with their caregiver has a very different experience. This is a child whose caregiver struggles to meet their needs, emotionally and physically. When the child displays an attachment need, like being hungry, tired or upset, the caregiver may be unresponsive, absent, angry, withdrawn or unpredictable in their response. It might be that when they cry for food, nobody comes, and they are left for long periods in a hungry, distressed state. It might be that when they are struggling with their feelings and become upset and 'misbehave' the adult shouts at them and pushes them away. It might be that they fear their caregiver because they are often drunk and aggressive.

There are three types of insecure attachment, and I am going to briefly touch on them here. I think it is helpful for us to look at the styles that can develop in relationships to help bring the stories of the children we know to life. However, my advice would be that you don't need to remember each of the names of these three styles for you to be able to apply this theory to your practice, because there is never a clear black and white line between these types of attachment styles, they can blend into each other. I also think it is important we are careful not to get into the habit of trying to diagnose or label children with an insecure attachment style. This is not a disorder to assess, diagnose and treat. Instead, it is their experience and part of their story, and we should use our understanding of attachment to inform how to cultivate our own relationships with them and inform how we respond, guide and teach them in an effort to support their development. We should always be framing research around how *we* can help make a difference and to inform our understanding of a child's frame of reference, not on what is 'wrong' with a child. A child is only a product of the environment, experiences, and relationships they have had up to the point where we meet them. It is our job to acknowledge that and avoid blaming them for the failings of adults or systems around them.

The three types of insecure attachment are:

Ambivalent attachment
Avoidant attachment
Disorganised attachment

Ambivalent attachment

The word ambivalent means having mixed feelings or contradictory ideas about something or someone and that is very much how a child experiences the caregiver in an ambivalent relationship. In these relationships, the caregiver might be attentive sometimes, but then other times they might be unavailable and detached. They are inconsistent and unpredictable, and this can make a child feel unsafe and overwhelmed. The child is never sure how their parent will respond and it makes it difficult for them to predict an outcome and keep themselves safe. Typically, insecurely attached children will try to be one step ahead of their caregiver and may even adapt their behaviour to meet the caregivers needs in an effort to stay safe and avoid being rejected or harmed. However, for a child in an ambivalent relationship, this can often be unachievable and so the child is left in state of high anxiety, never knowing what will happen next.

An ambivalent caregiver might:

- Respond sometimes but not others
- Be under involved with their child
- Be slow to notice the needs of their child
- Be preoccupied with their own needs

Sometimes the caregiver is so focused on their own needs that they miss the cues their children are displaying. This is not necessarily on purpose but can often be because the carer is focused on themselves.

For children who experience this type of attachment, they are often in a high state of anxiety, not knowing what to expect from the people around them or whether adults can be trusted. They may learn that to get the attention of their caregiver, they need to increase their display of distress to ensure that they are noticed. They might cry, demand and have melt downs to try to 'win' the attention of their caregiver. They may acknowledge their internal need for a relationship but fear they will be rejected or harmed and so push people away to protect themselves. Children who have experienced an ambivalent attachment often become stuck in this pattern:

They are overly demanding>win the attention>fear the attention will be quickly lost>push people away>and then feel the rejection they were afraid of getting in the first place. This can be a pattern they carry into adulthood.

 Real life

Have you ever had that friend who rings you constantly with a drama or emergency? You try to respond by being a supportive caring friend but their needs become too demanding and draining and so you begin to distance yourself? That is an example of this insecure attachment style. Unfortunately, they fear rejection the most and so do everything they can to keep you focused on them, for fear of you abandoning them, but their strategies become so overwhelming that you do detach – and their greatest fear is realised. This can often be a cycle they repeat in all relationships.

Avoidant attachment

Caregivers who have an avoidant attachment style with their child often struggle to respond to the attachment needs of their child. When the child needs them and is distressed, dependent or vulnerable, the caregiver is experienced as distant or dismissive. The caregiver themselves my feel anxious, angry, and overwhelmed when their child is 'needy' and they avoid intimacy, appearing emotionally distant and even uncomfortable. Parenting a child is emotionally demanding and this is true for any parent but for the avoidant caregiver, the constant demands cause them to go into survival mode and their flight mode response is activated, they then do anything they can to avoid the feeling of overwhelm, even if that means pushing their child away. The rejection is not of the child, but of their attachment behaviours – such as crying, persistently needing the caregiver, asking questions, needing help, wining, wanting support and coming for comfort. The child learns to adapt to this relationship style by rejecting their own need for care, learning to be independent wherever possible and downplaying any feelings they have. They know that if cry or ask for help, they are more likely to be told off, ignored, or rejected and so they avoid these scenarios by getting on with things themselves. They learn to 'be good' and 'be quiet' and avoid their feelings to keep themselves safe.

The avoidant caregiver might:

- Not respond to their babies' cries or their child in distress
- Avoid physical contact and closeness
- Belittle or make fun of children's feelings or struggles
- Discourage a child's display of emotion 'Stop crying,' 'Grow up'
- Only seem to accept the child when they are 'good'

Children who experience avoidant parenting styles are often met with rejection when they need emotional closeness the most. The very person who should be helping them understand their emotions is instead angry and frustrated by them. The child learns that there is a direct correlation between displaying the need for connection and rejection. They quickly learn to avoid closeness and even reject it themselves as they develop.

Disorganised attachment

This form of insecure attachment is usually developed in conjunction with abuse and trauma, the caregiver themselves is often a source of fear. This might be due to factors such as: drugs, alcohol, domestic abuse, depression or sexual, emotional, or physical abuse. The caregivers' responses and behaviours are unpredictable and frightening and often harm the child, emotionally, psychically or sexually. As a result, the child is unable to adapt or develop a strategy to best stay safe. This leaves them in a high state of stress and means they are constantly working from a place of survival, always trying to figure out how best to cope. A child with disorganised attachment is unable to seek comfort from their caregiver and is unable to trust them, this is difficult when the very person who is supposed to protect you, is the one hurting you. The child fears the erratic, unpredictable abusive behaviour, but at the same time, must depend on that very person for survival.

The carer might:

- Harm the child emotionally or physically
- Be erratic and unpredictable with their behaviours and responses.
- Invite unsafe people into the child's life
- Display contradictory behaviours such as being kind one moment and abusive the next
- Be intoxicated and helpless
- Be unkind, mock and shame the child

Disorganised attachment is usually a result of the carer themselves struggling with unresolved trauma which impacts their ability to be fully attuned, sensitive secure parents to their children.

Important note: It is important to note that although there are three styles of insecure attachment, they are not this clearly defined in a real relationship. Caregivers may display behaviours that are both disorganised and avoidant for example, or a child may have two caregivers who have different attachment styles.

Insecure attachment can also develop on a much lower level. A caregiver who is constantly on their phone, avoiding eye contact and interactions with their child might trigger an ambivalent or avoidant parenting style with their child. A parent who is overly critical and pushes their child in to things they might not want to do, like sport or high academic outcomes, may develop low level insecure attachment styles in their relationship. It doesn't always have to be rooted in trauma.

How does this impact the child?

Attachment is a complex, multifaceted construction that can be difficult to unpick and understand – especially when you are presented with the outside of a person or child and cannot see their inner workings. Yet, the impact of our attachment experiences wires our brains, informing our beliefs and our thought process and responses. Attachment impacts every single one of us in some way shape or form because we have all been influenced by the relationships in our childhoods. You might recognise that you struggle to trust people because your dad left and you fear abandonment, or that you struggle with intimacy because your mum didn't hug you much as a child, or that you find it hard to use your voice because you were not listened to. Whether you grew up with trauma and adversity or not, there are aspects of your early life that still inform your behaviours today. This is a normal part of our development but one that plays a key role in our future relationships and sense of self.

The same is true for every child in your class, especially those who are struggling.

What behaviours might you see in school?

In reality, the list is endless and although I will list some things here, it is important to remember that the behaviour is just the outward symptom that you see and that the most important thing for you to consider is the inner thoughts and belief system of the child. That is where the real understanding comes from. That said, this will be helpful, and you might find yourself linking some of the behaviours you see in your class to this list (remember though, it is not black and white or clear cut, remember also that these behaviours could be signs of other things too):

- Angry outbursts
- Struggling to control emotions
- Struggling to navigate social interactions
- Struggling to recognise their effect on others
- Struggling to connect to teacher and peers positively
- Sabotaging nice events, trips or treats
- Struggling to follow the rules, sit still or listen
- Often in trouble and sent out
- Lots of low-level disruptions and behaviours
- Does not display empathy for other children or understand their feelings
- Struggles to concentrate
- Doesn't 'try' with work or seem to want to learn
- Struggles with transition and changes in the day (big and small)
- Can't explain their actions or reasons for their actions
- Lacks self-awareness
- Has very little sense of self
- Is superficially charming
- Is overly affectionate with strangers
- Is overly demanding or clingy
- Constantly questions/continuous talking
- Lack of cause/effect thinking
- Pseudo maturity
- Abnormal eating patterns
- Struggling with peer relationships
- Poor impulse control
- Avoiding eye contact
- Telling lies and/or stealing
- Low self-esteem
- Struggling with shame
- Doesn't respond to behaviour management strategies
- Controlling behaviours
- Being compliant to get their own needs met
- People pleasing

Children show us they are struggling through their behaviour, and the reasons for that behaviour are often complex, however I hope this list helps.

Here are some ways this might show up in school for a child:

Secure attachment:
  Can work independently and with others
  Can concentrate on tasks
  Has good social skills and high levels of self-esteem
  Can cope with difficulties that they might encounter at school
  Tries new things even if they are challenging
Avoidant attachment:
  Does not like the teacher to get to close
  Want to do tasks alone, even when they don't know what to do
  Finds it hard when they don't know the answers
  Struggles to discuss a problem
  Struggles with group work
  Rips up their work, saying it's rubbish, before a teacher can comment on it.
Ambivalent attachment:
  Needs constant reassurance
  Struggles to work alone
  Is overly dependent on the teacher
  Struggles to focus on work for fear of losing the attention of the teacher
  Struggles to work in groups and hear different opinions
  Can be controlling
  Can be dependent
Disorganised attachment:
  Displays aggressive behaviour towards the teacher and children in the class
  May hurt themselves when distressed – banding head on wall or scratching/picking skin
  Controlling of relationships with others
  Struggles to trust the teacher
  Struggles to follow the rules
  Needs to be in control

Living with insecure attachment changes the brain and wires children to survive, some children spend so much energy and time trying to stay safe and manage the relationship with their caregiver, that they have very little time to play. Their brain also spends very little time developing that rational thinking part of the brain, the prefrontal cortex, and this can negatively impact their ability to understand, process and manage their emotions and reactions. The survival part of the brain is often on hight alert, as child tries to adapt to find ways to manage and cope, they are also frequently responding with their survival, fight flight and freeze responses. As a result, children will often develop coping strategies that work within the relationship, but do not work outside of it. For example, it makes complete sense for a child to avoid eye contact and emotional closeness with an abusive parent (flight mode) because it helps keep them safe and reduces their likelihood of being harmed. However, it becomes difficult in later life when as an adult, they cannot make eye contact or allow emotional closeness with their partners. It becomes even more of a problem when they begin to push partners away when they get too close, for fear of being emotionally vulnerable and then being rejected themselves.

Children who have experienced an insecure attachment in their early life can be impacted long term, often right the way to adulthood. Everything they know about love and relationships, themselves and others is informed by the early relationships in their lives, and it forms something called their internal working model. However, that said, it is important to know that through things like self-development, therapy and learning we can become aware of our insecure attachment styles and still go on to form happy secure attachments with people in our futures.

 Real life

When I was growing up, I learnt very quickly that my Mum and Dad couldn't be trusted. I knew that no matter how much I loved them (and deep down how much they loved me) I would need to rely on myself. I learnt that my dad couldn't protect and look after mum, even if he might have wanted to, and so somewhere deep inside me, I developed a belief system that I couldn't trust men and they couldn't protect me. Now, all these years later, I have a healthy, happy marriage but I still have a deep-rooted instinct within me that tells me I have to look after myself. As a result, I ensure I earn my own money and provide for myself, and I have to be in control of everything as much as possible. This comes from that early wiring, keeping me in control so I don't have to depend on anyone . . . just in case.

Internal working model

Understanding attachment in childhood is essential for anyone working with children, because it informs who they become and how they show up in the world (and at school!). Bowlby (1969) believed that our experiences of attachment in childhood develop something called our internal working model. This means that as a child experiences the relationships around them, their brain begins to internalise what they have learnt to create a sort of blueprint or picture of themselves and others. They begin to develop a sense of what is likely to happen if they behave in a certain way so they can predict the actions of those around them, which helps guide their own behaviour, beliefs and expectations. Children then use this to help guide them in the future, a bit like an inner road map.

This helps inform:

- Their sense of self
- Sense of others
- Expectations of relationships and how others are likely to react

Unfortunately, this means that for those children with insecure attachment, their predictions and beliefs are based on difficult or harmful relationships that may not be a true representation of other relationships they could develop with people. Their blueprint is faulty, and children begin to believe things like: they are unlovable and unworthy or that people will harm and hurt them. They might have intrusive thoughts that tell them, 'I am not good enough,' 'I am not valued,' 'people will harm me,' 'people will leave me,' 'I am not safe,' 'I can't trust anyone.' This then sabotages the relationships they could develop with others. In contrast, a securely attached child who may have internalised things like, 'I am lovable,' 'adults can take care of me,' 'I am safe' and 'I can trust those around me' will be more likely to develop happy, healthy connections.

A child who experiences unconditional love will know what love is and will be able to love others. A child who experiences a love that is conditional or who is harmed or rejected may not. How can you love if you have never been loved? How can you have empathy for others if nobody ever had empathy for you? Feeling emotionally safe, loved, and protected as a child has a direct impact on how you see the world, yourself and the people around you and this programming will follow you throughout your life. It is so important to recognise the significance of this on our children. Our brains are designed to help us survive, if they are programmed to believe that relationships are dangerous and that they often end in loss or pain – they will do everything they can to stay safe and avoid that perceived danger, these beliefs will be applied to every aspect of their lives– including in school.

> **Important note:** It is important to say here that an experience of insecure attachment doesn't have to be long, for it to have a lasting impact. A baby can be born into an abusive family and then be removed at a few days old, but can still show signs of insecure attachment style behaviour when they are five, eight and twelve, I have seen this repeatedly in my work. My company, TPC, supports many families who are struggling and some of these included adoptive families. Adopted children might be referred to us for therapy because they are displaying dysregulated behaviours. Adoptive parents might report things like aggression, running away, 'melt downs' and refusing to follow instructions. Some will be struggling with bedwetting, not eating and self-harm. Others will be shut down and push people away. Many of these children were adopted at birth or at very young ages, others may have been in the care system for a short time before being adopted. Although they are placed with safe, caring families, the impact of those very early experiences have wired their brains for survival and despite their external environment changing, their brains are still responding with a trauma/insecure attachment response. This is also true for some children in school, you might see their external behaviour and forget that it could be related to a traumatic experience or insecure attachment that happened years prior. I have had countless discussions with school staff who tell me the child they are struggling with in year 6 has had no triggers or trauma, but after some questioning, they mention that the children's parent separated when they were in year one. Our stories and experience make up who we

are and our bodies and brains remember our experiences, even if we don't!

It is often very easy to miss this in day-to-day life, especially when we focus our attention on the outward behaviour. We can miss what is going on internally and those feelings, belief systems and perceptions that are deep rooted and linked to our early life experiences.

Remember, although we are talking about trauma and adversity here, don't forget that insecure attachment isn't always developed from complex trauma. Insecure attachment styles can develop in any relationship at lower levels and will still inform our beliefs and thoughts. You could have a parent with very firm boundaries or parenting styles, so you become fearful of letting people down or doing the wrong thing. You may have a parent who doesn't cuddle much, or one who is overly protective. Insecure attachment can also develop due to lack of input from parents, maybe because they are too busy with work, or have a large family where it is hard for the child to find their place. Parents might be separated or be living with extended family where there are different rules and boundaries with multiple adults. In truth, many of us will have experienced some level of insecure attachment in our lives which makes the teaching in this book more relevant, at some level, we should all be able to resonate with this. It is not just about those children with trauma – although those children's needs must be always considered!

You are not doing it all wrong

If you are reading this as a parent and are suddenly finding yourself panicking that you are creating an insecure attachment style with your child, or you are worried you are traumatising them because you tell them off, please do not worry! Whenever I teach this, there are always people in the room worrying that they have traumatised their child! But don't forget that the connections we create with our children are part of the parent – child dynamic and we are all going to have tough days! We are all going to get frustrated, shout, tell children off and say things we don't mean. We are human and we all have emotions. The roller-coaster of ups and downs in parenting is normal and your child knows you love them and that you are there for them, that is what matters. That re-building and reconnection is what makes the difference here. Take some deep breaths and know you are doing okay! Parenting is tough, be kind to yourself!

Insecure attachment at school

School is a difficult place to go if you struggle with insecure attachment. It is a place filled with structures that constantly challenge and trigger children throughout the day, increasing their feeling of stress and keeping their survival part of the brain on. As a result, they spend much of their day in survival mode trying to find ways to cope. There is very little opportunity for them to feel calm and safe enough to access their rational thinking part of the brain (which they really need to be able to learn!)

School itself

Some of the very basic structures of the school system can be a real challenge for these children. The demands of school are in direct conflict with the needs of a child with insecure attachment. School is asking the child to allow adults to lead and have authority over them. It sets rules and expectations that the child must follow and puts conditions on their behaviour. School itself is full of children in large groups, expected to confirm to the social norms of what school demands of them each day and to share the attention of the staff around them. The insecure child, however, is constantly battling their survival instincts, and is triggered by authority, rules, sharing attention with others and conditional relationships, and yet they are expected to engage in this environment and academically and socially perform. In truth, we are often setting the child up to fail.

Rules and authority

School requires a child to be able to follow rules and authority whist the child has an innate need to keep control and power to ensure others don't harm them. They cannot trust adults can keep them safe and so they struggle to allow adults to be in control. This is reflected in their behaviour in both small and big ways in school. For example, not being able to sit down on the carpet like the adult asks or refusing to go into the classroom at all.

Relationships and working together

School requires children to work together, listen, collaborate, sit in close proximity, play on the playground and share their space with others throughout the day. It requires them to build a relationship with peers, teachers and staff. All of which is very difficult and often scary for a child with insecure attachment. They might want friends but push them away when they get to close, for fear of being hurt. They might like the teacher, but sabotage the relationship for fear of being rejected or not loved. They might want to play a game but are triggered by the feeling of being left out and so lash out. School also demands a constant change of relationships as they move from teacher to teacher each year, perpetuating the child's fear of abandonment and rejection.

> What is the point of making a close relationship with Mrs Smith when she is going to leave me at the end of the year? It is much easier to stay disconnected to make it easier when I leave her class.

Conditional exchanges

The conventional school system expects that children will 'perform' and meet expectations. It tests, monitors and grades children on their ability, behaviour and personality. This ingrained culture of the school system is like torture for children with insecure attachment and trauma, as it reinforces their core beliefs and perceptions of the world: 'I am not good enough,' 'I am a failure,' 'I am unlovable,' and 'adults with control harm me,' 'adults cannot be trusted with the power,' 'adults believe I am bad.'

Imagine living with parents who only fed you when you were quiet and 'good' or who seemed to care for you more when you were easy and cute. This is a conditional relationship. If they are good, they are fed. If they are quiet, they are not harmed. If they are cute, they might get noticed. Internally they have come to believe that adults will only accept and love them when they are a certain version of themselves. Their true, authentic self is not lovable, wanted, or worthy. When you are constantly having to please the adults around you to get your needs met, you can begin to refuse to engage all together, getting pulled into a power struggle instead.

I see so many children hold on to as much power and control as they can at school because they don't have that control outside in their day to day lives. School is filled with adults expecting them to listen and follow their rules, meet their expectations, and perform for them, and this can be overwhelming and create an internal sense of feeling emotionally unsafe and anxious. Common school norms like stickers, reward charts, behaviour charts and phrases like, 'If you do this piece of work you can go on the iPad' or 'If you behave this week you can come on the trip' trigger children to recall that conditional dynamic and they respond with a survival response. Being valued for performance and meeting expectations can be very hard when you have learnt not to let adults have control. It is also hard when your core belief is 'I am not good enough' or 'I am not lovable' because many children believe they will inevitably fail, disappoint, and let down adults and it is much easier to opt out of learning than it is to try but fail because that reinforces a very painful core belief.

Work

The school system expects children to challenge themselves, overcome failures and have the resilience to try again. It expects children to be open to learning new information and being taught by the adults around them. However, when you have spent years living in a state of stress, constantly scanning the environment for the next sign of danger it is impossible to access the part of the brain that is required for learning, problem solving and memory. Children are working from a place of survival not the rational part of the brain and therefore learning itself is a challenge. Another factor to consider is the act of completing work that is hard or challenging. When children spend most of their time trying to predict what will happen next, it can be very unsettling to be in an environment where you don't know things. Having gaps in your knowledge, not knowing the answers, and not knowing what will happen next can all make a child feel very unsettled and anxious indeed. Why would they put themselves in that situation? It is the opposite of keeping safe.

It can also feel overwhelming to be at the mercy of the school day and to feel constantly challenged and expected to learn and adapt. Not only does this mirror the trauma you have experienced, but it also feeds into the core belief that you will fail. When your life is full of challenges and difficulties, the last thing children need is more challenge and difficulty. That is often why children opt out completely of learning, because it is too much to have to battle something else. Pair that with lack of sleep, food and increased stress and it is literally impossible.

The school system also expects children to be able to ask for help from the adults around them. This is extremely tricky for a child who doesn't trust others. If the core belief is that adults don't care, adults can't help and adults can't meet their needs. If their experience tells them that needing help equals rejection or pain, then why would they raise their hand to let you know they are struggling? It is much easier to ask to go to the toilet five times or distract their peers or not to try at all (flight mode).

Group work and team work

The school system expects children to be able to work as a group or team in a variety of scenarios. It might be whilst working with others around a table on a science project or on the football pitch in the playground. It might be during a PE lesson or whilst sat around the dinner table. For children with insecure attachment, working in a group can be very difficult. Listening to others, working as a team, sharing and turn taking, listening to opposite opinions and knowing how to navigate when to talk/lead/listen, can all be overwhelming and demands you to be using your rational, thinking brain. Not only are they unable to access this part of their brain, but often, a child's internal driving belief is that people don't like them, they are not worthy and they are not valuable. Their life experiences have taught them that people will reject them, so being part of a group comes with the expectation that they will be left out, not listened to, or rejected in some way.

They may also have a core belief that when they are with other children, there is more risk of being harmed, ignored or abandoned. Imagine being a child in a large family, having to compete for the attention of your caregiver to get your needs met. Struggling to figure out ways to stand out from the other children, so that you can stay safe. For some children, this can be the difference between having some level of love and having none at all. For others, it can be the difference between feeling heard and seen or being fed or left hungry. Being part of a group can create high anxiety levels in a child, where their survival responses are triggered and you may see them display behaviours such as shouting out, arguing, being silly or even having all the answers and becoming the leader. These are often survival mechanisms to help them cope with the fear of being abandoned or 'lost' in the group. Teachers will often describe it as 'attention seeking' behaviours but in fact, it is a child who is trying to manage some really big feelings and who needs to be 'seen' by the adults for fear of being forgotten.

These are just a few of the many difficulties children with both trauma and insecure attachment may face in a school setting. However, although we can't change some of these things, we can adapt things to become more attachment aware and that starts with looking at conventional behaviour management strategies, which we are going to do together in the next chapter. We will then move on to look at how we can support children through our responses and behaviour policies a bit later in the book.

References

Ainsworth, M.D.S., Blehar, M.C., Waters, E., and Wall, S. (2015). *Patterns of Attachment: A Psychological Study of the Strange Situation.* Psychology Press and Routledge Classic Editions.

Bowlby, J. (1969) *Attachment. Attachment and Loss: Vol. 1. Loss.* New York: Basic Books.

Bowlby, J. (1982) 'Attachment and loss: Retrospect and prospect.' *Am J Orthopsychiatry,* 52(4), 664–678.

6

Re-defining Behaviour Management

The most crucial and significant aspect of the school culture that we need to consider here is how we approach children's behaviour. Given everything, we have learnt this far in the book, it is essential we begin to redefine 'bad behaviour' and the systems and procedures we follow.

To recap, we now know that:

1. All children go into survival mode wherever they feel stressed, emotionally unsafe, threatened or attacked. This is a developmentally appropriate response. Those with trauma and insecure attachment will do so more frequently, often numerous times in a day.
2. Feeling 'threatened and attacked' at school could be anything that is emotionally challenging or stressful, such as not being able to score a goal, a loud dinner hall or struggling with maths work.
3. Children will automatically respond with fight, flight or freeze behaviours such as lashing out, running away or shutting down in order to help them cope with the situation and stay safe.
4. When in survival mode, children will not be able to control their emotional responses or behaviour and will struggle to listen, follow instructions or think rationally, they will struggle to reflect and have empathy for others, and memory and recall will be affected. The rational thinking part of the brain will be shut down.
5. Children need support and guidance to calm down, regulate and feel emotionally safe, for them to be able to access the part of the brain that helps them problem solve and use tools to manage the situation (their rational thinking responses).
6. The more we help guide children to calm down and access the rational thinking part of their brain, the more they will begin to learn to self-regulate and manage their own emotions and behaviour in the future, thus developing self-awareness and emotional intelligence.

DOI: 10.4324/9781003410652-7

So, to help children learn and access the rational thinking parts of the brain, we must help them reduce their perceived sense of threat, fear and attack around them and increase their feelings of safety, both physically and emotionally. The more we focus on helping a child calm down their emotional, survival brain, reduce stress and help them manage their emotional states (and in turn their mental health) the more likely it is that they will learn. Now, when I say learn. I mean both academically and developmentally. Yes, they will be able to access the part of the brain that helps them engage and learn in the classroom. But more importantly than that, they will be learning about their emotional responses and behaviour and begin to develop the skills needed to manage them.

> As we move through the next chapters in this book, we are going to keep stopping and questioning the norm. Reflecting on current practices that are in place because of a generational culture, and asking ourselves whether this is the best we can do for our children and whether it is reflective of their needs and society today. If not, we are going to be brave enough to reject the cultural norm and instead, re-define what it means to be a teacher and what is means to be a school!

Behaviour management

Let's start by looking at 'behaviour management' in more detail and wind the clock back a little bit. Behaviour management has been a focus in schools since the beginning of the school system itself. From the cane to detention, society has always tried to find ways to 'manage' difficult behaviour. It is easy to see how this has developed with schools being expected to teach so many children at once. Age is also a factor, and since children are still developing, it is inevitable that there are going to be challenges with behaviour. However, one of the most important things we can do collectively, is to stop and ask ourselves two things:

1. Why are we telling children off in the first place?
2. Do our methods work or are they outdated?

This is a very important question we need to ask ourselves, because the answer impacts our responses, policies, procedures and culture. Stop for a moment and ask yourself why you tell children off? What are you trying to do?

Usually, our efforts to 'tell a child off' are coming from a good place, we have the intention to help a child learn from the situation they are in, make amends or do better next time, we might also be trying to keep them safe. However, if we are brave enough to look closely at our common responses, we might see that they are stopping us from being able to achieve those goals and instead focus on rejection and punishment. Similarly, when a child's behaviour is challenging, or there are several children struggling repetitively, if we are honest with ourselves, sometimes our intention becomes more about just stopping the behaviour which is not necessarily helping the child.

If we look back at historical behaviour management methods, we see things like:

- The cane
- The dunce cap
- Writing lines
- Sanctions
- Facing the wall
- Being told off or 'shouted at'

More recently we do things like:

- Time out
- Sending them out
- Sanctions
- Detention
- Exclusion
- Telling them off
- Taking things away

When we respond to children's behaviour, we communicate a set of intentions, and we are teaching them something. As adults, every interaction and response communicates something to the child and they learn from this. It is therefore important to reflect on these lists and ask ourselves *what* we are teaching children here, because, we are *always* teaching. If we look at these two lists, not much has changed. Although times have moved on and we are no longer physically hitting children to stop them from misbehaving, the root of the behaviour management method is the same. It is rooted in disconnection and punishment. Unfortunately, when we resort to methods rooted in rejection, punishment and disconnection, children are being taught:

1. Their struggle to self-regulate, understand their feelings, manage their feelings and feel safe is not your focus or concern

Our focus is on their behaviour and not on them and their inner state, which silently communicates that their feelings don't matter to us.

2. They are 'choosing' to misbehave, rather than learning it is a developmental stage

By not rooting our responses in neuroscience, we wrongly teach children that they have control over their emotions and should be able to 'stop misbehaving.' Communicating that their behaviour is a cognitive rational choice, rather than a survival response.

3. That your relationship with them is conditional

Telling children off, sending them away and asking them to sit in a corner with a timer, models a relationship that is conditional. 'I will accept you and care for you when you are 'good' and reject you when you are 'bad' and 'in order to receive my love, you must be a certain version of yourself.' This is very damaging to children with insecure attachment, but is also difficult for all children.

4. That they need to figure it out for themselves

When we fail to help a child through whatever difficulty they are facing, we fail to recognise the science and acknowledge that children need a caring adult to help them calm down before they can learn to do this for themselves. They must have a period of co-regulation with a safe adult, before they can self-regulate, sending them away to 'calm down' doesn't give them any tools or strategies and often resorts in them escalating the behaviour to the point that they burn out (we will talk more about regulation later in the book).

Real life

Let's look at how this might play out in real life. Eesa is outside playing football with a group of friends – he is annoyed that he hasn't been picked to be in goal and begins shouting and pushing others. You go over and say, 'Eesa, stop pushing Adam! Go inside and calm down!' Eesa becomes angrier and storms inside, pushes chairs over and refuses to listen to anyone. His behaviour escalates and he ends up in the Head's office.

Behind the behaviour: Eesa feels rejected, left out and devalued when he isn't picked to go in goal, that is where he feels his strength is and he wanted to contribute to the team and help them win. Eesa isn't aware of these feelings but knows he is getting angry. He doesn't know how to manage the feelings and his survival brain kicks in, so he pushes Adam and shouts at the other boys. When the teacher comes over, she focuses on his behaviour rather than helping him make sense of what is going on, she sends him away and he feels further rejection and now feels attacked from all sides. He gets angrier and responds with fight mode, pushing over tables. He doesn't know how to calm down and feels overwhelmed. All the adults talk *at* him about what he could do better and ask questions about why he got so angry. Eesa doesn't know why he got so angry, other than the fact that the boys didn't let him in goal. Their questions feel like further attack. The only thing he can do is continue responding with fight mode until he burns out because he isn't sure what else to do. He ends up shouting and being angry for 25 minutes until he loses steam and sits on the Head Teacher's floor with his head in his hands.

5. To feel guilty or shameful for having big feelings rather than learning to manage them

When we punish a child for struggling, we silently communicate that they are 'bad.' For many children this develops feelings of guilt, for a great many more children this communicates a feeling of shame, again communicating the problem is with them.

The difference between shame and guilt

Sometimes when we tell children off, we want them to feel guilty for what they have done and hope that this teaches them to not do it again. This method can be damaging for children, especially those struggling with insecure attachment, prolonged stress and trauma because they do not feel guilty, they instead feel shame. When we feel guilty, we feel bad about our actions and behaviours but this is not rooted in who we are, but instead what we have *done*. We can separate our sense of worth from our mistakes. When we feel shame, it is linked to deep feeling of not being good enough, we are not feeling bad about what we have done, we feel bad about who we *are*. For children who have struggled with insecure attachment, the rejection of their behaviour is internalised as rejection of them, it is more proof of them being 'bad' which is damaging to their sense of self and perpetuates trauma cycles.

So many of our common behaviour approaches will trigger children's insecure attachment or trigger a survival response in children. It is therefore important that we consider what isn't working so that we can meet all children's needs in an inclusive, effective way.

The problem with conventional behaviour management strategies

We now know that in any class, many children will have developed insecure attachment in varying degrees and many will be struggling with adversity and trauma in their lives. There will also be children who are struggling to understand and manage their feelings. You might notice that Chen rips up his work before you can see it, or Jasmine wants to control everyone around her. You might wonder why Joseph sabotages good things or why Sira pushes you away when you get to close. Why do children do these things? Simply put, they have developed ways to keep themselves emotionally safe, but often, these coping mechanisms don't fit into the conventional school system. When children 'misbehave' or are struggling, conventional behaviour management responses can actually make things worse not better. Let's look at why conventional behaviour management strategies are not trauma-informed or attachment-aware, but, as we move through this chapter, remember that these methods will also unsettle *all* children not just the most vulnerable.

Let's look at what doesn't work and why:

Putting names on the board

The problem: This is a behaviour management strategy that is underpinned by guilt or shame

This method picks out children and puts a tick by their name each time they do something wrong. Usually, the child is then given some form of consequence when a certain number of ticks are reached, for example four ticks equals four chances. When they get to tick four they might lose breaktime or be sent to the Head Teacher.

This approach will unsettle most children but is particularly difficult for children with insecure attachment. It is a guaranteed way to pull them into insecure attachment coping behaviours. For them, this technique does not elicit a feeling of guilt and 'make' them what to behave. Instead, it triggers the survival response, and it perpetuates feelings of shame. Putting their name on the board singles them out and sends a message that says, 'You are bad and I want everyone to know it, so your name is going to be displayed for them to see.' This causes them to feel emotionally unsafe and vulnerable, which will remind them of times when they felt unsafe in the past, triggering a series of responses designed to help them feel safe again or to gain some control. This common behaviour management strategy can trigger children's internal belief systems, reinforcing beliefs like, 'I am not good enough,' 'He doesn't like me,' 'I am bad,' 'I am not worthy.'

Seeing their name on the board triggers a stress response and a sense of being overwhelmed and it is very likely that they will then escalate their behaviour, suddenly becoming more disruptive. This is common for children with insecure attachment because you have pulled them into a power struggle. Remember, these children have experienced some difficult things in their lives, some might have witnessed domestic abuse or experienced abuse, some may have experiences of adults who harm them, or struggle to respond to their needs, others might not have a present parent. The child has an internal belief that they cannot trust adults to look after them or keep them safe, so must do that for themselves. When you take their power away, there is an overwhelming need for them to take it back. If they know that when you put five ticks by their name, they are sent out of the room, then they will take as much control over that as they can. They already anticipate that you will be sending them out. You have shown them that you believe they will fail, just by putting their name up there. So, there is no point trying to 'be good,' they are no longer working from their rational thinking part of the brain, they are now responding with their emotional brain and survival responses. The only way they can take control is to get to tick five before you do. So, their behaviour gets worse, they refuse to engage. They will do anything to get to tick number five, because if they have control over it then it won't hurt as much when you tell them they have failed. The faster they get there, the faster they can relax and reduce the anxiety.

It is important to note here that this behaviour management strategy will unsettle any child, even those who are generally well behaved. If you put their name on the board for talking for example, this is still likely to trigger a sense of embarrassment, shame or guilt which could trigger negative self-talk or anxiety. Remember, even if the strategy 'works' and they stop talking, it doesn't mean they are not now struggling internally.

Rewards

The problem: Rewards are conditional

Rewards are often conditional, and that can be hard for children with insecure attachment, especially if rewards are used as a bartering tool: 'If you are good, you can have golden time on Friday.' 'If you do this, you can have this.' Things like stickers, treats, reward charts and working toward a reward can all trigger insecure attachment responses. The children interpret this as another situation where they will fail or be disappointed, especially if the reward is delayed. Having to 'behave' for a period of time, before they can get something good can cause overwhelming feelings of anxiety. They don't believe they can get to the reward and they often believe they have failed before they began. Even if they try, you will probably take it away from them. So, what is the point in trying? This is so overwhelming that they end up self-sabotaging so that they have control. Remember, these children may have had repeatedly tried to please care-givers in the past and never won. They were always left vulnerable and hurt, so they have learnt to protect themselves by not allowing adults that control anymore. It is much safer to not look forward to good things, to expect good things to be taken away and to sabotage them before someone else does. Unfortunately, with the best of intentions, you have trapped them, and they have no choice now but to ruin it for themselves.

Using rewards to try to help children stay on-task can also trigger survival responses. You might devise a timetable where a child does a short blast of work and then is rewarded with 'choosing time" before they are asked to do more work, maybe they get to play on the iPad or play a game. This method might be effective for a short time, because, initially children want the reward. But as soon as they have an emotional need, they cannot sustain it, so it stops working. This method expects children to be able to make the choice to behave well – which they can do if they are feeling calm and happy. They cannot do this when their survival brain takes over and they are struggling with their feelings, as a result this method almost sets them up to fail. Timetables or reward charts activate a child's insecure attachment response because, again, you are not focused on their emotional need and trying to help them to manage their difficult feelings, instead you are focused on their behaviour and the intention is to get them to do what you want. You are not emotionally attuned to their needs, and this reinforces their insecure attachment experienced with others. As a result, they may interpret the reward chart as a means of control. You are trying to find a way to 'make' them do what you want, this could be experienced as manipulation or trickery, they have experienced unattuned adults before and it often resulted in pain or hurt. So, they respond by finding ways to stay in control or emotionally safe. They might refuse to use the timetable or use it to their advantage when they want something, or they may not seem interested in the rewards at all. It is important to note that these responses are not conscious and deliberate, but instead are triggered by the brain who recognises the emotional threat and responds in the best way to protect the child from further emotional harm.

> **Important note:** My work is focused on children with social, emotional, and mental health needs. Reward charts may work effectively with children with special needs who respond well to small, bitesize activities and need brain breaks between lessons. If you have a child with special needs and a specialist has advised a visual time table, this is likely to help! However, for a child with high levels of stress, ACES or insecure attachment or any other emotional need, I would advise against it.

Using rewards for children in general can also be counterproductive, causing a 'good' vs 'bad' culture amongst the children. If they get a sticker then their work was good, if they don't it must have been bad or not good enough. Children can then begin to believe things like: if 'someone else is chosen for a sticker, that must mean my work (or I) am not good enough or as good as that person'. This can begin to erode self-esteem and confidence without us realising even in the most competent of children. It can leave children worrying about their performance, comparing themselves to others and leaving school disappointed, which overshadows the day. Their work might have been really good and they might have worked very hard, but the external gratification becomes more important than their personal achievement. This reinforcement of a compare culture is something I would love to see eradicated from school, especially when it is so ingrained in things outside of school like on social media. We will talk more about this compare culture in our behaviour policy chapter.

Sending children out/away

The problem: This approach is rooted in rejection

This approach has been a staple behaviour management tool in schools for years. When I was at school, children had to stand and face the wall if they were in trouble. Now, children are sent out, taken to the Head Teacher, put in time-out or put on the 'sad cloud.'

The thing is, when a child is sent out or sent away, what we are doing is rejecting them for having an emotional need. This again, activates their insecure attachment responses or survival response and it doesn't have the effect we want. Every time we push a child into survival mode, we lose an opportunity to teach them. That is why a child will exhibit the same behaviours repeatedly. We are not teaching them anything valuable about their emotions or how to manage them, nor are we helping them feel better – which is what they need in that moment. We are simply reinforcing the internal beliefs that they are bad and confirming that adults don't care and can't keep them safe. Imagine being a young child and feeling scared. You are in a loud room and it feels overwhelming. You grab your parent's hand, give them a hug or snuggle into their chest until you feel safe. You know you can rely on them to help you until you feel better. What happens if that parent pushes you away? Doesn't recognise your need? Tells you to grow up. Or leaves you there alone? That is what we are doing every time we send a child away. We are leaving them with intense feelings and emotions that are overwhelming. We are rejecting them for struggling to manage their feelings. We are teaching them that their emotional state is irrelevant. No child chooses to get so angry that they lash out. No child wants to feel so unsafe that they hide under a table. No child wants to feel so anxious that they cannot concentrate and so they get up and distract others. They need help. When we send a child out, we teach them only that we won't help them.

Praise

The problem: This approach can be rooted in the power dynamic

Now, this might seem like a strange one, but it is another important thing to reflect on when considering our 'normal' approaches. This doesn't mean we shouldn't ever praise children of course, because lots of children thrive of it but we do need to reflect on how some children might struggle with it. When we praise children, we do it with the intention of making a child feel good. You might say things like, 'Well done, I love your colouring' or 'good girl' 'good boy' 'brilliant work' we might offer them a sticker or a certificate, but our efforts to praise can only be effective for those children to have self-belief, confidence, and a positive internal working model. Remember, our internal working model is our inner voice, that belief system that we develop about ourselves and the world based on our experiences. For children with secure attachments, their internal working model is likely to be a fairly positive one. People have made them feel loved and worthy, they have built them and made them feel good. They believe people like them; they believe what people say is true and they have a positive self-concept. When you praise these children, they feel positive about themselves, they may also want to continue to please you and receive your validation. This may not be not the case for children with insecure attachment or ACES, they are likely to have a negative internal working model, their self-talk reflects the way people have treated them, spoken to them or responded to them. It is likely to be negative and focused on not being good enough, not being worthy and not being loved. They do not trust what adults say, because they have so often been let down. They may also find themselves rejecting the need for your validation as a result.

When you praise a child with insecure attachment, it can trigger a few different responses. The first, and most simply, they won't believe you. They may also reject it. You might say, 'good boy' and shortly after you notice their behaviour isn't very good. This is often because they cannot accept your praise, they believe they are bad, they have been told they are bad all their lives in different forms and so your praise may make them feel unsettled or anxious. You have shown some affection and your views of them do not match that of others. Many children believe that sooner or later, adults who are nice to them will stop liking them, let them down or reject them. So, they find themselves sucked into negative behaviour, almost to prove to you and to themselves, that they are not good. They may even find ways to be 'rejected' by you, such as being sent out of a room or given a consequence. When you finally tell them off, they can settle emotionally, because their internal belief has been proven. It is almost like they think, 'They don't really like me, they will reject me like everyone else. I am not good, I can't keep up with being good, when I make a mistake or I am bad they will reject me (they then sabotage and are told off), see! They didn't mean it, they don't really think I am good. They rejected me just like everyone else, I am glad I didn't fall into the trap of trusting them and being vulnerable, they would have let me down like everyone else.' These thoughts are not likely to be conscious and in a child's awareness but rather, subconscious ones that drive them internally.

Praise may also trigger a power dynamic for some children. Some children may believe that when adults are nice to them, they want something. They don't believe that the praise is genuine or a reflection of them and what is good about them. Instead, it is a sign that you (the adult) are in a place of power. You can pass judgement on them for being either good or bad and the praise indicates that they have succumbed to your direction and control. It may also make them feel anxious to be constantly trying to perform to receive validation and praise. This can trigger the survival response in many children, because if they allow you to have the power, they are vulnerable. They therefore become less cooperative and stop doing whatever it was you praised them for, some may do the exact opposite.

 Real life

It is morning assembly and Elliot has just been given the 'star of the week' certificate. He stands up to collect his certificate and the hall give him a clap. Elliot had a positive start to the week and although he sometimes struggles with his behaviour, his teacher wanted to reward his efforts, she also hoped it would help him stay on track for the rest of the week. When they get back into the classroom Elliot seems unsettled, he becomes disruptive and isn't listening to the rules, this escalates and by break time, Elliot has been sent in for fighting on the playground. In the staff room, the teachers comment on how much of a shame this is when he just received a certificate that morning.

Behind the behaviour: Elliot is in assembly and his name is called for the 'star of the week' certificate. Elliot is happy for a moment, but he suddenly also feels anxious and his heart beats really quickly. Mrs Bell has chosen him? why? He hasn't been much of a star. His mum has been shouting at him all week and he was in trouble on Monday. He is always in trouble. His mum is always saying he is naughty. Elliot collects the award, but he is feeling emotionally unsafe, he doesn't deserve this award and he feels unsettled. Elliot isn't aware of it but deep down he is worried about letting Mrs Bell down, she thinks he is good, but he knows he isn't. How is he going to keep being good when he always let's people down? Elliot feels overwhelmed and stressed and his survival response is activated. He goes into fight mode and without being cognitively aware he begins to sabotage. He knows he will let Mrs Bell down, he knows he doesn't deserve this award, she will probably take it off him or regret giving it to him and there is no way he can keep being good for her. Before he knows it, he is fighting on the playground and is sent inside. That afternoon Mrs Bells says, 'It is very disappointing Elliot, especially after you got the certificate this morning.' Elliot feels intense shame, he knew this would happen but he also feels relief that it is over.

Shouting/showing anger

The problem: This approach is rooted in disconnection and rejection

Now, the truth is we all get frustrated with children from time to time, it can be emotionally draining to care for 30 children in a classroom every day and it is only human for you to become tired and frustrated. However, we do need to look at the impact shouting and anger can have on a child in order to truly make a difference to the way we approach behaviour and our responses. I have delivered hundreds of CPD sessions with teachers where

I have raised the issue of shouting. I always ask the same question, 'Why do we resort to shouting?' and am often given the following responses:

- To show my authority
- To get them to listen
- To show them I am serious
- To keep them safe
- To scare them a little bit into listening
- Because I am angry by that point too!

These are really honest answers which I always appreciate, and some are very valid! There are occasions where we might shout to get children's attention, for example if they are doing something dangerous or if we need to get someone's attention across a playground. There are also times we kind of 'put on' an angry voice to communicate we are not happy with certain behaviour. Whatever our reasons, it is important to recognise that sometimes, shouting and anger can cause more damage than good and if we are really honest, it might get the better of us!

WHY HAVE YOU BEEN FIGHTING IN THE PLAYGROUND? HOW DO YOU THINK JOHN FEELS NOW? YOU WOULDNT LIKE IT IF HE DID THAT TO YOU! LOOK AT ME WHEN I AM TALKING TO YOU, STAND THERE AND STOP FIDGITING, HOW OLD ARE YOU? YOU ARE YEAR 5 NOW BUT YOU'RE BEHAVING LIKE A RECEPTION CHILD, MAYBE YOU NEED TO GO BACK TO RECEPTION FOR THE AFTERNOON . . .

We have all been here at some point right? We have all heard this teacher or been this teacher at some point and said something along these lines to a child. Why? Probably because this is what was said to us, but we must ask ourselves whether this response gives us the outcome we want for our children?

Remember, when a child is 'misbehaving' they are struggling with an emotion or a feeling that they are unsure how to manage. When we respond with anger, raise our voices, or shout we can trigger survival responses and coping mechanisms which have a variety of effects (even if we are 'putting it on' as part of our teacher responses).

As soon as we raise our voice and show anger, we are creating disconnection between us and the child. Imagine there is an invisible string between you and the children you are caring for, you are responsible for their physical and emotional safety and are the person they go to if they have any sort of need, including an emotional one. Within a day you might talk to them, read to them, hold their hand in the playground, help them with their work, make sure they have had their dinner and so on. For the time you are with them, you are adopting a parent role (this is regardless of the age of the child.) As soon as you raise your voice and shout at a child or respond to their behaviour with anger, you cut that invisible string and you disconnect. The child is displaying an emotional need and is struggling but instead of helping, they experience you as angry and telling them off. This is difficult for any child when they are distressed or upset as it stops them feeling emotionally safe, but it is especially difficult for children with insecure attachment or ACES, because your response is replicating previous relationships they have had with adults where the relationship felt insecure. It reinforces their belief that when they are struggling, adults won't or can't help. Or, that when they are struggling, they are told they are bad. This makes it harder for them to be able to trust you, feel safe with you and to be their true authentic selves without conditions. Ultimately, they are only accepted when they are a certain version of themselves, if they cannot sustain that version, they are rejected. This doesn't just impact them in that moment, but their perception of the whole relationship and therefore their sense of emotional safety in it.

Shutting down the brain

Shouting and becoming angry will also cause children to feel attacked and threatened, this will activate their survival response and shut down their rational thinking part of the brain. They will then be unable to manage their emotions, reflect, reason, have empathy and problem solve. These are often the very skills we are demanding of them when we say, 'How do you think that made Jack feel?' or 'Why did you do that?' 'What happened?' Our angry response, switches off their ability to manage the situation and to learn from it, which is the opposite of what we are trying to achieve. We want them to listen and to stop the behaviour they are displaying, but we are pushing them further into a place of survival and making them feel more and more threatened and attacked. Responding like this will only make it harder for them to calm down and regulate their emotions and is more likely to escalate things.

Modelling

It is really important to remember that you are modelling all of the time. In a child's eyes, we are the experts at life! They believe we have it all together and that whatever we do, is the way it should be done. When we respond to a difficult situation (even if that is their behaviour) with anger or shouting, we are silently communicating that this is an appropriate response to have when things are challenging or hard. In truth, we are responding from a place of survival ourselves and are having an emotional response to the situation, but the child sees this as normal, and therefore will come to learn that it is okay to shout and display anger when they are struggling with something too. This again is the opposite of what we are trying to teach children. We are modelling responses that are fuelled by emotions and survival at the same time as they are experiencing a challenging situation and their responses are fuelled by emotions and survival. Regardless of what we are *saying,* we are *showing* that this is an appropriate response. If it is okay for you to be cross and shout when you are upset, why can't they? Instead, we want to be modelling a secure attachment style response that is calm, emotionally intelligent and rooted in problem solving and empathy, ie. using our rational thinking part of the brain! Remember, we are always teaching.

Here is a table of common behaviour management strategies we might use in schools and a quick reference to how they can be unhelpful.

Time out	Rejection/increase levels of stress and anxiety
Ticks by name/chances/ warnings	Rejection/shame/feeds into negative self-concept/ increases anxiety
Behaviour charts	Power and control dynamic/reinforces a conditional relationship
Sending them away/out	Rejection, power and control dynamic, increases stress levels, increases anxiety, leaves them in a state of dysregulation, increases shame
Shouting/'telling them off'	Rejection, shame, power and control dynamic, triggering, increases stress levels
Bargaining/coaxing	Power and control, conditional relationship
Threats	Power, triggering, increases anxiety and stress
Reward charts	Power and control dynamic, reinforces a conditional relationship

When glancing at this table, we can begin to build up a picture of how our conventional behaviour management methods, do the opposite of what we want. Instead of helping children feel safe and guiding and teaching them to manage their emotions and behaviours, or even encouraging children to 'behave' and 'make better choices,' we instead shut down the part of the brain that allows them to do that and perpetuate survival responses. In many children we may also be triggering their insecure attachment and trauma responses. This is not only damaging for children's development and sense of self, but also for their mental health and coping mechanisms for the future.

Behaviour and mental health

Remember, at the start of this book, when we talked about the issues our children and young people are facing with their mental health? We must recognise here that behaviour and mental health are linked. If a child is struggling with their behaviour, then it is a sign they are struggling with a thought, feeling, experience or belief, all of which stem from a child's brain and will be impacting their wellbeing and mental health on some level. If a child is struggling with their mental health, it is going to show up in their behaviour. The two things are not separate.

Remember this:

All behaviour is linked to a feeling
All feelings are linked to thoughts and beliefs
Our thoughts and beliefs can impact our mental health

For example:
Behaviour: Sam is outside playing football with the other children. He gets angry and kicks Leo in the shin and storms off.
Feeling: Sam was playing football with the other children, he was trying to score a goal because other children had scored and he wanted to show that he could do it too, but nobody would pass him the ball and he began to feel frustrated, left out and unseen, he didn't feel valued in the game and felt rejected.
Thought and belief: Sam began thinking, 'nobody likes me,' 'they don't want me on the team,' 'they don't think I am good enough,' 'I am being left

out!' this linked to his belief system which is rooted in beliefs like, 'I am not worthy,' 'I am unlovable,' 'I am always rejected'

Mental health: The longer Sam has these thoughts and beliefs which are reinforced in his perception of experiences he has, the more likely they will become rooted in his core concept of self. The more he thinks/believes these things, with no adult guidance or input to unpick them and make sense of them, the more that they will begin to affect his mental health long term. This will continue to impact his behaviours in the future. He might begin to struggle with meeting new people or trying new things for fear of being rejected, he might become angry and argumentative easily when someone seems to disagree with him, he might behave in ways that seem to be attention seeking to try to keep people around him or reject/ constantly seek validation from others.

All behaviour is linked to a feeling, all feelings are linked to thoughts and beliefs, all thoughts and beliefs can impact our mental health.

The school system doesn't always make this link

I see many wonderful ways schools are focusing on supporting mental health and wellbeing. They might run meditation clubs, mindfulness lessons, PHSE lessons, have a sensory garden and therapy interventions taking place. These are all fantastic offers to the children, but what I tend to find is that the same school's behaviour policy doesn't align with those efforts. They still have a traffic light system, put ticks by children's names on the board and use rewards and sanctions as a method of behaviour management. This is where we are often going wrong! It is great to have the incentives, lessons and wellbeing offers throughout school, but if you are still practicing punitive based behaviour management strategies, those efforts are not going to have lasting impact on a child. Think about Sam above, he would benefit from meditation lessons and some PHSE lessons, but they will probably be delivered when he is calm and using his rational thinking part of the brain. This is all just concept and will not be something he can apply when he needs it the most, which is in the moment when he feels unheard and not listened to by his friends. He will continue to argue and respond with fight mode, unless we recognise that our most important contribution to his wellbeing and mental health is actually in that moment, through our own responses and guidance. It is with the feelings, thoughts, experiences and beliefs where the real work needs to be done!

Are we contributing to the problem?

We now know that the connection between the emotional and survival parts of the brain are still developing and that all children can feel overwhelmed by their feelings, it is developmentally appropriate for children to be unable to manage them without help. We see this struggle in their behaviour. If they knew how to manage things better, they would, but instead they lead with their feelings.

So, what is the lesson here for us? If they lead with their feelings, so should we!

Yet, the frustrating truth is that although this is all based on science and research. It is not reflected in our standard behaviour policies or responses. Our approaches in school do not consider what is going on internally for the child but instead focuses on the external. We still tell children off, refer to behaviour as 'misbehaving' and we still punish. We focus so much of our attention on the behaviour itself, sending a subconscious message to the child that their behaviour is a choice (we now know it is not) and as a collective society, we fail to focus on the feelings, thoughts or beliefs the child is having which is causing the behaviour in the first place.

If we step back and truly look at the situation, maybe we are contributing to the problem, both at school and also with regard to mental health on the whole. On the surface we acknowledge that children's mental health is declining and that it is a national issue. Yet we continue to punish and reject children when they show us they are struggling through their behaviour. We must remember that as adults, it is our job to guide our children and to teach them. They are always watching us and we should be modelling healthy responses to difficult situations through *our* own behaviour and responses – even if that difficult situation involves them and their behaviour! It is important to consider our contribution to the problem and realise the more *we* ignore children's feelings, the more *they* will. As a society we are indirectly teaching our children and young people to avoid their feelings. We are teaching them that when they struggle with something emotionally stressful that they don't know how to manage, they will be told off or punished. We are not offering any skills or strategies to help them, and we are not offering the nurture and emotional guidance they need. Then we wonder why we have teenagers bottling up their feelings and struggling to share their problems. Often, issues like self-harming, drinking, using drugs or even overusing technology become a means to cope, which makes sense when they feel have nowhere else to turn, and many young people are in a constant state of avoidance. If a child cannot express how they feel in a safe environment with adults who can help, then all they are left with is increasing intrusive thoughts and beliefs, hard feelings and experiences bottled up inside them with no healthy strategies to express them or manage them. We might see a depressed, isolated or angry teenager on the outside, but it is important to ask ourselves whether this is the result of a 5-year-old boy who was not supported with his feelings and given the insight or tools he needed. I recognise fully here that there are many children and young people struggling with a diagnosable mental health issue that will have developed over time because of many factors and I am by no means suggesting that our approach to behaviour is the cause of mental health issues. However, it is important to consider how our approaches to behaviour are contributing to the problem and may perpetuate difficulties. Telling children off when they are struggling is damaging to their sense of self and communicates that they are the problem, and they should be able to do better. These are children trying to cope with tricky emotional situations the best they can, without the strategies and awareness they need to rationally problem solve and regulate and yet we are leading them to believe that the fault is with them. Our social norm is to tell them off or give them consequences and punish which silently communicates to the child that they are to blame. If they cannot manage their feelings, it is their fault. If they cannot 'behave' it is somehow a reflection on them. Yet we as adults are offering no life lessons, support or guidance in the moment when they need it most. This is actually a reflection on us! We are sending children out into the world with the belief that they are the 'naughty' one or the 'bad one' who is always in time out or detention. The one who was always told off and told they were not good enough. This is so damaging for our children when in fact, they were responding in a developmentally appropriate way, many from a place of survival with very little control over their responses. Their responses and behaviour were scientifically expected and yet the child has no awareness of this. This is a tragic failure on our part and something we must begin to change. I am not blaming anyone here, but instead highlighting a national culture that has developed which doesn't meet our children's needs and has become a generational norm. This is ultimately impacting our children's development and mental health long term. It is especially concerning for those children who are also struggling with adversity, stress and trauma in their lives – which, make up a large percentage of the children who are 'misbehaving.'

Children need emotionally attuned adults who recognise difficult behaviour as a sign that they need help and to guide them through whatever it is that is difficult. Remember, an adult modelling secure attachment responds with care and empathy, regardless of what the child has done. The child learns that they can make mistakes without being rejected. Children need our approaches to be rooted in the neuroscience, working *with* their internal responses, not against them. We must begin to respond with connection rather than disconnection.

Connection vs disconnection

To begin to change your approach, you must begin to focus on cultivating connection with children. When we feel connected to someone, we feel heard and seen and we feel safe, connection also calms the brain and helps children access rational thinking. A therapeutic teacher cultivates connection through their day-to-day interactions with children, recognising that the child is often expecting disconnection due to their previous experiences of both relationships and behaviour management strategies. Leading with connection helps to:

- Raise emotional intelligence
- Keep the rational brain on
- Calm down and access our rational brain
- Encourage learning
- Encourage new patterns of behaviour

When we lead with disconnection, we:

- Keep the survival brain on
- Send children into FFF
- Strain the relationship
- Develop mistrust
- Reinforce old patterns of behaviour
- Stop learning

Being brave enough to face cultural norms and question them is difficult but it is the first step to being able to shift from old patterns of behaviour to new ones. It is easy to feel defensive when someone challenges the way you do things but that is often the barrier to change. We like what feels familiar, but that doesn't mean it is right. Pushing past old beliefs, learning new things and striving to truly meet children's needs will make all the difference here, not only in the lives of the children you know but beyond that too! From now on let's lead with connection, both in our thinking and our actions. But where do we start and how do we embed changes as a teacher and as a school? Let's find out . . .

PART 2

The 'How': What You Can Do to Make a Difference

7

The Therapeutic School Approach

How are you feeling? I know sometimes it can all feel a little overwhelming at this point and although you may feel inspired to make a change, you might be wondering how in the world you are going to do it and where to begin! Or maybe you are very familiar with the theory and are already on the journey to becoming more trauma-informed in your school, and you are reading for new nuggets or are keen to find out how to bring the rest of your team on board! In the chapters to come, we are going to explore the 'how' and my aim is to leave you feeling empowered, upskilled and confident to make changes either in your own school or within your own practice, and the remainder of this book will be your guide! It will be full of strategies, steps and processes to help you and your team get there.

So, let's first establish what I mean by therapeutic school and therapeutic teacher.

A therapeutic teacher

> Be the change you wish to see in the world
>
> Gandhi

For change to happen in the world, it first begins with the individual. Every person can make a real significant difference, even though that can often feel small. Who you are, how you show up, how you respond to things, your values goals and ethos are all essential in helping make a difference. Why are you doing this job? Who are you doing it for? What do you want to achieve? Why? How will you do that?

DOI: 10.4324/9781003410652-9

A therapeutic teacher is someone who knows the answers to these questions and:

- Put's children's mental health and wellbeing at the core of all they do
- Considers the whole child – their experiences, mindset, internal processing, beliefs and ability to regulate their emotions
- Acknowledges child development, trauma and attachment theory, SEN and SEMH needs and meets them in practice
- Knows how trauma and stress impacts the brain and how insecure attachment impact's relationships
- Recognises that they are a key part in moulding children socially and emotionally and uses emotional intelligence as a foundation for success
- Considers what is going on behind behaviour and guides and teaches children rather than punish and reject
- Is brave enough to challenge the status quo and raise standards
- Recognises that their role is to be a safe, caring, secure adult who helps children feel emotionally safe
- Recognises that their own triggers and traumas can sometimes impact their responses and reactions

A therapeutic school

A therapeutic school is a term I use to describe a school which includes therapeutic teachers and:

- Embeds a whole school approach, ethos and culture that puts children's mental health and wellbeing at the heart of everything they do
- As an organisation and collection of people, considers the whole child, specifically with regard to their internal processing, mindset, belief system and ability to regulate their emotions
- Takes responsibility to help guide their children through their formative years, helping develop emotionally intelligent children who have the ability to understand their own feelings, how those feelings impact their behaviour and then what they can do to manage that for themselves
- Acknowledges that they are a key part in moulding children socially and emotionally and that is a foundation for success and their offer to

children evidences this throughout their practice and runs through the whole school

- Is brave enough to question the norm and to say, 'This isn't working' and to change the status quo by doing things differently, using the children as their moral compass at all times
- Considers the world we live in today, and prepares the children to be able to access that world and flourish in it, regardless of their experiences
- Are trauma-informed, attachment-aware and therapeutic in their approaches and they are forward thinking enough to break the mould
- Invests in their staff's skillset so that everyone feels empowered and confident to make a difference in the children's lives, every single day. A culture is created where staff feel supported enough to embrace change and practice self-reflection, without fear of judgement, helping them to shred old 'teaching responses' that have been handed down to them by previous generations and no longer work, and develop new 'therapeutic responses' that make a tangible difference
- Help teachers become attuned to the children's emotional needs and respond in a way that meets those needs
- Applies trauma-informed approaches to the teaching staff as well as the children

They know:

- Feelings, thoughts, beliefs and experiences inform behaviour
- That struggling with behaviour is a developmentally appropriate response to a difficult situation and not a bad choice
- That children cannot learn if they do not feel emotionally safe
- The significance of the relationship between children and staff

The therapeutic school approach can be categorised by six areas – these are especially helpful when thinking about how to apply this to a whole school.

1. Overall ethos and school culture
2. Teacher skillset and development
3. The behaviour policy
4. The environment
5. The children's skillset and development
6. Therapeutic support

Overall ethos and school culture

Whether you are a leader in the school or a member of staff, it is important to ask yourself about the overall culture and ethos of the school you have chosen to be in. How somewhere makes you feel, what they prioritise and what their values are, says a lot about the culture that has been created. It is important to be part of a culture that resonates with you, increases your own sense of wellbeing, happiness, and emotional security, and makes you feel inspired to be there. If you work in a school that isn't aligned with your own values, your own wellbeing will be affected which means you will not be able to offer the children the level of emotional support they need. This is the place you choose to work every day; you should be excited to go to work, feel valued and seen, you should enjoy the company of the people you surround yourself with and believe in a shared vision and ethos. In many ways, school can be akin to a family home, the building and environment is like the house and the people within it, are like the family. The overall feeling of that home and the people within it are essential to how nurturing and safe that home feels. What is the school's overall priority for the children and adults within it? Is wellbeing and mental health at the core? Are the people safe, nurturing, loving and kind? Do they encourage and support one another, listen and value each other? Is there a common set of values and beliefs that are embedded into the way things are run and managed? Does everyone share the ethos and work together to make things the best they can be? This is what a successful family household does every day. A school that welcomes children into its doors every day and houses routine, teachings, relationships, and basic needs is the same in many ways.

To roll out a whole school approach for wellbeing and mental health, everyone must have the same understanding of the reasons why this is important and shared knowledge of what they can to do help. Everyone must believe in the values and ethos of the approach and want to make that difference. There must be guidance, training, and support along the way to make sure everyone feels supported and can shred old beliefs or reactions and be open to learning new ways of being, with recognition from leadership that this might be hard and they may need ongoing support to embed new skillsets. Whole school approaches need leadership to drive change, be consistent and reliable and guide and teach throughout.

Self-reflection

Ask yourself these questions:

What does the school value?
What is the overall culture and ethos?
How do you want children and staff to feel when they come in to school?
How do you want parents/visitors to feel when they come in to school?
How do you personally make children/staff and parents feel?
Does the school put wellbeing at the core of everything?
Do you put wellbeing at the core of everything?
What is your goal every day when you go into school?
How do you contribute to the whole school culture?

Teacher skillset and development

To have a shared culture and approach that runs throughout a school, it is important that every adult working there has a shared understanding, goal and skillset. If you truly want to support children with their mental health and wellbeing, if you want to be trauma-informed, attachment-aware, inclusive and therapeutic, and if you acknowledge that this starts with supporting behaviour (because behaviour is a sign that children are struggling), then every teacher need to be upskilled with the relevant training to ensure each person is contributing to the overall goal. Much of this work is about changing mindsets and perceptions about what teaching should be, especially when we begin focusing in on behaviour. It is often easier to understand the concept and to whole hardily agree with the 'why' once you understand the science and research, however, it is a lot more difficult to try and shift practice, responses and the engrained cultures both within teaching itself, and also the overall concept of the school system. Teachers, TAs, support staff, one to ones, lunch time organisers, office admin, Deputy Heads, Head Teachers and anyone else that works in a school should all have access to the same training to truly understand what you are trying to achieve. It would be a real shame if the teaching staff are responding to children's behaviour therapeutically within the classroom, but the lunchtime organisers are still shouting or sending children away, or for the receptionist to be talking about 'naughty' children in the staff room. To make a true significant impact on every child's wellbeing and mental health, everyone must work together to help guide and teach children. This not only encourages a strong staff ethos and set of values but also helps every child feel emotionally safe. This communicates to the children, through consistent, shared approaches, that every member of staff is modelling a secure attachment style and leads with connection. The foundation of a successful school is relationships, and each member of staff can cultivate meaningful, nurturing, safe relationships with the children so that every child feels seen, valued and cared for. This is the first step to them feeling emotionally safe enough to learn – this is worth investing in training for!

> **Quick side note:** If you are reading this and you are not part of the leadership team, please don't be discouraged. Although the ideal model is for everyone within school to adopt the therapeutic school approach, it isn't always achievable. This book has a dual purpose, the first is to detail how to become a therapeutic teacher and the second is how to embed a whole school approach. You have so much power in the role you have with children and by adopting the therapeutic teaching skillset I am about to guide you through; you can make a huge difference on the lives of the children in your care and that is significant to every child you interact with!

The behaviour policy

Another important factor to consider in the therapeutic school approach is the behaviour policy. Does your behaviour policy focus on helping the children learn from their behaviour, so they can change things for next time, or is it purely there to stop challenging behaviour and make sure everyone is following the rules? This is key question when looking at the therapeutic school approach. It is important that the leadership team create a whole school behaviour policy that reflects the emotional needs of the children which is trauma-informed, attachment-aware, inclusive and therapeutic. The behaviour policy should be designed to *support* children with their behaviour, to teach and guide, and help develop each child's emotional intelligence by using behaviour incidents as a tool for teaching. Remember, giving children insight and awareness into their feelings, thoughts, beliefs and behaviour in the moment is key. It isn't enough to roll out wellbeing workshops, PHSE lessons and mindfulness sessions if the children are being told off or punished when they are struggling with their behaviour. Both the behaviour policy and the mental health and wellbeing agenda should be aligned.

The environment

The environment plays a key role in the therapeutic school approach because it acknowledges that the external environment has a significant impact on children's feelings of emotional safety as well as their emotional wellbeing. It also has a significant impact on behaviour! Being a therapeutic school means being brave enough to question the norm, re-frame your perception of a 'classroom' and a 'school' and put children at the core of the environment. Classrooms, intervention rooms, corridors, outside spaces and staffrooms should feel safe, welcoming, calm and nurturing and silently contribute to cultivating an environment conducive to learning. A therapeutic school is brave enough to do things differently and raise standards, pioneering a new concept of 'classroom' that meets the needs of children today. We will discuss this much more in our therapeutic environments chapter.

The children's skillset and development

When cultivating a whole school approach, it is important to remember the children! As adults we often spend a lot of time making decisions on behalf of children, talking about children and learning about children but we often forget to include the children themselves in all of this! I have spent a lot of time in staff rooms hearing caring members of staff commenting on children's behaviour, they might say, 'I can tell Jack is tired today after being at his dads at the weekend, he said he was gaming all night, he will struggle today' or 'Camilla is really struggling this morning, she is fidgety and teary already, because mum had the baby this week.' These are examples of adults who are in tune with the children and their emotional states and who have some insight into the potential reasons why they are struggling, but they don't communicate this to the child. Jack doesn't realise he is tired and so is more likely to struggle, but when he is reminded to listen four times, he begins to feel attacked and threatened and he disengages. Camilla isn't aware she that she is feeling unsettled because of the new baby and so feels rejected and alone when she falls out with her friends on the playground because she is feeling a bit more fragile than usual. Neither have insight or self-awareness and neither know how to deal with their emotions! This is such a shame, and we are doing a disservice to our children. For them to understand themselves, develop self-awareness and become emotionally intelligent, they have to be part of these conversations and understand the 'why' too!

The therapeutic school approach teaches children about their own feelings, emotions, thoughts and beliefs and gives them insight into how they are impacting their behaviour and mental health and wellbeing. The approach gives them the power back and helps them develop the life skills they need that will take them beyond the classroom. Focus is placed on children's emotional intelligence as part of the commitment to developing the whole child and the children are taught through things like: specific PHSE lessons, interactions with adults, conversations with adults, school incentives and the behaviour policy.

Therapeutic support

This approach also acknowledges the value of therapeutic intervention within school. So many children and young people are struggling with adversity, trauma and insecure attachment and they have very little time to make sense of their experiences and process them. To be able to understand and explore their experiences children often benefit from therapy or therapeutic interventions to help them. Remember that due to the fast pace of life today, children have very little time to stop, reflect, find peace and stillness and to organise their thoughts. Therapy gives children the space and time to process life in a safe space with a safe person. I always encourage non-directive creative therapies in primary schools such as play therapy or art therapy. These interventions allow children to explore their feelings without the need for language or cognitive conversation. They often do not know how they feel and sometimes, the difficult or traumatic experience was so far in the past that it doesn't feel linked to their current struggles (even though it almost always is!) Play and art therapy allow children to explore the resources in the room freely allowing their inner thoughts and feelings to be expressed through the medium of play or art. I recommend therapies such as art, creative, music and drama therapy in secondary schools for very similar reasons.

Having therapy on site gives children and young people opportunities to partake in therapy, which they might not be able to afford later in their lives. It also promotes early intervention which is more likely to reduce risk factors in later life. It is important to remember that although therapy can be expensive, it is an investment into the emotional wellbeing of the children and is likely to have a long-term impact on:

- Their sense of self
- Their self-awareness
- Their self-belief
- Their emotional intelligence
- Their relationships
- Their coping strategies
- Their ability to recognise and regulate emotions
- Their ability to navigate future stresses and challenges

Focusing on these key areas will help you to create a culture that runs throughout the school so that you can be confident that emotional and mental health are running throughout the school eco system.

Side note: Although I am not going to cover therapy in this book, I encourage you to consider it as an intervention at your school.

So how do you pull all of this together? In this part of the book, I am going to guide you through the therapeutic school approach step by step to help you begin to embed these changes in your practice or you're setting.

The intention of this book is to:

1. Help you understand the 'why' behind becoming trauma-informed, attachment-aware and more therapeutic in your approaches is essential both as individuals and as a whole school
2. Give you specific strategies and processes to follow to begin to make a difference in your practice as individuals and as a whole schools

The following chapters lay out how to implement the therapeutic teaching/ school approach and are designed to be referred to regularly to help guide you as you begin to adapt your way of working. I invite you to make notes in this book, highlight specific areas, leave bookmarks, bend pages and carry it with you for reference! When you have a tricky incident with a child, pull out this book and flip to the relevant section, reflect on the scenario and think about where you could have tweaked things. If you are a leader in a school then share this book with your team, encourage them to read it, read out sections in staff meetings and use different sections as an area of focus each half term. Embrace this as a tool for teaching and be brave enough to try the advice in this book with the children each day, building on your skill-set until you are confident that this has been embedded into your practice. You might be surprised at the outcome even in the early stages!

This book runs alongside our online therapeutic teaching course, which is comprised of six modules that we roll out in schools with the whole team. If you have signed up to our whole school course – then this book is the perfect accompanying resource for you! Reading this book after the course modules will help you embed the changes we outline in the modules. I have also included more information about specific strategies and commonly asked questions to help you all on the journey.

> **Remember:** It takes time to adopt a new way of thinking, working and responding and it will take time to feel fully confident in your own practice, especially when it comes to the language you use with the children and new responses to difficult behaviour. When you begin, it might feel a bit alien and uncomfortable even, and you might won-der if it is working, you might find yourself slipping into old patterns but that is normal and to be expected. It will have an impact straight away, which is great, but don't stop there – keep going. If you can be consistent and committed to the approach and if you are always try-ing to improve your responses and understanding, you will see a huge difference in not only the behaviour of the children but the quality of your connection and relationships with them and their overall hap-piness and wellbeing. You might even find yourself shifting how you speak to the other children in your lives, and the adults too!

I hope that whatever your role, you find useful strategies within these pages that help you truly impact the lives of the children in your care.

8

The Therapeutic Teaching Approach

Therapy vs therapeutic

Although I have called this approach the therapeutic teaching approach, it is important to highlight here that therapeutic does not mean you are being taught to become a therapist. A therapist is a clinically trained professional who has studied for a number of years to gain the qualifications and the experience necessary to deliver therapy sessions or services. When we think about therapy it could be things like: Counselling, Play therapy, Psychotherapy, Drama therapy and so on. A clinical therapy involves a client and a therapist meeting at certain time each week. This approach is not that, however it does draw on therapeutic techniques that will help you develop a way of being and communicate and build relationships with the children around you (and probably some adults too!) I have drawn on my own experience as a play and creative therapist in the development of this approach, as well as my extensive experience with children, and I am going to be sharing with you the things I have learnt along the way. I have been practicing this way of being with children my whole life and have seen the positive power of it time and time again.

The first thing to consider here is *you*. How does it feel to be around you? What is it like to interact with you? What is your impact on someone when they spend time with you? Can you be trusted when things get hard?

You are the most important part of this whole approach, and this is where the idea of being therapeutic comes in. When something is therapeutic, it helps us feel better, a bit like helping us remedy something we are struggling with. It feels nurturing, safe and wholesome to do something therapeutic and often, it has a healing effect on us, helping us to feel healthier and happier, calm, relaxed and at ease. Interacting with something therapeutic often help us feel more in-tune with ourselves.

DOI: 10.4324/9781003410652-10

When we think about things that are therapeutic, we might think of: going to the spa, having a long bath, talking to an empathetic friend, going for a long walk, having a swim, meditation, gardening or listening to relaxing music. It might be doing some art or engaging in an exercise class or sitting quietly in the garden listening to the birds.

After we have done something therapeutic, we often feel:

- Ready to get on with things again
- Supported
- Recharged
- Better about ourselves
- Calmer in body and mind
- Able to see 'the bigger picture'
- At pace or settled
- Balanced
- In control
- Clearer in our thoughts
- Ready to support others
- Reading to think about others and reflect on our behaviour
- Ready to try new things or face difficult things
- Ready to listen and learn

Engaging in things that are therapeutic helps us feel able to be the best versions of ourselves and tackle the tough stuff, and this is exactly what we want to achieve for our children. All my approaches and support start with the word 'therapeutic' for this reason! I have the therapeutic school approach, therapeutic teaching approach and therapeutic classrooms, and now you can see why. If our aim is for the school, ourselves and the classrooms to be therapeutic, then we should be able to elicit those same feelings and benefits for children.

You are the central pillar of this. If *you* are therapeutic then just being with you should help children feel better and be a remedy for something they are struggling with. Being around you should feel nurturing, safe and wholesome. You should have a healing effect and help them feel healthier and happier, calm and relaxed and help them feel more in-tune with themselves.

Now that, is pretty powerful!

The power of you

Working with children can be hard work, it can feel tiring and sometimes emotionally draining but the power you have on the lives of the children you support is significant. Working with children is very much like parenting, after all you are moulding and guiding children through your work and for this reason, it isn't just a 'job' whatever your role and it is important to remember that.

 Real life

Oprah Winfrey, talk show host, producer and actress lived in poverty in a small farming community when she was young. Her mum was only a teenager and so Oprah lived with her grandmother where she experienced domestic violence and physical and sexual abuse. When she was six she went to live with her mum at a boarding house but was made to sleep outside on the porch at night. At 14, she went to live with her dad in Nashville. He was her one caring adult. He was strict but he provided stability, rules and structure and helped her focus on her education. She said (Stump, 2022) 'Respect, character, honour and doing the right thing no matter who is watching – these are the foundational values we learned from my father. I don't remember ever seeing him angry.' She went on to become the first black news anchor before the age of 20 and later went on to be one of the most successful show hosts of all time. During an interview (Winfrey, 2021), Ophrah highlighted the significance the people around you can make to your outcomes. She said, 'Why don't I have more problems? It's your relationships with people who cared about you other than your family members, that changes the way you view yourself and view the world.'

Oprah experienced severe, repetitive trauma in her life yet has become an emotionally intelligent, empathetic caring adult who is extremely self-aware and successful. Her outcomes were shifted by significant people around her. Don't underestimate the power you have to change lives!

It is easy to downplay your impact on children and question what influence you can have but the truth is, whatever you do, however you show up, whatever you say – you are already impacting and influencing children. We all remember that teacher in school who made us feel like we could do anything, who believed in us and made us feel good, even if it was as simple as knowing that teacher liked you! The one who helped transform your beliefs about yourself and planted seeds of confidence! Similarly, we all remember that teacher who wasn't very nice, who didn't like us and who negatively impacted our experiences at school! The one who left us with bad memories and maybe some negative beliefs about ourselves!

 Self-reflection

Look back on your own time at school for a moment, connect with the memory of one of the teachers you had, did you like them? Why? What did they do to impact or influence your life?

Now think about this, what is stronger for you – the memory of the teacher themselves or the memory of how they made you feel? For many of us, it is about how they made us feel and that is the key here – it is all about feelings! How you make a child feel, communicates so many silent messages to them without you being aware of it. Becoming therapeutic harnesses this and will help you communicate the things that really matter.

Looking after yourself

To become a therapeutic teacher, you must be able to first learn to look after yourself! In this busy, fast-paced world it is far too easy to leave yourself behind and get pulled into the narrative that we should be chronically busy and chronically stressed! Pull yourself out of the matrix and focus on the things that make you feel good. Apply the things we learnt in previous chapters to your own life and make looking after your wellbeing and mental health a priority. This is a step that will be crucial in ensuring you can show up and be your best self for the children you support – especially the ones who are struggling most!

Being self-aware and reflective in your practice

Part of being therapeutic in your approach is also about being able to self-reflect and become self-aware enough to recognise that sometimes, you will be responding from a place of survival yourself when interacting with children, it might not always be about them, sometimes, it will be about you. Remember, we all carry around our own histories, experience, and trauma too! We were the children once, learning from those around us, creating a blueprint we now apply to the world and developing a set of ingrained beliefs. The way you respond to children and interpret what they say or do might be influenced by your own history, thought process, perceptions and triggers! So, in the journey to becoming more therapeutic, it is important you are conscious and aware of your own responses and what might be impacting them. Because these can sometimes spill out without you realising.

 Real life

Terry is teaching Year 5 their English lesson but Ethan, a boy with a reputation for being disruptive, is calling out, making silly noises and disturbing others. Terry is getting annoyed and is struggling to teach the other children, some of them are getting restless and unsettled by the disruption. Terry gives Ethan a warning and explains that if he continues, he will need to stay in at break. Terry tries to teach the rest of the class, but Ethan's behaviour becomes more difficult to manage and Terry is losing patience. Eventually Terry raises his voice and tells Ethan he will be staying in at break. Ethan then begins to argue, 'What have I done!' Terry says, 'Ethan you are stopping everyone else from learning and I have given you several warnings! You are staying in at break to make up for your lost learning time.' 'That isn't fair!' Ethan shouts as he kicks the chairs in front of him. Terry then asks one of the children to go and get Mrs Davidson to come and help with Ethan. Ethan is taken out of class to calm down and Terry continues to teach the rest of the children.

Break down: Let's look at what is going on for Terry in this situation. When Terry was a child, the house was often chaotic and loud, Terry's parents worked a lot and were not at home much. They had three children. Terry was the oldest, but the younger children were often difficult to be around, they would argue a lot and fight with one another and although Terry's grandmother was usually there to babysit, she would get agitated easily and give up, so Terry was left to sort them out alone. Terry often felt anger and resentment toward the adults around him and was frustrated by the constant noise and responsibility. When Terry was older, he challenged his parents about it but was met with arguments and conflict.

In the classroom, Ethan's disruptive nature triggered a subconscious feeling in Terry of overwhelming frustration and anger. Due to his history, Terry needs order and control to help him feel emotionally safe and reduce the sense of being overwhelmed. Ethan's behaviour elicited feelings his body recognises as threatening, overwhelming and unsafe and so responded with his survival, emotional part of the brain. Terry found himself becoming hot and flustered every time Ethan moved around the room without asking or when he talked to another child and shouted out. Terry was hyper aware of Ethan's behaviour and it felt like a personal attack. The feeling of things being out of control triggered Terry to respond with a fight response. He raised his voice and issued a warning to try and regain some control, but this was anchored in his own emotional responses and was reactive, rather than being a reflective, rational response that was centred around Ethan. In truth, Terry wanted Ethan out of the class and was relieved when Mrs Davison came to get him. With Ethan gone, the sense of threat was also gone and Terrys body began to calm down and release the stress hormone, Terry was then able to access his rational responses and continue to teach the rest of the class.

This sort of scenario plays out regularly when we are around children. It could be something that links to your own triggers like this example with Terry, but it might also be that you haven't slept well that week and so are feeling more irritable and are more likely to respond with a survival response rather than a therapeutic, rational one. It might also be that the child's anger, distress or dysregulation causes you to also then feel that same distressed and dysregulated. Maybe you don't know what to say or how to handle the situation, maybe it feels like nothing is working or maybe what they do when they are dysregulated makes you feel unsettled too!

Often when I see adults responding to a child in distress, the adult is quickly triggered into a dysregulated state themselves. Suddenly both the adult and child are responding to their own emotions through survival fight flight or freeze and there is nobody to help bring calm to the situation. This can all feel emotionally draining and causes the adult to dread the next time the child is dysregulated because it makes them feel unequipped. The brain begins to link the child's distress or behaviour to feelings of overwhelm and it creates a trigger that signals the adult's brain to move quickly into a survival response at the first sign of a reoccurrence. So, in our example, the next time Terry teaches Ethan, as soon as Ethan begins to move around the room without asking – even if he is calm and just sharpening his pencil, Terry will feel the frustration more intensely than he should and may respond with fight mode (telling him off) or flight mode (sending for help) much quicker.

 Self-reflection

Have you ever been in a situation like this with a child? Where your emotions hijack your responses and mean you respond in survival mode? Can you think of a scenario that reoccurs regularly and where you quickly get stressed at the first sign of it happening again? If you are a parent, you might experience this very phenomenon at bedtime because asking a child a million times to brush their teeth and being met with refusal and delay tactics can quickly cause us adults to dread bedtime!

Of course, this is all totally normal – we are human and our brains are just kicking in to help! However, when you are working with children, especially vulnerable children, it is your job to stay out of the chaos and dysregulation and be the one to bring calm to the situation. Imagine yourself as the place of warmth and refuge in a storm, or a calm paramedic in an emergency – that is the goal here.

From now on, when you find yourself with a dysregulated child, I want you to step back for a moment and recognise what is going on in your own body.

Notice your feelings: Are you feeling overwhelmed and unsettled, do you feel anxious or frustrated or teary?

Notice your body: Is your body responding to the situation with physiological things like sweaty hands, a faster heartbeat, heavy breathing, feeling hot?

Notice your thoughts: What are you thinking? Are you worried you can't keep control, are you hearing intrusive thoughts? Are you hearing yourself think 'I don't know what to do!' are you arguing with the child in your head or playing out a conversation In your mind?

These are all signs that your own feelings are triggering an emotional response and you are likely to move in to a survival state. The trick is to become self-aware and conscious of your own reaction internally before it spills out externally and you also become dysregulated. This is not an easy thing to do, especially if you have your own history of trauma, but this is where the self-care things come in – the more you are doing in your life to help calm your mind and reduce those stress hormones, the more control you have over your emotional state. When you are stressed – everything feels more stressful, and your tolerance and threshold is lower. This isn't going to help you or the children. But when you feel good, and your stress hormones are kept low – you will find you can deal with the tough stuff much better (both in your job role and outside of it!)

Remember: Taking care of your wellbeing is an ongoing practice and requires you to constantly 'fill up' your own cup with daily and weekly practices and routines. When you stop doing the small stuff – you begin to feel it and see it in your behaviours, thoughts, and feelings.

It isn't personal

When a child is struggling with their behaviour, they are struggling with their own emotions, thoughts, beliefs and experiences. This often has very little to do with you! You might aggravate responses through how you react or be part of the situation, but it is rare that the actual issue is about you. It isn't personal, they are being hijacked by their own emotional responses to whatever the situation is – whether that is not being able to play football, struggling with the chaos of the dinner hall or being annoyed due to lack of sleep and too much gaming! You are a separate entity to this – so don't join in with the chaos.

So, from now on, when you find yourself in a situation with a dysregu-lated child – ask yourself, are my responses about me or about them?

Cultivating emotional intelligence

Both the therapeutic school approach and the therapeutic teaching approach acknowledge the fact that children are still developing, and it harnesses the opportunity to help mould well rounded, happy, emotionally safe little humans who can go out into the world and flourish in whatever way is best for them! This might not always be academic and although there is so much value placed on outcomes and attainment in education as a system, the actual child we are producing, and their development is an integral part of what schools should be contributing to. Children's emotional intelligence, sense of self, worth and value and their relationship building skills are a foundation for success for therapeutic teachers and this is built into the way in which the teaching is delivered.

Emotional intelligence is the ability to be aware of, control and express emotions and navigate through relationships with empathy. Simply put it is the ability to identify and manage your own emotions and the emotions of others. Daniel Goleman, a psychologist who studied and wrote about emo-tional intelligence, transformed people's awareness of the significance role emotional intelligence plays as part of our development and overall success in life. He demonstrated that in order for us to be successful in life and navigate the many challenges, emotions and relationships we encounter, emotional intelligence must be established. Learning to be emotionally intelligent should begin in childhood, but unfortunately it isn't reflected enough in education, where the primary focus is on children's IQ (intelligence quotient) instead.

Intelligence Quotient (IQ):
Is how well someone can solve problems, use logic, and grasp or communicate complex ideas.

Emotional intelligence (EI):
Is how well someone can recognise the emotions in themselves and others, and to use that awareness to guide their decisions and responses. EI informs how someone deals with challenges, conflict and difficulties.

Interestingly, Daniel Goleman suggests that emotional intelligence is actually a better indicator of success than IQ and when we link this with the research we have covered on the brain, stress, trauma and attachment – it is hard to disagree! Why then is this not an integral part of the education system and included in standard qualifications and courses we take when training to work with children?

To help us understand the important role emotional intelligence plays and why this is so integral to our approach, we can refer to Daniel Goleman's emotional intelligent quadrant (Goleman, 1988):

Self-awareness (self)	Social awareness (others)
Emotional self-awareness Accurate self-assessment Self-confidence	Empathy Organisational awareness Service
Self-management/self-regulation (self)	Relationship management (others)
Emotional self-control Transparency Adaptability Achievement Initiative Optimism	Influence Inspirational leadership Developing others Change catalyst Building bonds Conflict management Teamwork and collaboration

Self-awareness

This is the ability to identify your own emotions and thoughts and understand how they might impact others. It is our understanding of what we feel and why. If you have developed good emotional intelligence, you will be more aware of your emotions and therefore be able to manage them better. This is a core goal of the therapeutic teaching approach and is the first step in our seven-step model.

Self-management

Self-management is another way of saying self-regulation, which is the ability to manage your own emotions, thoughts and feelings and calm yourself down in a healthy way. When you have developed a good level of emotional intelligence you can support your own feelings of wellbeing by 1. sensing when you are becoming overwhelmed and moving in to your survival brain.

2. Using self-regulation skills to calm yourself down enough to be able to activate your rational thinking part of the brain and feel in control. This then means you have more control over your behaviour and connectedness to others which is a core goal of the therapeutic teaching approach and is also part of the seven steps.

Social awareness

This is the ability to identify the emotions of those around you and 'read' social situations intuitively, sensing what is going on and applying empathy to support or understand them. To do this, we need to able to identify the possible emotions of those around us. This is why we name emotions in our therapeutic teaching approach to normalise feelings and emotions and help bring them to everyone's awareness (more on this later!)

Relationship management

This is the ability to use what you know about your own emotions and the emotions of others to manage social relationships successfully. Having relationship management skills helps you deal with conflict, disagreements and barriers and overcome them with kindness and an awareness of others. Having a good level of emotional intelligence and development of the other three quadrants means you are more likely to be able to deal with conflict and listen, empathise, resolve issues with others and work as a team. This is an essential skill for our children to develop not only for school but for their future lives both in work and relationships.

Empathy vs sympathy

It is important to note here that empathy is a very different skill than sympathy. Empathy is the ability to connect to the feeling someone else is having and truly feel that feeling. Their feelings/story or distress activates something within you that is linked to a time where you also felt that way and so you use your own experience to support, guide and understand the person. You are responding with your heart and an inner knowing and connection. This doesn't always have to be the exact same feeling or experience but something within you recognises how that feels.

Real life

Sarah is eight and is in Year 4 at school, she has had a difficult morning and has been in trouble on the playground. Mrs Dawson has bought her in for some reflection time. Sarah does some quiet drawing and then begins to tell Mrs Dawson about home. Sarah has been taken into care and has been separated from her parents. Part of her is happy to be away from her parents because they used to hurt her and there was always a lot of shouting, but she also feels guilty for enjoying living with someone else and is worried about her mum. Mrs Dawson has never been in care but she feels the pain that Sarah feels and truly connects with what she is going through. She is reminded of her own losses in life and can connect with Sarah's feelings because of that. Mrs Dawsons parent's divorced when she was around Sarah's age and her mum and dad used to argue a lot. She remembers feeling guilty about enjoying living with Dad more than Mum. Mrs Dawson can apply empathy to the situation to help her connect with and support Sarah. She says, 'It is so hard when you feel torn between two things!' rather than, 'Don't feel guilty, it is okay.'

Sympathy is very different to empathy, empathy requires you to feel the feelings and identifying with those feelings within yourself, which requires you to be vulnerable. Sympathy, although an important skill, is more like feeling sorry for someone or having concern for them. Sympathy is more about acknowledging someone's feelings but not necessarily connecting with them. Brene brown, author and researcher of empathy say's sympathy is 'I feel bad *for* you' and empathy is 'I feel *with* you.' She teaches that empathy fuels connection and is vital for relationships and for a therapeutic teacher, connection is everything!

As therapeutic teachers it is important, we lead with feelings and develop a sense of empathy with our students but it is also vital we help them develop a sense of empathy toward others. Naming emotions and helping create those cognitive connections between shared feelings is part of the therapeutic teaching approach.

Important note: Sometimes it might seem like a child doesn't care about how another child feels and that might very well be true! Childhood trauma can impact a child's ability to have empathy for others.

A child who experienced neglect and abuse may have lower levels of empathy for others because they never received it themselves. A child who was raised by a depressed parent or alcoholic may have higher levels of empathy for others because they had to learn how to read people's emotions to survive. This of course is not so black and white, and every child is individual, but it is important to be aware of this and to acknowledge that some children won't seem to care about how others feel. That isn't because they are a bad child or unkind, it is because nobody ever cared about how they felt, if nobody ever showed empathy for them, how can they know what it is and show empathy for others? You must experience it to learn it, like unconditional love.

Emotional intelligence is a core part of child development and one we must harness and cultivate in the school years. This is in everyone's best interest, the child's, ours and Ofsted's! Children with higher levels of emotional intelligence are more likely to have a better quality of life, better quality relationships and be more likely to want to learn and achieve in school.

These four quadrants are enveloped into our therapeutic teaching and therapeutic school approach both in practice and strategies and also incentives within the classroom. The goal is to help every child you support to develop their EI through your interactions, guidance and support as well as the culture you create. In this chapter we will look at how you can increase children's emotional intelligence through your own practice. In the chapters to come, we will look at how you can improve emotional intelligence through incentives and ideas within the classroom.

How therapeutic teaching helps

Therapeutic teaching pulls everything you have learnt so far together in a step-by-step approach.

When you begin to practice the approach, it will help:

- Calm children's brains so they are ready to learn
- Identify their feelings and understand how to manage them
- Help them feel emotionally safe
- Re-wire their brains and perceptions of themselves/others and situations
- Establish healthy good relationships they can apply to future relationships

- Help them feel ready to learn, challenge themselves and achieve
- Raise their self-esteem, self-belief and self-concept!
- Empower them to be their best selves and believe that they can be
- Develop their emotional intelligence skills

It will also help you:

- Embed therapeutic, trauma-informed, attachment-aware approaches that are inclusive
- Feel more in control of your own emotions and responses
- Respond to difficult situations in a rational, thought-out way rather than a reactive one
- See behind the behaviour a child is displaying and support the real problem
- Develop healthy, connective relationships with the children
- Make a real impact in your job (which is the whole point!)

From now on, we are going to lead with connection before anything else, coming away from the typical 'normal teacher' responses and moving into therapeutic ones. Have a little look at these two diagrams and how we can make that shift.

Leading with disconnection

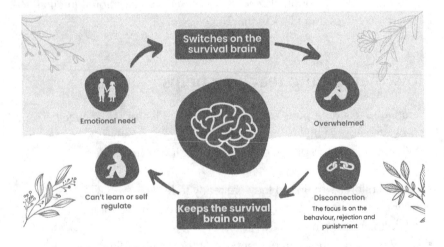

Figure 8.1 The process of leading with disconnection

Emotional need

The child is struggling with something which means they are experiencing some tricky feelings, emotions, thoughts or beliefs that are making them feel overwhelmed.

Jack is playing football on the playground with some other boys, he isn't able to score a goal and nobody is passing him the ball, he is getting frustrated and feels left out. Jack's body responds by getting hot, his heart beats more quickly and he begins to get intrusive thoughts like, 'I am not good enough' 'Nobody likes me' 'Nobody thinks I am a good player' as the game progresses and more boys score, he feels more and more attacked and emotionally unsafe.

Switches the survival brain on

This turns on the survival part of the brain and activates a fight flight freeze response.

Jack's brain interprets the situation as something overwhelming and potentially threatening and so shifts into a survival response – fight mode. Jack grabs the ball and throws it over the fence in anger and kicks another peer in the shins.

Overwhelmed

The child's behaviour is an outward sign of their inward overwhelm.

Jack is shouting at the other players, telling them that they are not playing as a team. He begins to insult them and is becoming more and more dysregulated. His feelings of overwhelm look like 'bad' behaviour.

Disconnection

The child is met with disconnection, rejection, punishment or consequence or an adult who isn't attuned to their emotional state or needs.

The teacher comes over to Jack looking cross. 'Jack,' he is shouting across the playground, 'Calm down Jack! What is going on? Why have you thrown the ball over the fence?' He gets to Jack and sees he is angry, 'Stop shouting and calm down! You have ruined the game for everyone now and you've hurt Rio's leg! Come off the pitch, you can't play football for the rest of the week!'

Keeps the survival brain on

The response of the adult or people around the child, perpetuates their sense of threat and overwhelm and keeps them in a state of survival and stops them from being able to regulate, learn or calm down.

Jack feels even more attacked and overwhelmed now and feels like this whole thing is unfair. He is disappointed and angry that he can't play football this week and doesn't feel like it is his fault. Nobody was passing him the ball – that was *their* fault not his! Jack is unable to reason, reflect or problem solve because the thinking part of his brain isn't on and so he just becomes more dysregulated at the injustice of it all. Jack doesn't want to hear the teacher telling him off anymore, it feels like everyone is against him. His body responds by sending him in to flight mode to get away. He runs off the playground to the fence and begins trying to climb it.

Can't learn or regulate

The child is left in a state of dysregulation where they are left with their overwhelming feelings, thoughts or beliefs without any guidance or understanding of what is going on for them. They have no skills or strategies to 'calm down' or regulate and so use whatever coping mechanisms they can, often burning out instead.

Jack is now in a state of dysregulation with no skills or tools to calm down or understand what has happened here. He feels like he is always in trouble and feels like everyone thinks he is 'bad.' Jack wants to get away from everyone now and doesn't trust the adults around him to help him. He continues to try and climb the fence, run away from staff and ends up crying in a corner. The staff spend 45 minutes trying to calm him down and he misses part of the afternoon which leaves him in a state of anxiety until home time.

Conclusion

Sadly, this is a common situation that happens time and time again in schools. Jack just wanted to play football and feel connected to his team, but he didn't have the skills to successfully do that yet and needed some guidance. This was the perfect opportunity to teach Jack how to manage the challenge of playing football, working with others, dealing with failure or challenge and to give him insight into his emotional responses when he feels overwhelmed. It was also an opportunity to give him the strategies to manage those feelings without judgement or rejection. With a little guidance and support, this could have had a different outcome.

It doesn't mean Jack wouldn't have been angry or frustrated and it doesn't mean Jack wouldn't have thrown the ball or kicked someone, but it would have helped him feel understood, connected and supported and would have helped reduce his sense of threat and overwhelm enough for him to learn from the situation and apply some healthy coping skills to the next time. It is also very likely that he wouldn't have got to the point where he was trying to climb the fence and he wouldn't have needed 45mins of input from staff. Instead of connection at the point of overwhelm, he was met with disconnection which perpetuated the situation and stopped him learning anything from this life lesson.

If Jack hasn't learnt anything, there are no insights or tools he can apply to this situation for next time. So, the next time he is struggling with football at break time – what will he do? The exact same thing.

Leading with connection

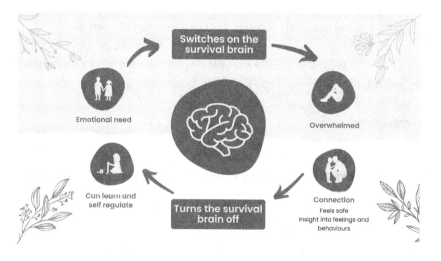

Figure 8.2 The process of leading with connection

This second diagram leads with connection. Here is how we want this to play out:

Emotional need

The child is struggling with something which means they are experiencing some tricky feelings.

Jack is playing football, he isn't able to score a goal and nobody is passing him the ball, he is getting frustrated. Jack's body responds by getting hot, his heart beats more quickly and he begins to get intrusive thoughts like, 'I am not good enough' 'Nobody likes me' 'Nobody thinks I am a good player'

Switches the survival brain on

This turns on the survival part of the brain and activates a fight/flight/freeze response.

Jack's brain interprets the situation as something overwhelming and potentially threatening and so shifts into a survival response – fight mode. Jack grabs the ball and throws it over the fence in anger and kicks another peer in the shins.

Overwhelmed

The child's behaviour is an outward sign of their inward overwhelm.

Jack is shouting at the other players, telling them that they are not playing as a team. He begins to insult other players and is obviously dysregulated. His feelings of overwhelm look like 'bad' behaviour.

Connection

The child is met with empathy, understanding, connection and guidance by a calm, in tune, (but still assertive) teacher who gives appropriate boundaries to help the child stay emotionally safe but not punishment or rejection.

The teacher comes over to Jack and recognises he is overwhelmed. 'Okay boys, okay,' he says to the boys shouting about what Jack has done. The teacher has taken some time to assess the situation in the few minutes it's taken to walk up to the pitch, look around and hear what the boys are saying. This space means Jack feels able to say something: 'They wouldn't pass me the ball, Sir!' 'They were not playing as a team!' The teacher doesn't know the full situation but from the limited information can conclude that Jack felt left out and moved into a state of survival. The teacher can also see that Jack must be in fight mode because he kicked someone and threw the ball. The boys are all gathered around the teacher now and he says, 'Right, it looks to me like Jack really wanted to score and be part of the team but felt left out. Boys, I know you didn't mean to leave him out but feeling left out isn't nice and Jack felt over-whelmed. Jack, you are very frustrated and angry and have ended up hurting Jason and throwing the ball over the fence, let's go and have some time to calm down and then we can sort this out' (this would then be followed up by more steps in our approach which I will re-visit later – including boundaries).

Turns the survival brain off

The response of the adult or people around the child, creates enough con-nection that the child doesn't feel as emotionally attacked. This begins to reduce the stress hormone and turn on the rational part of the brain.

Jack feels like the teacher gets it and feels validated enough to not feel as attacked. He is still not calm, but he feels that he can trust the teacher enough to help him regulate. The teacher suggests they go and get a drink of water and then come back to sort things out. The break from the situation helps jack calm down and his rational, thinking part of the brain becomes more available to him. He can begin to think more clearly, problem solve, reason and have empathy for the other boys in the team.

Can learn and regulate

The child feels emotionally safe enough to begin to regulate with the help of the teacher. This turns on their rational thinking part of the brain and helps them learn and embed the insight, understanding and skills to learn from the situation. Meaning they are more likely to be able to manage the same situation better in the future.

With the help of the teacher, Jack learns that coming away from the situation for a moment and having a drink can help calm his brain. Through the teachers' therapeutic responses, Jack begins to understand what happened on the playground and make sense of his emotions. He doesn't feel judged or punished but he is able to see the other children's frame of reference and the impact of his behaviour. Jack is soon ready to make amends and sort this out with the boys. Jack has more clarity and understanding and has learnt a lot from this situation.

Conclusion

In this scenario, Jack has had the emotional support and guidance he needed to be able to learn from the situation and gather some insight and skills. The more experiences like this he has, the more likely it is he will develop his emotional intelligence and be able to manage his responses better in future. This scenario meant Jack spent less time in a state of dysregulation and meant less input was needed from other staff members, it also meant he was able to continue on with the rest of his day without this overshadowing things or becoming a bigger issue than it needed to be.

> **Note:** I am aware that in this scenario, the other boys were also frustrated, and one boy was hurt. As we move through the steps below, we will discuss how the teacher in this scenario would have approached this, offering safe, fair consequences to ensure Jack was able to make amends and the other boys also felt validated and heard.

The way we communicate and respond to children can be the biggest catalyst for change both in the moment and long term for the child's development, learning and skillset. This is where our therapeutic teaching steps come into play. This is a way of responding and communicating with children that helps you constantly connect, guide, and teach whilst also helping children develop their emotional intelligence and regulate. This approach will help every child and I encourage you to use it with everyone, but it will also help ensure you are responding in a trauma-informed, attachment-aware way which means regardless of the child's background and experiences, your response will be relevant and supportive.

9

The Therapeutic Teaching Steps

The seven therapeutic teaching steps are:

Step 1: Name
Step 2: Feeling
Step 3: Behaviour
Step 4: Encourage
Step 5: Regulate
Step 6: Boundary
Step 7: Teach

These seven steps form a complete approach when thinking about both general communication with children and approaching difficult behaviour. It is important you learn each step and begin to embed these into your practice but with the awareness that you may not need every step in every interaction. See each step as a tool for you to apply using your judgement and awareness of the child and scenario.

Initial therapeutic response

Step 1: Name
Step 2: Feeling
Step 3: Behaviour

The first three steps in the therapeutic teaching approach are anchored in how you talk and respond to children in general, both when they are struggling and when they are not. It is important to think about how you are communicating with children on a day-to-day basis with your aim always to

DOI: 10.4324/9781003410652-11

create a caring, connective relationship in which the children feel safe and can trust you. It is no good just being therapeutic when a child is struggling with their behaviour because it won't feel authentic and genuine to the child. The basics of any relationship is to feel liked, seen and emotionally safe first, otherwise you have no foundation to work from. These initial therapeutic responses are to be used all the time, as much as you can, and the key here is tuning into the child's emotional state, potential thoughts, beliefs and experiences. Remember, if they lead with their feelings – then so should you!

From now on, from the moment you are in the presence of the children, I want you to be using all you have learnt here to inform the way you communicate with them. Ask yourself, what feelings might the child be feeling, what beliefs might they have about themselves, what experiences might they have had that are forming their behaviour and emotional state? It could be as simple as Milly coming into school and putting her head on the table in the first lesson. It is the first day back after Christmas break and although you don't know what her holiday was like, you can guess that it was chaotic and loud and that Milly spent a lot of time watching TV or playing on her tablet. Your normal teacher response might be something like, 'Come on Milly, it's English now, sit up straight and open your book' – the focus is on the behaviour and the outcome you want. Instead, from now on, you are going to focus on the feelings first and say, 'Milly you are feeling a bit tired this morning, it is hard to come back to school after a long break.' The skill here is in noticing the behaviour and trying to put yourself in the child's shoes and see their frame of reference and then verbalize what you see. This is the first part of our therapeutic teaching approach.

The art of listening

When we speak to children (and adults too) our responses often shut them down without us realising it. We might respond with offhand comments or dismissive statements, or we might jump in with our own opinion or experience. We might also be too quick to offer advice and solutions. When we do this, even in small exchanges that seem to not matter, we can shut down potential connection and a feeling of safety. We also miss things when we respond like this and loose our ability to be in tune with the child.

A child might be talking about what they did at the weekend, their favourite game or what happened on the playground and to you, it might feel long winded or trivial and sometimes you shut off and are just waiting for them to stop talking. Unfortunately, most children experience adults that are too busy or distracted to really listen, to children this communicates a silent message that adults don't care about what they are saying, or that our goal is to stop them talking and make them do something we want instead. We might say things like, 'Oh well, never mind,' or 'It will be okay,' or 'I am sure your mum does play with you!' or we might say, 'I told you to ignore them,' or 'Wow really, okay, can you get your coat on now please,' responses like this shut children down and this can create a feeling of disconnection. Now, I am aware that we often don't have the luxury of listening to an hour-long monologue about a child's favourite game, especially when you have a class to teach or work to do, but by developing the art of listening and some strategies to cultivate connection, children can feel heard and validated in every interaction, whether it is them talking to you about their favourite game or talking to you about their behaviour.

The art is in *how* you listen. It begins first with body language, eye contact and your tone of voice and expressions and then becomes more about how you respond.

 Self-reflection

Imagine you are in the staff room, and you've had a bad night with your child. You are pouring a cup of tea and Sally comes in. She asks how you are, and you say, 'I am exhausted, I was up all-night with Alex, he was having nightmares again, I don't know if they might be night terrors because he was literally shaking and it took me ages to get him back to sleep. I struggled to get out of bed this morning, it is like having a newborn again!'

Whilst you are talking, Sally is moving about the staff room and busy with other things, she responds to you by saying, 'Jack used to have bad dreams too. Have you tried meditation before bed or stopping him from going on his tablet before bed?' She then goes on to talk about her own child before walking out the room.

Although this might feel like a normal exchange, your feelings were not validated, and you didn't feel listened to.

Jackie was sat in the staff room whilst you were both talking and she comes over to you and says, 'You sound exhausted, it is so hard to see your child distressed like that and not know what to do. It sounds like you supported him well though.'

Suddenly you feel heard, seen, validated, and understood, you pour your coffee and head out of the staff room to face the day! That small tweak is the difference between a therapeutic response and a normal teacher response. Jackie connected with your feelings, Sally didn't.

Body language/eye contact

Walking around the room or doing other things is necessary sometimes when a child is talking, especially if you have lots of children to support. But when a child is talking to you or struggling with something, be mindful of how much you do this and be intentional about stopping and using your body to show you are listening. If they are sat on the floor, can you sit down next to them instead of standing over them? Can you move your body to be 'open' rather than 'closed' by turning yourself to face them and creating a connective energy? Can you make eye contact with the child and show you are engaged and present? Can you read the child's body language to sense what feels comfortable and what doesn't to them? Some children might like you sitting next to them, others might need you to sit a little bit away from them. Some will want eye contact; others might want you to look away but sit close, so it doesn't feel too intrusive. Use your intuition to 'read' the situation and use your body language as a tool to communicate connection to the child even before you say anything.

Tone of voice/expressions

Whenever you are with children, think about the power of your expressions and tone of voice. It is no good saying things that are therapeutic, with a look of anger or frustration on your face. Children are very good at 'reading' adults – especially those who have been through trauma. To them, it isn't just about what you say, it is about what you do. They will learn very quickly to read your body language, expressions and tone of voice to determine your emotional state and they will respond accordingly. Your tone when speaking is another great tool to build connection so use it as part of your tool kit. When you are asking a chid to do something in the classroom, is your tone calm and caring but instructional or is it hard, frustrated, and instructional? The tone in which you say things makes a huge difference even when it is the exact same sentence.

> Try saying the following sentences with a totally different facial expression and tone of voice and see how different the very same thing can feel when you change how it is said.
>
> Calm, caring but instructional
>
> 'Come on guys, let's focus on the work and stop chatting, save your chat for breaktime.'
>
> Hard, frustrated and instructional
>
> 'Come *on* guys, let's focus on the work and *stop* chatting, save your chat for breaktime!'

For children who are always 'reading' the adults around them and who are expecting disconnection, and challenge – this can make a big difference to how they receive and interpret what you say.

Once you are being intentional with your body language, expressions and tone of voice, the next thing to be intentional about is what you say, this brings us to the start of our seven steps.

Step 1: Name

Step 1 is nice and easy and is simply saying the child's name in your response or interaction with them. Saying their name before anything else can help you get their attention and connect to them, especially if there are lots of people around or if their emotions are very heightened. It might be that a child is very upset so you use their name to connect and show empathy whilst touching their shoulder before you move on to Step 2, but sometimes it might be more natural to move straight to Step 2, so use your judgement with this one.

Step 2: Feeling

Step 2 is about naming the feeling a child is having. Feelings are a huge part of my work because as we established in previous chapters, we are all lead by our feelings on some level. Understanding our inner state and being able to identify our feelings, understand them and then manage them is the key to being able to navigate your mental health and wellbeing, social skills and emotional development. However, children are not being given enough feedback about their feelings and many of them have no idea how they feel! I can't tell you the number of children I have met who are feeling anxious or nervous, but they think they have tummy ache or are hungry! In fact, I remember visiting a school who were struggling with a little girl in Year 3, she was pulling out people's chairs, trashing classrooms and running away. When observing her, I noticed that every time there was a transition during the day she would suddenly say she was hungry and wanted a snack. This was not only for big transitions, like when the lessons changed or when it was breaktime, but also when the game changed in PE or the activity shifted in maths. Because she hadn't been given the insight into what anxiety or nerves felt like, she assumed she was hungry! We could also acknowledge here that wanting a snack was a form of flight mode to help her get out of the situation that was making her feel uncomfortable.

When you ask children to describe how they felt in a particular situation, they will usually say things like happy, sad or angry but these are not sufficient words to describe the multitude of feelings they will be having on a daily basis. Without being equipped with the right feeling words, children are disempowered and will not be able to develop their emotional intelligence skills and their own self-awareness. This is why some children confuse their feelings- like the child who says he is angry in a lesson, when really he is embarrassed about not getting a question right. The most important part of the therapeutic teaching approach is to begin to name feelings for the children around you, so they can identify what the feeling is and how it feels when they are having it. To do this, you must learn to 'read' the feelings the child might be having and tell them! Within our responses, we are going to harness the power of some therapeutic skills that are common with counsellors and therapists, but with a twist. As I mentioned previously, we are not training to become therapists here, but will adapt some of the therapeutic techniques into our work.

Remember: Although I am talking about feelings, we must also be recognising the child's potential frame of reference, beliefs, thoughts, and experiences at the same time.

Reflection

Mastering the art of reflection is one of the main skills in our therapeutic teaching approach because it means you are constantly focusing on the feelings and frame of reference of the child. This is where you recognise what is going on behind the behaviour or words a child is saying. It is about:

1. Noticing what is actually being said or what is actually going on, almost like reading between the lines and identifying what the real issue is
2. Noticing the feelings that are linked to what is being said

You then use what you have identified and reflect it back to the child (tell them) so they get some insight into what is going on for them. At times you may reflect both the feeling and what is going on for the child, or just one – use your own judgement in each situation. It is also important to develop the right time to reflect, without interrupting or taking the child off track. It's your job to fully listen, observe and empathise and really try to *feel* what the child is communicating to you.

Example 1:

Child: 'I hate that teacher. He doesn't like me, so I don't like him either!'

Normal teacher response: 'Mr Ross does like you! He just gets annoyed when you don't listen and have to be asked the same thing over and over again. If you listened to him, he wouldn't tell you off!'

Reflective response: 'It feels like Mr Ross doesn't like you, so you don't want to like him either . . .'

Example 2:

Child: 'Why are we not doing PE with Mr Ross? We always do PE with Mr Ross? I don't want to do it!'

Normal teacher response: 'Mr Ross isn't in today, but Mr Jackson will be teaching you. He is really nice, give him a chance. I bet you love the lesson once you are in there!'

Reflective response: 'It is hard when things change, and you are not sure what is happening! You really like Mr Ross and are a bit unsettled now . . .'

Using reflection skills in this way will help you create that initial connection which will then begin to calm down the brain and help them feel heard, but the key is to name those feelings as much as you can! Then the other steps follow. Let's break this down even more.

Naming feelings

Naming feelings is an essential part of your skillset and should be done both generally with children and when they are struggling. This is the key to connecting and helping to calm down the brain.

From now on, I want you to focus on feelings first in as many interactions with children as you can! Whether it is a child who is excited about the school assembly, a child who has come in withdrawn and quiet or a child who has just punched someone in the face. Before you do anything else, you begin with feelings first, this is powerful for all circumstances but especially those where a child is struggling. As we have mentioned in the behaviour section of this book, we usually focus our attention on the behaviour or the outcome we want. We might try to have a conversation, offer suggestions, advice or guidance, we might jump to a consequence or a telling off, but we now know that none of these things will work because the child is usually in their survival brain. If you refer back to Figures 8.1 and 8.2, naming feelings is the first thing you do to break away from the normal response that is anchored in disconnection and instead, lead with connection. When you recognise the child's feelings you are communicating that you understand what is going on for them, you have no judgement and can see it is hard for them, you are here to help, and you are here to guide and teach. You'll be surprised just how much difference this small tweak makes.

So, from now on:

- Reflect feelings before you do or say anything else
- Acknowledge their frame of reference (even if you don't agree or it isn't fully true)
- Override your 'normal teacher response' and focus on a therapeutic response

Try saying things like:

'You are feeling . . .'	'You're feeling really frustrated with this maths' You are feeling left out, and like nobody is listening to you'

Or

'It is hard when you feel . . .'	'It is hard when you feel stuck and don't know what to do' 'It is hard when you feel like nobody is listening'

Or

'Feeling (X) can be . . .'	'Feeling worried can be really unsettling' 'Feeling left out can be really upsetting' 'Feeling angry can make it hard to think straight'

Or

Describe the difficult situation/ their frame of reference	'This room is so warm it is putting us all to sleep' 'You have got lots on your mind and it is hard to concentrate.' 'It is hard to know what to do' 'It feels strange when the day gets mixed up'

Try to remember as many feeling words as you can and use them with your children whenever they crop up. Avoid using sad, angry and cross and really expand your own use of feeling words. The more feeling words you use, the more they will recognise within themselves.

Change your practice top tip

To help you figure out what to say, use the information we learnt about trauma, attachment and stress to inform your therapeutic response and meet their emotional needs. Whether you are dealing with a child who is fidgeting on the carpet or who has kicked over a bin, the process is the same. This will help you embed a trauma-informed, attachment-aware approach that will support the child's emotional intelligence and development.

Before you respond, try to figure out if the child just needs some general reflection or re-direction, or if they need you help with dysregulation. Do a quick mental check list in your head. Ask yourself these four key questions:

1. Are they in fight, flight or freeze – how do you know?
2. What is their frame of reference or belief in this moment?
3. What might they be feeling?
4. What might they be thinking?

Then use what you can see, what you know about the child and what you can pick up from the scenario you are in to respond.

 Real life

Ambreen is doing some group work with four other children on her table. She is swinging on her chair and trying to pull other children into conversations about other things, she then takes Jessica's rubber and flicks it across the table toward Oliver. Oliver shouts you over, but you had already noticed the table was unsettled. Although you didn't see everything, you can draw some conclusions from what the children have said, what you can see, and from what you know about Ambreen.

1. Are they in fight, flight or freeze – how do you know?
She is in flight mode, because she is avoiding participating in the session and working with the group by distracting herself and trying to distract others. This increases when her efforts don't work.

2. What is their frame of reference or belief in this moment?
Ambreen has a core belief that she is not good enough, she believes she is always left out and will be abandoned. She always struggles with group work.

3. What might they be feeling?

She might be feeling anxious, overwhelmed, unsure about how to fit into the group, worried about not being listened to or have anything good to contribute, uneasy about dividing her attention and dealing with different opinions.

4. What might they be thinking?

She might be thinking she isn't good enough to contribute, that her voice isn't worthy of being heard, that she is going to be left out (so she may as well not join in), her ideas are not good enough (maybe she has said this in lessons before). She might be thinking that she needs to be in control here and not let anyone else lead because it makes her vulnerable.

From this quick pause and assessment of the situation, you will feel more confident about responding therapeutically. You will also feel more connected to Ambreen and her frame of reference – rather than seeing the behaviour first and you will be informed enough to use your therapeutic teaching responses, not just with Ambreen but the other children as well.

'Ambreen, you are feeling a bit unsettled about this group work. It can be hard to work with others sometimes . . . maybe you are worried nobody will listen to your ideas . . .'

Now this isn't all we would say to Ambreen if we were following the seven steps, but right now, this is an example of how you would reflect back using her name and her feelings. We will come back to Ambreen as an example in other steps. In this exchange you might also reflect Oliver's frame of reference and say 'Oliver is a bit frustrated now, he was trying to concentrate but that rubber just hurt his hand . . .' you would then go on to the behaviour, encourage and boundary and teach steps.

A common question: What if I tell them the wrong feeling?

People often worry about naming the wrong feeling and making children angrier. However, it is important to remember that naming a feeling is more beneficial to a child than avoiding it. If you have used your judgement in the situation and asked yourself the four key questions above, then you are in a strong position to make a reflection. The truth is, there are usually several different reflections you can make in any given situation. In the above example, we reflected that Ambreen was unsettled and worried, but we could have said feeling left out, anxious, unsure, tired etc! Don't worry about getting it wrong, instead focus on fine tuning your judgment in the situations with children and practice! If a child does happen to tell you that your reflection is wrong, then this just a great opportunity for them to reflect on what they *are* feeling.

When I was working as a play therapist years ago, I found myself in this exact situation. I was working with a boy in Year 5 who always looked angry and frustrated with everyone. He was referred to me to help him process his feelings and understand them, and to become more self-aware. One day, in our session he was creating something at the art table, and he looked so angry.

I was early on in my training, so I reflected this back to him saying something like, 'Abdul, you are feeling angry with this art work right now.'

He looked at me in surprise and said, 'No I am not, I am concentrating!'

I responded 'Oh!! You looked angry but you're just concentrating!'

This was a mini breakthrough for us both because although I had reflected his feelings incorrectly, he was given the opportunity to

1. Get insight into what he was communicating through his body language and facial expressions
2. The opportunity to voice his emotional state for himself

From this point on, he never looked angry again when he was concentrating, and I assume that was because he was more self-aware.

Things to avoid

One of the things I notice in the schools who enrol in my therapeutic teaching course or award is their tendency to start saying 'I *know* you are feeling . . .' 'I can *see* you are feeling . . .' and 'I *understand* you are feeling . . .' when they begin to name feelings. Although this is with all the best intentions and may have come from other approaches/therapeutic ways of working, in this approach, I want you to try to avoid using these statements as much as possible. The therapeutic teaching responses should feel natural, fluid, and authentic. They are designed to become part of your normal way of talking and communicating and they should feel like you. When you say things like 'I understand you are feeling . . .' it can sound forced or scripted, a bit like when a therapist says 'and how does that make you feel . . .' in a movie. It can bring with it a bit of an eye roll as if to say, here we go again. You want to avoid that in your exchanges with the children. As I have said before, you are not a therapist, but instead a therapeutic adult who is creating the feeling of connection and safety through this way of talking. It should feel real and genuine. Adding 'I understand,' or even, 'I can see . . .' makes it all feel a little stiff and rehearsed. Similarly, try to avoid saying 'I know you feel . . .' because this can trigger children to respond with, 'No you don't know!' They might feel that you are being intrusive and making assumptions and that might shut them down or create disconnection. Be brave enough to name the feeling without these crutches as your way 'in' to the reflective response.

 Develop your practice

As you begin to name feelings with the children and even adults around you, try to reflect on how you responded after each interaction. If you catch yourself using 'I know you feel . . .' 'I can see you feel . . .' 'I understand you feel . . .' sit down and write out what you said, and then write out what you could have said instead. Keep doing this until it feels second nature to respond with feelings first as described in the tables above.

Important note: Although Step 2 is called 'feeling' it doesn't mean you have to use a feeling word every time. Sometimes you might describe the difficult situation the child is.

Here are some examples of where you might adjust your response:
A child is unsure about their work so is giving up and putting their head on the table

'You are finding this a bit tricky, and it is frustrating . . .'
'It's hard when you feel stuck and don't know what to do . . .'
'You feel unsure about the work this morning . . .'

A group of children are arguing about who will be the 'mum' on the playground

> 'You feel like nobody is listening and it's hard to hear each other . . .'
> 'It is hard to play together when everyone has different ideas . . .'
> 'It feels frustrating when nobody listens to what you'd like to do . . .'

A child is refusing to do their work and has walked out

> 'The questions are hard today, and it feels overwhelming . . .'
> 'It can feel overwhelming when the work is hard'
> 'These questions are tricky, and it is making you feel like giving up'
> 'You have had a late night, and it feels hard to concentrate this morning'

Scribbling over their work before you can see it

> 'You are not sure about that one . . .'
> 'You are worried that one wasn't good enough and don't want me to see'
> 'Sometimes you scribble out your work when you think I will say it's wrong'

Daydreaming when you are talking

> 'Jack, you are tired today and it's hard to concentrate'
> 'This room is so warm it is putting us all to sleep'
> 'It's hard to listen this morning'
> 'You have got lots on your mind and it is hard to concentrate'

Step 3: Behaviour

Once you have named the feeling, the next step is to link that feeling to the behaviour the child is displaying or the situation they have found themselves in. This helps to connect their feeling to their behaviour and bring it to their awareness and is important for their emotional intelligence. Making this link is uncommon in the way we interact with children but an essential piece of the puzzle. Remember, it is about naming what you are seeing and helping the child to develop some insight into what is going on, so they can see how it is impacting their actions, thoughts, behaviour, response or the situation itself. This should always be done without judgement, ensuring you are aware of your own emotional response and keeping that in check. This isn't about you; it is about them, so keep it about them and try to stay neutral (even if they are spitting or hitting out, which I know is hard!) This doesn't mean you are 'airy fairy' or 'soft' in your approach, you can be firm and kind keeping your body language open and your tone connective.

In our example with Ambreen, we can move to Step 3 by saying:

'Ambreen, you are feeling a bit unsettled about this group work. It can be hard to work with others sometimes, you are worried nobody will listen to your ideas and so you are distracting others and messing with this rubber . . .'

Name: Ambreen
Feeling: You are feeling a bit unsettled about this group work. It can be hard to work with others sometimes . . . you are worried nobody will listen to your ideas
Behaviour: and so you are distracting others and messing with this rubber . . .

Or

'Ambreen, you are feeling a bit unsettled about this group work, so you are struggling to get involved.'

Name: Ambreen
Feeling: You are feeling a bit unsettled about this group work.
Behaviour: So, you are struggling to get involved.

Here are some bridging statements to move into the behaviour step. Remember this comes after the feeling/reflective response:

'So you are/have/ need/want . . .'	'You're feeling really frustrated with this maths and *so you keep walking around the room to get a break . . .*' 'You are feeling left out, and like nobody is listening to *you so you don't want to play anymore . . .*' 'You feel a bit embarrassed about getting the answer wrong this morning and *so you've stopped joining in*'

Or

'So it is/so it's . . .'	'You're so angry right now, *so it is hard to listen to anyone or think straight*' 'You are unsure about the new teacher, *so it's hard to settle*' 'You are tired and haven't slept well, *so it's making you teary and unsettled*' 'You are shocked and hurt that Jack kicked you *so it's making you want to hurt him back!*'

Or

'and/so now . . .'	'It is hard when you feel stuck and don't know what to, *and now you want to give up . . .*' 'It is hard when you feel like nobody is listening, *so now you don't want to join in . . .*'

Or

'I can tell because . . .'	'You are feeling left out and it's hurting your feelings, *I can tell because you've stopped joining in . . .*' 'This work is frustrating, and you don't want to do it, *I can tell because you keep going to the toilet . . .*' 'It feels hard to play with the others today, you are feeling frustrated, *I can tell because you keep walking away from them*' 'You are annoyed and don't want to listen to Sarah anymore, *I can tell because you are turning your back to her when she speaks*' 'Feeling angry can make it hard to think straight, *I can tell because you are finding it hard to tell me what's happened*'

Or

'It's making you . . .'	'You are worried about your mum and *it's making you want to go home*' 'You are disappointed that you didn't get chosen this *time and it's making you want to walk out*' 'You feel so mixed up and angry *and it's making you kick others and hurt them*'

Using name, feeling and behaviour in a group

Reflecting back feelings and linking them to behaviour is not only something you do with individuals but also with groups of children who are struggling. This might be during an argument or conflict or when children are not thinking about each other. When children have fallen out over something, it is common practice to ask everyone what happened or to write down what happened. Although the intention here is to be fair and give every child a voice, in truth it rarely solves the problem because each child is only able to see their own perception of the situation. When children are stressed and overwhelmed, they get tunnel vision and can't see or understand the frame of reference of those around them. Their memory is also compromised, and facts can become blurry or distorted. Asking them to recall what happened can become confusing and difficult to decipher and takes a lot of time and effort. It also doesn't always appease the group! In a group situation, it can seem like the most important thing to do is figure out what happened but in truth, it isn't. The most important thing is to validate everyone's feelings and help them feel heard. Have you noticed how children can't forget about an incident and move on, even if it happened at dinner and was dealt with? That is because they didn't feel heard. As soon as you validate a child's emotions and frame of reference, they are more likely to be able to move on and make amends. They are also more likely to be able to see the other children's side of things. Children often don't need us to solve their problems for us, they just need us to listen to how hard the situation was for them and how it made them feel.

Use therapeutic responses after big arguments or small disagreements by verbalising each child's feeling and frame of reference in the situation.

 Real life

The class are doing group work on different tables, Sarah thinks she is on the blue table so she goes over to them.

In an irritated voice Patrick says 'This isn't your table! You can't sit here with us! Go over to that one.'

Sarah feels upset by his response and feels rejected. She is sure she should be on that table. She comes over to you and says 'Miss, Patrick isn't letting me sit on his table and he told me to go away.'

Your response could be, 'Oh, Patrick that wasn't very nice, Sarah you are on this table, come on get on with your work.' But instead, you can see how upset she is. Patrick is now also annoyed about being told off too. You use your therapeutic responses to name both of their feelings and bring their behaviour to their awareness.

'Sarah, you feel upset and a bit rejected because of how Patrick spoke to you. Patrick, you didn't mean to upset her, you just noticed that she was supposed to be on the yellow table but the way you spoke to her was a bit abrupt, it made Sarah feel like you didn't want her over here.' You then might add a 'next time try' statement which we will discuss later in the book to help him figure out what he could have done differently. You might then get them both on task by saying 'Sarah you are on this table here lovely, come and sit next to Oliver.'

The trick to reflecting to more than one child is to name everyone's feelings and help raise their awareness as a group so that though you they can understand each other's intentions or feelings. It doesn't have to be long winded either, for example if a child is upset that they are not being included in a game you might say.

'Charlotte you are feeling left out, you really want to play but nobody is listening to your ideas. Jessica, you are enjoying leading the dances so much that you are forgetting to listen to Sarahs ideas. You are so good at doing dances, just remember to work as a team.'

It is important to note here that when children struggle in a group, your job isn't to make it better or solve the problem for them. It is to give them enough insight and awareness so that they can solve the problem for themselves.

 Develop your practice

The best way to get comfortable and familiar with Steps 1–3 is to practice! You can do this outside of the classroom as well as inside, and with adults as well as children. Responding to people using these skills will strengthen your relationships and are a brilliant tool when facing anyone who is struggling with their emotions – including an angry neighbour or frustrated grandparent! A simple way to embed the language is to write out as many statements as possible based on real life scenarios you have found yourself in. Get yourself a notebook and take some time now and then to reflect on the week you have had. Were there examples in the week of times people were using their survival brain and responding with an emotional/stress responses? What did they say? What were they doing? What did you say? What could you have said? Write out different potential versions of steps 1–3 and say them out loud to yourself. This will help you get used to speaking in this way and will make it feel more natural. Then try and use the phrases in all of your interactions, whenever you can.

Always remember, name, feeling, behaviour. If you take nothing else from this book, this alone will have a significant impact on those around you.

Step 4: Encourage

Step 4 is an optional step depending on the situation you are in and is a good step to add in for lower-level situations, like when a child is struggling with their work or has a small fall out with someone. If the child is too overwhelmed or dysregulated, then it is better to use an encouraging statement later in the steps when you get to the 'teach' response. This just gives the brain time to calm down and hear what you are saying without triggering the need to reject it or processing it as a tactic to get them to do something.

This step is about continuing that feeling of connection with a child and helping to raise their self-belief and self-concept in the moment. It also helps re-wire their brain by subtly offering a different response to the one they are expecting. One that focuses on positives even when they are expecting to have done something wrong. You would still start with a reflective response by naming their feeling, you might also name their behaviour and then use the encourage step which allows them to hear something positive and reassuring about themselves that links to the situation.

For example, you might have a child in reception who is doing some colouring and is snatching all the pens. Your therapeutic response might be:

Name: Sarah

Feeling: You are really enjoying colouring in this morning and are working hard on your picture

Behaviour: but you are so busy that you are taking all the pencils and Charlie hasn't got anything to use

Encourage: You are a good friend to Charlie and are good at thinking about other people's feelings

Then you might follow on with a boundary like, 'pop some in the middle for him to use too . . .' (we will talk about boundaries soon!).

Encouraging statements can be focused on:

- Something they do well
- A personality trait they have
- A skillset they have
- Something they did well previously
- An affirmation that they can aspire to

They might sound like:

You are/you have/you can . . .	You are good at figuring things out You have got great problem-solving skills You can solve problems really well You are so good at helping other people You are good at helping people feel better

Or

You/You had . . .	You had a great football match yesterday and you scored two goals! You played so well together yesterday making up dances You had such a positive mindset yesterday about it and you did really well You love playing with Jack and he loves playing with you . . .

Make your encouraging statement even stronger by linking it to a specific time or event that backs up your statement. This will help the child believe in what you are saying and begin to shift their own frame of reference, sense of self and self-belief.

'You are such a good friend to Charlie, yesterday I saw you getting his coat for him.'

'You can solve problems really well, remember yesterday when you figured out how to make a house from Lego?'

Putting it all together:

Name: Ambreen

Feeling: You are feeling a bit unsettled about this group work. It can be hard to work with others sometimes . . . you are worried nobody will listen to your ideas

Behaviour: and so you are distracting others and messing with this rubber . . .

Encourage: You have brilliant ideas though, remember yesterday when you said about the tree? That was a great way of thinking about it. Oscar was so impressed with that answer, weren't you Oscar? He even wrote it down himself!

(You might then remove the rubber from the table visibly but without saying anything which is part of our boundary step)

Remember: Using the 'encourage' step is often helpful for low level behaviours to help a child refocus or move on from whatever they are struggling with. This should often be followed up with a gentle boundary which we will discuss soon.

Important considerations

When using the encourage statement it is important to remember that this should be a genuine statement that is specific to the child rather than being a flippant statement used to appease them. They will know the difference! Make it personal and specific to connect to *this* child and help shift them into the rational thinking part of their brain.

Use your judgment and what you know about the brain to determine whether the child is ready for an encourage statement straight after a reflective response, or whether they need some time to calm down first.

Positive affirmation

The encourage step can also be used as a tool to shift the child's thought and belief system, a little bit like a positive affirmation. An affirmation is a phrase or statement that challenges your negative thoughts and the more you repeat them to yourself, the more your brain begins to believe them and will accept them as reality. Saying positive affirmations to yourself helps improve mind-set and mental health and can replace negative self-talk. We know that so many children are struggling with their thoughts and beliefs, so this is a good tool to help you address that in your day-to-day interactions with children. Children believe and accept what they are told about themselves and then they live up to that expectation. If we tell a child they are naughty, never listen and hurt others – it is very likely that this is exactly what they will do. Our characterizations (or labels) become self-fulfilling prophecies. So, let's flip the narrative for these children and give them something more empowering to live up to! Tell the children they are helpful, kind and honest, tell them they are great problem solves, brilliant thinkers and good team players and watch how their behaviour suddenly shifts to meet that expectation.

If Jack is struggling to take turns, say, 'You are so good at listening to others . . .'; if Sarah is angry with Tilly, say 'You are such a valuable part of that group and the girls really like you . . .'; if Tyrone is finding his work hard say, 'You are great at solving problems and figuring things out . . .' Go ahead and try this out with the children, even if you don't believe it yourself! You have the power to plant seeds of self-belief into the minds of the children you interact with, those seeds could mean a child blooms in ways you didn't expect!

Some children in some scenarios might be struggling a lot more with their emotional response than our example of Ambreen. They might be visibly angry or upset and might be displaying higher levels of flight, fight or freeze behaviours. This is where Step 5 comes in!

Step 5: Regulate

This is one of the most important steps of the approach and one that is rarely acknowledged in common behaviour policies (although I know that lots of teachers will naturally do this). We know that when children are overwhelmed, struggling with a big feeling, stressed or feeling attacked that their survival part of the brain turns on. We also know that this means their rational thinking part of the brain shuts off and they cannot think clearly, process the situation, reflect, problem solve, have empathy for others and so on. As we have established, our role as adults is to help calm the child and therefore their brain, so that initial emotional response reduces and the child feels emotionally safe and connected again, this will then shift them in to their rational, thinking part of the brain and help them to learn from the situation and manage it. However, in typical behaviour management approaches, there isn't a step to help the child calm down and instead the process is to jump straight to a consequence or sanction when the child is still dysregulated. In the therapeutic teaching approach, we prioritise calming the brain down above all else because we know that the child isn't going to learn anything from the situation if we don't! This will not only help them process, understand and manage the immediate situation but also give them skills for the future which, if repeated over time will contribute to increased emotional intelligence and better mental health.

So, once you have acknowledged the child's feelings and linked it to their behaviour (and possibly after an encourage response-but that isn't always needed or appropriate) your next and most important step is to help the child calm down!

What does regulation mean?

In the context of this approach, regulation is about helping the child to come back to a calmer state both within their body and mind. Remember, when a child is working from a place of survival, their body is also responding by increasing their heart rate, blood pressure and breathing. They might feel sweaty and hot. They will also be feeling intense emotions like fear, anger, frustration and anxiety and they may be experiencing negative or intrusive thoughts like, 'I am not good enough', 'nobody likes me', 'I am bad'. This is what is referred to as dysregulation. Being in this state of dysregulation means a child feels overwhelmed and is unable to control their emotional responses and this is when we see them get angry, run away or struggle to listen and process what we are asking them to do.

Being able to 'regulate' yourself is being about having the self-awareness and skillset to be able to acknowledge your emotional response and intentionally use techniques and strategies to help you take some control back and begin to calm down. It is about finding a way to get back to a calm, controlled state by processing and responding to what is happening, instead of reacting to the emotions and being hijacked by them. The strategies to self-regulate can be simple such as going for a walk at breaktime because you are feeling irritable and tired, or cuddling the dog on the sofa after some bad news. It might be taking control of your breathing when anxious by taking some deep breaths and going outside in the fresh air.

Although these things sound simple, we are not born with the natural ability to self-regulate, it is instead, something we are taught. To be able to regulate yourself, you need to have experienced someone helping you first, though 'co-regulation.' Co-regulation is when you experience a calm adult who feels safe, helping you calm down by soothing you when you are distressed and overwhelmed. Adults are co-regulating when they respond to the child by hugging them, by using a soothing calm tone and by acknowledging the child's feelings whilst modelling ways to calm down. They might get the child a drink or a teddy, or they might sit with the child quietly until they are feeling better. During these exchanges the adult is attuned and responsive and is acknowledging the child needs help with their feelings. They are not telling them off. When a child repeatedly experiences co-regulation, they can learn and internalise the understanding and strategies needed to help themselves calm down in the future. This is the only way they can learn to self-regulate. A child cannot be told how to calm down, they must be shown.

Important take away: A child cannot be told how to calm down, they must be shown. Without experiencing co-regulation, a child will struggle to self-regulate.

Every child needs to experience co-regulation with adults to develop healthy strategies for themselves and to learn that it is okay to feel your emotions. However, many children have not experienced co-regulation with a soothing adult. Some children, especially those living trauma or adversity experience anger, rejection, or abandonment when they are overwhelmed by their feelings and are often left dysregulated for long periods of time. This can often cause them to struggle to allow an adult to support them when they are overwhelmed because for them, adults are not associated with emotional safety. This is why co-regulation is such an important part of your approach at school, it is not just something they need from home, but from you, especially because you might be filling gaps for children who have never experienced it before.

152

Real life

Tahlia is having a difficult morning, she was late and is tired because her brother was unwell last night and it kept her awake. Tahlia struggles with her friends at break time and gets upset when someone says she can't be the leader in the game. Tahlia goes into the corner and cries by herself. Mrs Bell sits beside Tahlia and puts her arm around her.

'You are having a tricky morning,' she says, 'and so you are feeling a bit fragile, and it is hard to play, let's go and have a drink of water to calm down, come on.'

Mrs Bell takes Tahila inside for a drink, she knows it will give Tahlia a little break from the playground and help her gather her thoughts. Once she is inside, Mrs Bell gives Tahlia a hug and they have a chat about what is going on, they walk out on to the playground holding hands until Tahlia feels able to join in with her friends again.

In this scenario Mrs Bell acknowledged Tahlia was in flight mode and feeling overwhelmed. She verbally reflected her feelings and linked it to her behaviour, she then helped co-regulate Tahlia by sitting next to her, giving her a cuddle, giving her a break from the situation, getting her some water, talking to her in calm caring way and holding her hand until she felt better. She didn't ask Tahlia what had happened, make suggestions about how Tahlia could join in with her friends or call her friends over to solve the problem. She simply acknowledged Tahlia's emotional state and focused on that first. She knew there was time for conversation later but her first priority was to help Tahlia calm down.

> **Remember:** If we don't help children calm down when they are in a state of overwhelm (and are in survival mode), they won't be able to problem solve, reflect, have empathy for others, or learn from the situation. They must be in their rational, thinking part of the brain to do that and therefore we must help them calm down so they feel less overwhelmed and can access their rational thinking part of the brain. It is never about just stopping the behaviour; the child must be able to learn something in order for your input to have real lasting impact.

Helping children regulate

Adding a step in your response to help children regulate is essential. Here is how you can embed it into your approach:

Generally, if you work with younger children, then you will probably be using co-regulation most frequently. They will need you to help them calm their brain, soothe them and to be *with* them when they are struggling. Just as any young child would with a safe parent. That is why younger children are often holding hands with a teacher and why we tend to let children sit on our knees and offer hugs in nursery and reception. That said, regardless of their age, every child should be able to experience co-regulation if they need it. You can then build this up to help them find ways to self-regulate when they are ready. A four-year-old can still learn that hugging a teddy helps them calm down, even if they are on your knee whilst they do it, and a ten-year-old might still need to hold your hand when they are struggling. Don't be fooled by their age, even with teenagers! We all need help with co-regulation and self-regulation.

> **Remember:** When you help a child calm down with co-regulation you are helping them calm down *through* you, when you are helping a child self-regulate, you are helping them calm down by using a strategy or technique they can do by themselves but this doesn't mean you should leave them alone to do it.

Help a child calm down through co-regulation by:

- Simply sitting beside them quietly or being with them
- Holding their hand
- Putting your arm round them
- Giving them a cuddle
- Using a soothing tone of voice
- Bending down to their level and giving them eye contact whilst talking calmly and holding their hands or touching their arm
- Sitting them on your knee (if appropriate and safe to do so)
- Rocking them on your knee whilst hugging them (if appropriate and safe to do so)
- Reflecting back their feeling through connective language (the firsts steps of our approach)

- Reading to them
- Singing to them

Teach a child to calm down through self-regulation with:

- A teddy or blanket to cuddle
- A drink
- A safe place or tent
- Reading
- Listening to music (on headphones or without)
- Journalling
- Drawing
- Colouring
- Lego/Meccano or a construction toy
- Going for a walk
- Meditation
- Deep breaths or breathing strategies
- Space without judgement

The list could go on, but the idea is to have a range of resources and strategies to help a child calm down, remembering that every child will have a slightly different preference for what works for them. We all have different things that help us when we feel overwhelmed so you will need to use your knowledge of the child (if you know them well) and professional judgment in the moment.

Here is how it all fits into the therapeutic teaching steps

In the therapeutic teaching approach, we use regulation as part of the steps to help a child when they are struggling. This acknowledges that they are working from a place of overwhelm and survival and that their behaviour is a survival or stress response. Normalising self-regulation techniques outside of the times when a child is distressed is important. The more you help children feel comfortable to draw, write, listen to music or practice breathing techniques when they are in a state of calm, the more likely they will feel comfortable turning to these strategies when they need them. You could introduce journalling in the mornings for 5mins to help encourage children to express themselves through writing, you could practice meditation after break time to help children feel the benefits of calming their mind before lessons. However, it is no good just teaching children about meditation, drawing and mindfulness in PHSE lessons if you don't help them practice those skills when they need it most in real life. If wellbeing strategies stay within the remit of a taught lesson in PHSE, then it will only ever be a concept and children will struggle to apply it, especially when they are being hijacked by their survival part of the brain. Helping them regulate *in the moment* is the key here, to help them make a connection between the feelings, thoughts, or beliefs they are having and the emotional response of their body and giving them the tools to manage this.

Your job is to

1. Normalise self-regulation techniques when children are calm in their day to day lives
2. Help the child regulate through co-regulation when they need it (remember, you will be doing this through your therapeutic response too)
3. Offer the child ways to self-regulate in the moment, when they are struggling

For some scenarios and some children, just connecting with their feelings and offering an encouraging statement is enough to get them back on track. They might feel validated enough to keep working or to try to figure things out with their friends on the playground. However, some children will be in a visible state of dysregulation, they might be angry, crying, shouting, or turning away. Their body language and emotional state will be obvious, and their behaviour is likely to be either a fight, flight or freeze response. If the child is in a state of distress, whether that is low level (arguing back, turning away, sulking, struggling to get past an incident) or at a higher level (throwing, shouting, walking away) then helping the child calm down is the next natural step.

Important note: It is important to note here that if you approach any situation with a therapeutic response, naming feelings and behaviours and then offering some regulation – the child is less likely get into a state where they are running away, climbing fences or lashing out. Unless at some point their interactions with other peers or staff have escalated their sense of overwhelm. If a child *is* up a fence when you get involved, the best thing to do is use steps 1–3 (however feels most appropriate) and then stop until the child feels less threatened. Just let them know you are there for them when they are ready and allow them some time to calm down. They are in flight mode, so bombarding them with instructions or ideas might not be very helpful. After some time has passed and their sense of attack has reduced, you might suggest something they can do with you to help them calm down like, 'When you are ready, let's go and find Jack the school dog for a cuddle.'

Following your initial therapeutic response use connective language to help children move into the regulation step. Here are some ideas:

Let's . . . go/get/ take/have	*Let's* have ten minutes in the calm corner and *we* can come back when it is a bit quieter.
	Let's go and do some Lego for a bit to help you calm down, and then *we* can sort this out . . .
	Let's take five minutes to calm down and *we* will come back to this in a minute
	Let's get away from all of this for a little bit and go for a walk
	Let's go and calm down first and then *we* can come back to this
	Let's go and get a drink of water and take some deep breaths
	Let's get a drink before we carry on, it will help clear your mind
	Let's go and find Timmy (the therapy dog) for a cuddle and come back to this in a minute
Take some . . . / Let's take some . . .	Take some deep breaths and come back to it in a minute when you can think a bit more clearly
	Take some time to yourself for a little bit before we sort this out, you are too overwhelmed to think right now
Give yourself	Give yourself a two-minute break and then come back to it, it will help your brain calm down a bit

Children might not always be able to come with you or accept your offer to help them self-regulate. In these scenarios, you don't need to force anything, just offer or suggest ways they can calm down and make things available if possible. If they choose to accept the resource or suggestion that is great, if they don't, then they now know it is an option.

'Listening to music might help you shut things out and calm down' (offering headphones)
'You can use the calm box to help you feel better, I have Lego and playdough '

'Sometimes teddies help us feel better' (putting the teddy next to the child)

'When I am overwhelmed, blankets always help' (pulling a blanket around yourself and putting one near the child)

'Writing or drawing how we feel can help when we feel overwhelmed' (placing a pad and pencils near the child or starting to sketch yourself)

Once you offer these suggestions, you might sit alongside the child quietly (co-regulation). Avoid continuing to talk and prompt though, allow them to sit in the silence. You don't need to force anything, just being there is often enough. If a child is so overwhelmed that they don't want you next to them, like if they are crouched in a corner or hiding somewhere then leave them alone and sit with the silence, then tentatively and sparingly offer some thoughts 'out loud' that might help them. This works well with younger children.

You might:

Put on some calm music in the background
Sit and start drawing by yourself
Cuddle a teddy on a sofa and read something
Start sketching on some paper

If they look interested or look up, you might then say:

'Drawing helps me feel better, there is some paper here for you too'
'Reading helps us when we feel sad, this one is about . . .'
'This music is so calming . . .'

Then continue to do whatever you are doing. It is likely that most children will come and join you. It also takes the pressure off them having to 'come out' or 'behave' without them feeling like you have left them. Putting it all together:

Name: Ambreen
Feeling: You are feeling a bit unsettled about this group work. It can be hard to work with others sometimes . . . you are worried nobody will listen to your ideas

Behaviour: and so you are distracting others and messing with this rubber . . .

Encourage: You have brilliant ideas though, remember yesterday when you said about the tree? That was a great way of thinking about it. Oscar was so impressed with that answer, weren't you Oscar? He even wrote it down himself!

Regulate: Let's go and get a quick drink of water and take some deep breaths, so you can come back to this.

Important things to remember

Be mindful of your language

When you are faced with a child who is dysregulated, avoid saying 'calm down.' Remember that children have no idea how to calm themselves down. If they did then they would! No child wants to be in a state of overwhelm and dysregulation. We must remember that children are still developing, and using blanket statements like this can confuse a child into thinking they should be able to calm themselves down or should be able to 'behave.' This can cause them to believe something is wrong with them, especially when the adult is angry or frustrated. But the language here is misinformed and is another example of why we need to be careful about how we speak to children. What we say matters!

Give them space

If you have a very dysregulated child who has run off or is hiding, it is important to give them space. This is especially true if the child is shouting at you to go away, keeps running away from you when you get close or moves when you get too near. Your natural instinct will be to help or to go over and you might want to talk the child down but sometimes, the best thing you can do is to leave them. This doesn't mean ignoring them or being indiffer-ent but instead acknowledging they need to feel less threatened in order to calm down. Instead of getting too close and trying to talk to the child, say something like 'I am here when you are ready' or 'I am going to give you some space but I am here when you are ready' and then wait. If they are a runner, man the exists and allow the child some space. Try to avoid having too many staff watching or talking to others about what is happening in front of the child. Once they are calmer in their body language then go over to redirect them to some regulation time. Remember to wait before engaging in conversations or directions about their behaviour.

Here are some other tips

- Use 'let's and we' to create a feeling of connection and help children see that although they have struggled, they are not being 'sent' away to time out or to be on their own but instead they are with a safe adult who is supportive and nurturing
- Depending on the scenario and the child, you could take their hand as they say this as you begin to walk away from the situation.
- Avoid using phrases like 'shall we . . .' or 'do you want to . . .' because it is likely that some children will say no as a fight response. Learning to calm down, isn't a choice. You are the adult, and you are making and informed, judgement based on your knowledge of the brain, stress hormones and trauma which evidences that regulation time is needed. As the adult, your role is to help the child calm down when they need it, just as a parent would. Asking them is assuming they can make a rational decision informed by self-reflection and emotional intelligence whilst knowing their rational thinking part of the brain is shut down – that doesn't make sense.
- Remember to frame your response with them in mind and don't be afraid to highlight how it will help, 'Let's go and get you a drink and get away from this for a moment, it will help you feel less attacked' that doesn't mean you agree with what has happened or that the child is right, but you are leading with their frame of reference in the moment.
- Regulation time is for the child to calm down so whilst they are having a drink, drawing or sitting quietly it is important you do not interrupt their calm time. Asking loads of questions, talking at them, or giving them solutions and direction is not appropriate here. This is their time to calm down and you must respect that otherwise you risk them being triggered back into a state of survival.
- Adding '. . . before we sort this out' or '. . . then we can come back to this' after your regulation statement helps communicate gently that the problem or issue will still be sorted out and that regulation time doesn't mean that they are not expected to make amends for whatever they did when they were struggling.

- Avoid 'sending' a child for regulation time as a form of 'behaviour management.' 'Go to the reflection room and calm down!' or 'Go and calm down!' will just perpetuate a survival response and will create a negative connection for the child between calming down and punishment which isn't your intention. However, you might still say 'Go and grab a drink of water' to a child who is showing lower-level signs of struggling and can take some direction in the moment.

Once a child is calmer, you can then focus on how they can make amends if that is necessary in the scenario.

Once you have given the child/ren time to calm down, the next question is, how do you set boundaries or consequences that are not anchored in punishment or rejection? That is where Step 6 comes in!

Step 6: Boundary

We often hear the phrase, 'children need boundaries' but what does that mean in real life and how do boundaries differ from the rules we set? The easiest way to separate the two is to think of it in picture form: imagine a wire fence with a sign that says 'Danger, keep out!' The sign is the rule that has been set, but the boundary is the fence. The fence reinforces the rule in the moment, whilst the sign sets and communicates the rule.

Rules – are usually communicated before an incident or situation

A boundary – is how you reinforce the rule whilst the incident is happening, or after it. This might be through something you do or say to help the child understand the rule or expectation or to help them make amends for something they have done.

Rules vs values

The first thing is to determine what your rules are. These should always be communicated in a connective way that keeps channels of communication open. Instead of framing them around things we 'don't do' instead frame them around what you'd like them to do. Think of your rules as a set of values that are focusing on the child and not just the behaviour. This sets the expectations but also the tone for your overall ethos and culture as a school and informs your therapeutic school approach.

Rules

No swearing
No phones
No fighting
No running

Values

We listen to each other
We look after each other
We take care of our things
We support one another
We work as a team
We respect everyone's opinions

To effectively teach children, you must have both – the rules (or values) and boundaries together. You cannot have a rule if you are not going to enforce it and you can't enforce a boundary if the child isn't aware of the rule or expectation.

A boundary should never be a punishment or a sanction. These, as we have discussed, are rooted in rejection. So instead, boundaries should be linked to safety and not just physical safety, but emotional safety. Remember, as a therapeutic teacher the perspective is not that a child is 'misbehaving' it is instead, that they are struggling and need our help. We should therefore see boundaries as a means to help children feel emotionally and psychologically safe and to teach them, instead of a means to control or manage their behaviour.

Unlike the rules, boundaries are not separate to you, they are an extension of you and your relationship with the child. Whether *you* are boundaried or not communicates a lot to the child about whether they can trust you and that will determine how they behave around you. Being boundaried with a child is a bit like creating an invisible circle of safety around them that allows them space to move, run, play and explore but within the safe parameters you have allowed. If they begin to struggle, you will adjust that circle or step in to help. Children need the space to be able to experience their world and figure out how to exist in it, but with the knowledge that an adult is there to help them if it becomes difficult. You might do this simply by reminding them about the rules and expectations with words, or by reinforcing this through an action or decision you make. For example, you might give a child some pencils and a rubber to draw with, but if they throw the rubber at someone, you might take the rubber away or remind them about looking after people. You recognise they are struggling to independently manage in the moment, and so you step in to help guide and refocus the child.

When you are boundaried you:

- Follow through with what you say
- Reinforce the same set of rules and expectations
- Have consistent, predictable, reliable responses
- Stay attuned and empathetic and connected to the child whilst still reinforcing the rule or expectation

An adult who is unboundaried, however, might:

- Set rules and not follow through with them
- Change their expectations each time
- Change their responses each time
- Be experienced as unpredictable or inconsistent
- Become frustrated or annoyed whilst reinforcing a rule or expectation

Boundaries quite literally communicate safety and so communicating and reinforcing boundaries with children is a fundamental part of becoming a safe, trustworthy adult who is modelling a secure attachment style. When an adult is boundaried, it means the child knows where they stand, the adult is predictable, and the child learns to trust that the adult can keep them emotionally safe when they need it most. If they are overwhelmed or struggling with their feelings and behaviour, they can trust that the adult will step in and help them. They can also trust that the adult will help them take responsibility for their actions (when appropriate) and teach them natural consequences that mimic the real world. If a child experiences an adult who is unsure how to respond, tries different approaches every time, joins in with the dysregulation and responds with their own stress responses, then they cannot feel safe nor trust them to help. It can feel scary to be around an adult who doesn't know what to do when you are overwhelmed, and this can perpetuate the feeling of threat and danger which keeps them in a state of survival. This is especially important for those children who are struggling with insecure attachment and who may never have experienced an adult who is emotionally safe and boundaried before. What you do matters.

Insecure attachment and boundaries

Children who have experienced trauma such as domestic violence, abuse or neglect or who have been removed from parents and placed in foster care, might struggle with rules and boundaries, as we discussed in previous chapters. However, although it may seem as though they are pushing you away, *trying* to break your rules or 'pushing boundaries' they are probably more likely to be unsettled by them. It is hard to allow adults to have control when you believe they cannot be trusted with it, so they are likely to attempt to prove to themselves that you will let them down at some point and become unpredictable and unboundaried like the other adults in their life. It is easier to believe you will let them down, than to trust you and be disappointed or hurt by you. They don't want to believe you are safe, because that is alien to them and feels scary (even though they know deep down they are seeking safety and connection) so they will do all they can to push you into reactive responses to reinforce their belief system. This, however, just reinforces the need for you to remain boundaried and consistent! The more you respond using a therapeutic, boundaried response, the more likely they will begin to believe they can trust you. This takes a lot of time and repetition but is so worth it, and although it seems hard, it is achievable in a school setting if every adult is modelling a trauma-informed, attachment-aware response like this from nursery through to Year 6.

> **Remember:** It is very scary for a child to be so dysregulated that they are screaming, running, hitting and shouting with the belief that nobody can help. No child *wants* to feel so overwhelmed that they are that out of control of their responses and actions without any way to calm down. It might look threatening and volatile to you, but it is frightening and overwhelming for them. They desperately need you to help them feel safe and in control again!

Boundaries with low level behaviours

Reinforcing boundaries is an extension of your everyday teaching tool kit and should be part of your general interactions to help children learn the rules and expectations. Choosing when to enforce a boundary depends on the scenario you are in with a child and it might not always come after a full therapeutic response. In fact, a boundary might sometimes just be the way in which you redirect or remind them of things. For example, a child tapping their pencil on the table doesn't need a full therapeutic response, but you would still need to remind the child about the rules. In fact, being predictable and boundaried are over small things makes it less likely that the child will become dysregulated. It also makes it more likely that they will respond to you when they are dysregulated. That said, being boundaried doesn't mean constantly 'telling children off' though. What you say and how you say it matters!

 Develop your practice

The trick is to ask yourself whether the child's behaviour is a sign that they just need reminding about the rules – like lots of children do. If it is because they are already dysregulated, or if it is an indicator of them becoming dysregulated.

Low level behaviour that just needs a reminder

Let's look at some strategies for those lower-level behaviours where children just need reminding about the rules.

No, don't, can't and stop

If you are redirecting children or reminding them of the rules then a full therapeutic response isn't always needed, however, tweaking your language to ensure it is still trauma-informed is important. That change is really simple. Instead of using language that is anchored in disconnection and telling children what you *don't* want, focus on the key message and what you *do* want.

We often use buzz words such as no, don't, can't and stop when we are redirecting children.

'Don't swing on the chair Jack'
'Stop shouting out'
'No, you can't have the iPad'
'You can't have the bike, Taylor is on it'

But using these words is often problematic because they can be interpreted as negative and confrontational by the child. They also mask what we are really trying to say. When we say 'Don't swing on the chair' we are really saying 'Stay safe' but that is being missed. Children hear these 'No,' 'Don't,' 'Can't' and 'Stop' statements from adults lots of times a day, in various annoyed tones, and so their brain codes these words as threatening and associates them with disconnection, rejection or punishment. This can then trigger a survival response. Children are then more likely to respond by arguing back (fight mode), walking away (flight mode) or ignoring you (freeze mode). Unfortunately, we are then more likely to tell them off and become frustrated, not realising *we* have triggered them to respond in that way. Using language like this can mean the child doesn't hear the intention, message or direction behind what you are saying because they shut down as soon as they hear the buzz word. If our intention here is to teach and guide, we must avoid triggering an emotional or survival response and keep that rational part of the brain on, so that they can hear our actual message and then process and reflect on what they are doing and manage their responses.

It is much more effective to focus on the message or direction and reframe it by taking out those buzz words. Here are some examples:

With buzz words	Without buzz words
'Stop messing with that pencil' 'Stop shouting out Sarah!' 'Don't kick the chair' 'We can't go on iPads now' 'No, you can't have the bike' 'Don't interrupt Tom while he is talking' 'Stop running!' 'Don't lie on the floor!'	'Jack put the pencil down for me please' 'Sarah, let's listen now' 'Sarah just wait for me to finish' 'Keep your feet still for me Ben' 'Careful with that chair Ben' 'Look after that chair Ben' 'We will go on iPads later, it's PE first' 'iPad time is after lunch, let's wait until then' 'You can have the bike next, it's Sarah's turn first' 'Just wait 5 more minutes and it's your turn' 'Let Tom finish and then you can tell us your idea' 'Tom is trying to give his ideas, let's listen and then we can hear yours' 'Slow down guys' 'Be careful' 'Walk for me please' 'Jump up for me, Jack' 'Stand up, Charlie, so you don't get stood on'

Important note: Obviously if the child is in danger, you would still shout 'stop' to keep them safe.

These are all appropriate responses to low level behaviours and are still necessary alongside therapeutic responses. You might also remind the child of the rules and then follow it with a boundary – which is in this case a statement to help redirect or remind the child of the rules or expectations like this:

Remember we/it's	'Remember we listen to each other in this class, I will be two more minutes and then I will ask you for your ideas'
	'It's important to listen to each other's ideas, let Sarah talk and then you can share your ideas'
	'Remember, to take care of each other, be careful with Jacks leg'
	'Careful with that book Charlie, remember to take care of our things'
	'Remember, it's important to respect each other's opinions, it is okay for Jack to like something else'

For example, Ella is over excited in a lesson and keeps shouting out. You know Ella well and are confident her behaviour isn't rooted in a stress or survival response, instead she is just forgetting the rules. In this scenario you might say:

'Ella, remember, we listen to each other in this class, let me finish and then you can tell me what you want to say' (name, rule/value, boundary)

Start with the child's name, remind them of the rule (or value) you want to reinforce and then redirect them in a kind but assertive way. For many children, this will be enough to redirect them, especially if their behaviour isn't coming from a place of survival. You might also use your other teaching techniques like raising your eyebrows or raising your finger as if to say 'One minute.' Use your knowledge of the child, therapeutic approach and teaching in general to respond. If Ella does then begin to become unsettled, you might use some of the other therapeutic responses.

'You are worried I will forget you, so you are shouting over me, I am going to ask you next, wait one more minute' (feeling, behaviour, boundary)

Acknowledging Ella's frame of reference is important here and her feelings but that doesn't mean you stop speaking. Adding another statement that reinforces your boundary is important.

'I am going to ask you next, wait one more minute.'

If you are reminding children in this way but their behaviour continues, you can still move them or enforce another boundary but whilst avoiding buzz words and rejection. For example, if two children are still talking after reminding them a few times you might say, 'It is really hard for you to stop chatting so I am going to move you for a little while so you can concentrate' or 'Okay, you two, I have reminded you a few times now but you are still struggling to listen, Sarah can you move over there please for a little bit.'

Top tips

We and let's

Using the words 'we' and 'lets' with children helps to maintain a sense of connection and an air of 'togetherness' without making the child feel singled out or 'told off' which can, for some children, make them feel threatened or unsafe and trigger them to respond with an emotional, stress response like fight, flight or freeze. We want to make sure the children are directed in a way that still makes them feel included and connected to you.

Use words and actions together

When you are redirecting children, what you do is just as important as what you say. Your gestures and actions inform what you are saying and communicate your intention and boundary. If you are asking a child to put their pencil down, you might also move your hand across theirs as you speak to lower their pencil, this can help show them that you mean what you say. Asking a child to wait their turn for the bike can be done as you give the bike to another child and reminding a child not to walk on the mud might be paired with taking their hand and redirecting them away from it. This should always be done in a calm way and can make a huge difference to whether or not they follow the direction.

Special needs

It is important to remember that this approach makes up part of your overall teacher tool kit and should be applied when and where appropriate whilst using your knowledge of the children. Some children who have autism or special educational needs will still need direct instructions which may include, no, don't, can't and stop and so you would continue to use them to help them process the instruction or guidance given.

 Real life

I recently volunteered to be a DJ at my children's school disco. We had two cohorts of Years 3, 4 and 5 in the hall and I was leading the dancing at the front and prompting the children through a microphone. I love a good dance and so my school discos are less like a disco and more like a rave, with all the children jumping with their hands in the air. I love it, but I also love boundaries and it is important for me that there are rules and structure, especially with that many children. It is also important for the children to know what the boundaries are so they don't get overwhelmed, hurt, and can have a good time. I explained the rules as they came in and off we went! Now of course, in the excitement I had some children trying to roll on the floor and others doing piggy backs and so in order for me to communicate my boundaries I went over to them and instead of saying things like 'Don't roll on the floor' and 'Stop doing piggy backs' I said things like 'Stand up for me boys so you don't get hurt' whilst tapping them on the back or taking their hand, or 'Careful girls, you might fall' whilst putting my arm out to steady them and help one down. The children don't know me and I am always aware that they may have additional needs or be struggling with adverse experiences I won't be aware of. It is important to me that every child can access the disco and so I wanted to ensure I didn't make anyone feel singled out or stop their fun by triggering an emotional response but I also want to quickly redirect their behaviour. What I said was simple and it didn't include buzz words, it was to the point and direct and my actions helped them to understand my expectation over the noise without making them feel 'told off.'

Sometimes, a bit of redirection is all you need to gently get children back on track. This is more effective and connective than jumping in to giving them warnings or consequences. For example, 'Stop rocking on that chair, Ella, or I will put your name on the board' becomes 'Careful with that chair, Ella' (whilst you gently push the top of the chair down to steady it).

What happens though, when children are struggling with their behaviour and have broken the rules because they are dysregulated? Like Jack in our previous examples who has thrown a ball over the fence and hurt another child? How do you enforce a boundary without rejection and punishment but whilst still ensuring the children experience fair consequences?

Using a boundary after dysregulated behaviour

Remember, if a child is dysregulated, the boundary step comes *after* a child has had time to calm down and regulate. This might be through co-regulation (with your help) or through self-regulation (where you offer/suggest something they can do to help them calm down). It is important that the child feels emotionally calmer (and therefore safer) before the rules are reinforced and a boundary is put in place. If the child is still overwhelmed and struggling to manage their emotions, then they are still dysregulated and are responding from their survival part of the brain, and you can assume they are not going to handle your boundary very well. Children will not be able to rationally think, problem solve, have empathy or learn unless they are able to access their rational thinking part of the brain so calming them down is essential if you want any real learning to occur. If the child is still emotional or unsettled, they:

- Won't be able to follow your instructions or guidance
- Are likely to see your boundary as a punishment or rejection which will keep them in survival mode
- May respond with a fight, flight or freeze response to try and cope

Once you are confident that the child has calmed down enough to be able to access their rational, thinking part of the brain and that they feel emotionally safer, then you can remind them of the rules and give them a boundary.

When using the boundary approach, the idea is that you replace things like losing points, staying in at breaktime and missing golden time.

Develop your practice

This might sound like it makes sense as you are reading this, but it can be hard to do in practice, especially if you are used to giving a consequence as a direct response to a behaviour. It might take some effort on your part to try and re-program your 'go to' responses. To help you, try and identify where and when you might usually jump to a consequence or boundary even if the child might not be ready to receive it. Have a think about encounters you have had with children recently where they have been struggling with their behaviour. Write out what you said or did and think about what their response was. Maybe they threw their rubbish on the floor during a heated discussion, and you said, 'Er pick that up now Tom or you'll be missing break.' Or maybe they swore at you when they were cross and you said, 'Do not swear at me! Apologise please otherwise I will be ringing your mum.' Be honest with yourself here and think about whether they followed your instruction or consequence and whether it felt as though they learnt something valuable. Reflect also on whether it might have escalated the situation.

You might also need to enforce a boundary that keeps them safe in the moment but doesn't expect anything from them (for example removing a stapler they are snatching). In the therapeutic teaching approach, there are two boundaries to consider that could help depending on the situation. These are through limitation or through responsibility.

A limitation boundary (in the moment)

This is where you *need* to take something away from the child/children to keep them safe or defuse the situation. This is usually appropriate when the child is using an item to hurt others, in an unsafe way or arguing over something.

For example: fighting over a skipping rope, blocks or a toy; throwing a football, slamming down an iPad or throwing a rubber.

Important note: This is not the same as taking away golden time, stopping them from playing outside or taking away house points.

A boundary through limitation is relevant in the moment and is in the children's best interest because it takes away something that is causing the problem, it is not a punishment or a sanction.

A tool for teaching: whatever you take away, is only for a short time and is returned to the child so that they can 'try again' and figure out a way to manage the conflict or problem they were having when they are feeling calmer. It is a temporary measure to help the child calm down and refocus. You are helping shift them from dealing with the problem in survival mode, to dealing with the situation rationally. For example, if a child is arguing over a toy train, the train is gently taken away for a few minutes as you use your therapeutic responses and help the child calm down, it is then given back to the child so that they can figure out to deal with the situation in a healthy way, and solve the problem.

Sometimes this might be done silently without the need to say anything. Like with Amreen in our example, where we reflected back her feelings but also removed the rubber from the table at the same time. Or you might be suggesting some regulation time which naturally takes away the thing they are arguing about or struggling with. Other times you might explain to the children that you will be taking something away but they can have it back in a few minutes.

Here are some ways you might use a limitation boundary with the children. Remember this would be after your therapeutic, reflective response, name, feeling, behaviour and possibly the encourage statement too.

Limitation boundary (in the moment)	'Guys, nobody is being safe with this skipping rope (whilst taking it from a child gently) I am going to have to take it away for 10 minutes until you can use it safely, you can have it back in a little while to try again'
	'You are struggling to look after the iPad (while picking it up) go and have a quick drink and a five minute break and then you can have this back to try again'
	'Okay, that isn't safe, you can have this back in a minute just take a few moments to calm down and show me you can look after this'

Remember, a boundary through limitation is also where you silently remove the item whilst you are using your therapeutic response, name, feeling, behaviour:

Name: Ambreen

Feeling: You are feeling a bit unsettled about this group work. You are worried nobody will listen to your ideas

Behaviour: and so you are distracting others and messing with this rubber (whilst picking up the rubber and removing it from the table)

Encourage: You have brilliant ideas though, remember yesterday when you said about the tree? That was a great way of thinking about it. Oscar was so impressed with that answer, weren't you Oscar? He even wrote it down himself!

A responsibility boundary (after they are calm)

A boundary through responsibility is where you help the child figure out how to make amends for something they have done wrong. This is my favourite way to help a child feel boundaried and to teach at the same time.

For example: Picking up something they threw; cleaning up the water they poured on the floor; taping up the book they ripped; helping but the display they pulled down back up.

With a responsibility boundary, you would:

1. Allow them some time to calm down quietly
2. Acknowledge they feel better
3. Gently remind them of what happened/acknowledge their frame of reference or repeat your therapeutic response
4. Enforce your boundary by saying how they can fix things
5. Mention how you'll move on (this is important to help them see that you are focused on getting back to normal and not the punishment itself)

For example, after a child rips a book in anger and after your initial therapeutic response and regulation time you might say, 'You feel a bit more in control now, the Lego has helped. That was really tough. Let's go and find some tape for that book and put it back together and then we can go and do some PE.'

Important note: Children are more likely to accept responsibility for their actions and make amends when they are calm and feel safe, so this must come after regulation time. How you do this and what you say makes all the difference here. You are not demanding that they go and make amends or telling them to do it by themselves, you are using language that is empathetic and supportive but still giving them a boundary and an expectation of them to take responsibility for their actions. You are not saying – 'you chose to do something wrong and that is not okay, so now you have to be punished'. You are saying, 'I know that was really hard to navigate, you felt out of control, now let's make amends'.

Making amends *with* you: It is really important to acknowledge here how hard it is for a child to accept responsibility and fix it, this is often something they are forced to do when they are not ready and so it can feel huge for them to go and tape up a book they ripped, pick up something they dropped or clear up something they spilt. Navigating this through connection is key. Imagine a child has ripped down a display in anger, this is a big mistake to make and it can feel overwhelming for a child to take responsibility for it. However, it is really important that they do. We are not helping children by clearing away the mess they made and fixing what they have broken, because that means the lesson has been lost! In the same way, it doesn't help the child to be forced to clean something up or fix it by themselves in a way that might trigger shame. A really simple way to help children take responsibility without it feeling overwhelming is to do it with them, so using phrases like 'Let's go and . . .' helps. If they have trashed a whole room then we cannot expect them to clean the whole room by themselves, if they have pulled down a display we cannot expect them to put the whole thing back up again. So, instead, help them by saying 'Let's sort this display out, you stick the pictures back on and I will staple the border and then we can go and get lunch.' This communicates that before they can have lunch, they need to make amends but it also communicates they are not alone and it doesn't have to trigger a shame response. They made a mistake, they fix it with your help and move on! As soon as children realise this isn't anchored in punishment or anger, they will do it.

Have you ever had a child who tipped out the whole Lego box on to the floor and then when you ask them to clear it up, it just feels so huge to them, they refuse? Asking a child to do this with you is far more effective than making them to it themselves. It avoids them being triggered into a survival response and keeps that rational thinking brain on so that they can actually learn in the moment. That is the goal here!

Here are some examples of ways to communicate a responsibility boundary, again this would come after the other therapeutic teaching steps:

Responsibility boundary	'You feel much calmer now, let's go and clear up that water and have some lunch'
	'Do you feel a bit better now? It is horrible when you feel out of control like that and your emotions take over isn't it? Let's go and fix it so we can get on with the day (holds child's hand or touches arm to lead them out)'
	'Okay, let's go and find some tape for that book and put it back together and then we can go and do some PE'
	'I bet Sarah is wondering where you are, let's go and pick up those chairs and we can go and find her'
	'You were so overwhelmed before it was hard to think straight Now you are calmer, let's go and make amends, let's find the stapler so we can put those pictures back on the wall and then you can go out for a play'

Putting it all together:

Name: Jack
Feeling: It sounds like you really wanted to score but felt left out, you got frustrated and overwhelmed
Behaviour: and so that you threw the ball over the fence
Encourage: (Jack is too dysregulated for an encourage response – save it for later)
Regulate: Let's go and get some water and calm down a bit and we can sort this out when we are all thinking more clearly

(has time to calm down)

Encourage: Jack, you are a really good football player and the boys love playing with you, remember that pass you did last week? You are a great defender!
Boundary: Let's go and get the ball and make amends with James, I know he will want to play with you again at lunchtime . . .

Showing sorry

Another form of the responsibility boundary is helping children show sorry and not say sorry. Too often we force children to say sorry with no actual learning outcome or meaning. If we really reflect on it, when we ask a child to say sorry, we often get one of two responses.

1. A child will say 'sorry' in a voice that communicates that they don't really mean it
   or
2. A child will say, 'I'm not saying sorry!' and then you end up in a power struggle over saying sorry which has nothing to do with the thing they are saying sorry for!

When a child just says sorry but doesn't mean it, it is often because they have learnt that if they say it, the situation will be finished with and they can move on. Although it isn't conscious, this is not coming from a place of remorse, but instead from learnt behaviour or even a survival strategy. Saying sorry stops the uncomfortable situation, so they just do it. However, we now know that if children are apologising whilst still frustrated or upset, then they are very likely to be working from the emotional and survival part of their brain which means they cannot always feel the empathy we expect. This is another 'norm' that we need to re-think when approaching children, especially in our therapeutic teaching approach. If it doesn't have learning value for the child, then what is the point?

Instead of saying sorry, let's encourage the children to *show* they are sorry. This is a much better way to teach them how to make amends, rather than just forcing them to say sorry. Now this might not always be possible, but if it is I would encourage you to use this strategy as much as possible.

For example:

- Getting the person they hurt a drink or a teddy
- Getting them a tissue to wipe their nose or tears
- Giving them a hug
- Writing them a letter
- Doing something kind
- Using better phrases to communicate that they are sorry

Depending on the scenario there are lots of things you could encourage a child to do to help them show that they are sorry. Some children might be able to do this straight away, others may need to calm down first and then show they are sorry when they can actually feel it.

Showing sorry (after a therapeutic response)	'You were so frustrated and angry that you hurt Sarah, she is your best friend and I know you didn't mean it but she is really upset, could you go and get her a teddy to help her calm and show her you are sorry?'
	'Oh dear, Jack has a mark on his hand now, Toby you didn't mean to, but you hurt him, can you go and get the first aid box and some water to help him please?'
	'Sarah is hurt by what you said, how can you show her you are sorry? Maybe she could help you be the door monitor today?'
	'You were so cross you hurt Olivia, can you go and get her a tissue to help dry her eyes?'
	'Tilly is really upset that you pushed her. How could you make amends?'

Remember: You would only ask questions if the child is calm enough to use their rational thinking part of the brain, if they are also overwhelmed, they will need to calm down and then figure out how to show they are sorry later.

Learning through boundaries

Remember, everything we do with children should guide and teach them and promote skills they can use in their lives well beyond school. Every interaction is adding to a bank of lessons which will inform how they do things later in life. No teenager or young person is going to put themselves on time out or take away their own iPad when they do something wrong! So instead of giving children consequences anchored in punishment and sanctions that are punitive, let's instead focus on how we can help them learn to make amends and take responsibility for their actions. They are much more likely to adopt these lessons and use them later.

Being comfortable with no punishment

It can feel hard for some adults to accept that asking a child to tape up a book, or mend a display is a good enough replacement for a sanction like missing their break. Sometimes this is the hardest part of the approach for people to embrace. We have been programmed from our own childhoods to believe that a sanction or punishment is needed to be a sufficient consequence, but if we really take a step back and think about it, learning to tape up a book and take action to show you are sorry for something, is much more powerful that having to sit inside and miss break. It is also harder for the child to do, and a bigger step for the child when they do it. The learning and outcomes are far stronger and beneficial than the child receiving a random consequence or punishment.

Validating whilst keeping boundaries

Asking a child to make amends is a big deal and it can feel really hard for the child, and that might mean they are not happy about it. That's fine! They are allowed to feel cross about having to do it and they might even stomp about when doing it. When this happens, avoid being pulled into a fresh power struggle where this becomes a new source of disconnection and instead empathise with how hard it is whilst still maintaining your boundary. They might say, 'This is so unfair' but instead of saying, 'Adam, you threw the water so you need to clean it up, that isn't unfair, it seems very fair to me!' say, 'I know, it feels really unfair and you just want your dinner now' (whilst handing them the mop to wipe up the water they spilt) or 'It is such a big job it feels overwhelming!' (whilst kneeling down to help them pick up the Lego bricks they dropped). You might then follow this with, 'We can do it together. You get that side and I will get this side and then we can go and play.' Children won't always be happy about the boundaries you set, and that's fine. You can empathise with how hard it is for them without budging on the expectation or boundary itself. This helps validate the child's feelings but clearly communicates that you are sticking to your word (which means you can be trusted remember!)

Step 7: Teach

The teach step in the approach is where we might have a conversation with the child, explore that they could do better next time or offer a solution or guidance or ask questions. This is usually what we would jump to straight away but, in this approach, it comes last.

Remember, children must calm down that initial emotional response and feel connected and emotionally safe before they can access their rational thinking part of the brain – the prefrontal cortex. It is only when a child feels emotionally safe and calm that they can utilise skills like problem solving, empathy, reflection, reasoning, and their memory. The steps that come before this one are all guiding and supporting a child back to a place where they can then begin to feel in control and use those executive functioning skills.

Without this guidance from adults, children cannot develop or grow this rational part of the brain and cultivate these skills. By following a therapeutic approach, we are helping children to learn how to identify, understand and manage their initial emotional, survival or stress response that triggers them into fight, flight, freeze and move them into their rational thinking part of the brain. The more we do this with them, the more they will begin to be able to do this for themselves. The result will be children who are able to then access the skills to truly manage and cope with challenge and difficulties, social interaction and emotions and grow the part of the brain they need to make these skills for life. We will have children who no longer believe they are badly behaved or naughty with no control over their responses when they are stressed, and instead have children who recognise how they respond to stress and what to do about it! How you respond to their emotions and behaviour is literally shaping, growing and re-wiring their brains! This is an amazing contribution and impact that you can have on children's lives and is far more significant to their overall life outcomes than learning how to spell or do their times tables. Although the world will have you believe that the role of the teacher is to teach academically, I would argue that in fact the real role of the teacher is to teach them how to be emotionally intelligent. I recognise this can feel frustrating when you have tests and outcomes measuring children's academic achievements, but the truth is, children will not and cannot learn if they are overwhelmed and working from a place of stress anyway. Their brain literally shuts down, so the *only* answer is to focus on their emotional safety and to calm that survival brain down. Along with shaping them for the future and contributing to better mental health and wellbeing, this also means they also more likely to want to do their maths because their rational brain is on! Win, win!

Conversation

Teaching children about what just happened when they were overwhelmed is the last step in our approach. After the child is calmer and has made amends, you can then have a therapeutic, empathetic conversation about what happened or offer guidance or insight. Whatever you feel is most appropriate given the situation and the child. This is not a lecture, or a telling off, it is a way to help them have further insight into what happened, and to have help to think about what they could do next time. If your school follows the restorative conversation approach then this is where those conversations are most appropriate, not straight after the incident. Although it is important revisit the situation with a child, especially if they have hurt someone or something, this doesn't have to be in the form of a traditional sit down. You could mention it when playing alongside the child, eating, or chatting to help it feel less threatening. In the chat, you could ask them what is going on and whether they are they okay or you could explore what happened and asked why they think they responded in that way. It is here where children will feel emotionally safe enough to open up and aside from the scenario that just occurred, they might also talk about what is going on at home, intrusive thoughts, or a problem with a specific peer who is upsetting them. During these conversations it is important to help the child to feel validated and continue to use your therapeutic responses rather than just give suggestions. Always start with reflection, 'That sounds really hard,' 'It is tricky having a new baby in the house,' 'You sound like you miss your nana.' This will continue that feeling of connection and help the child experience a safe, secure adult who not only guided them through their difficult emotions and whatever the scenario was, but also offered a safe, nurturing space to talk too.

Aside from a conversation, it is important to offer some guidance to help them figure out specifically what they can do differently. In previous steps we have already highlighted their internal response, helped them manage it and also make amends, that in itself is a series of important lessons, the last bit is to help them figure out what they could do differently next time a situation like this happens again.

'Next time try' response

One of the other common 'teacher responses' that could use a little tweak is the habit of using blanket statements. We might say things like, 'use kind voices,' 'be kind friends,' 'play nicely,' 'I want to see good sharing,' 'work together,' but honestly, what do they even mean? If a child is struggling to navigate a tricky situation with a friend, hearing you say 'be kind friends' or 'play nicely' really doesn't help them in the moment. These statements have good intentions, but we forget that children need to be shown and taught how to respond or what to do and say. What do you mean by 'be kind friends?'

When a child is calm and in their rational thinking part of the brain, yes, they understand that they should be a kind friend but as soon as they are feeling stressed, overwhelmed or unsafe, however, they're not thinking rationally about how they can be kind, they are hijacked by their survival responses. Our job here is to help children reflect on the scenario to realise what they could have done and what they could say to handle the situation better in the future. If they could 'play nicely' in the moment, they would – but they can't!

The 'next time try' response comes at the end of our therapeutic teaching steps and helps the child to look back over what happened (when in their rational brain) and reflect on the situation with specific guidance from you about what they can do next time. It is linked to something they could have *done* or something they could have *said*. In some scenarios you might need to do this after following all six previous steps, for other scenarios you might just need to reflect back their feelings and behaviour and then go straight to a 'next time try' statement. Remember, these steps are fluid, and you can use them in whatever way best meets the child's needs in the moment.

When you are telling a child what they could say, you are literally telling them how to communicate what they felt in an emotionally intelligent way. This can be short and sweet.

For example: Connor is playing with the bricks in Year 1 and he is building a tower. Jenny comes over and starts taking the bricks away to play her own game. Connor is getting frustrated and snatches his bricks back from Jenny. You go over and instead of saying, 'Connor share the bricks please' or 'Don't snatch,' you say, 'Connor you are working so hard on this tower and Jenny is taking your bricks, it is frustrating you and so you are snatching. Next time say, "Jenny, I really want to build my tower but you are taking my bricks and it is frustrating"' – this connective response empathises with Connor, helps calm his initial fight response and also gives him the words he needs for next time. You could then follow on with a boundary or guidance for Jenny. 'Jenny, Connor is working really hard. Let's let him finish his tower, you play with these blocks.' Your 'next time try' response could be a variation of things depending on the situation. Here are some more examples of what you could say:

'Connor you are working so hard on this tower and Jenny is taking your bricks, it is frustrating you and so you are snatching . . .'	Next time say . . . 'Jenny, I am just finishing my tower. You can have these bricks instead (offering different bricks)' Or 'Jenny, let me finish this tower and then you can have the bricks' Or 'Jenny, I am getting frustrated because you are taking all the bricks I was using' Or 'Jenny, I just want to finish this and then we can both use the bricks together'

Start the sentence off with, 'Next time try saying . . .'	'I feel like nobody is listening and it is making me frustrated' 'I want to play but you are leaving me out' 'I am trying to help, but you think I am taking over' 'I feel like nobody is passing the ball to me and I am getting upset' 'I have tried to join in but I feel left out' 'I really want to play with you but you keep hurting me' 'I want to tell you my ideas but you keep saying no and I am getting frustrated' 'I am getting frustrated with this question and I need a break' 'I am worried about the new teacher and feel a bit unsettled' 'I need a minute to calm down, I am getting overwhelmed' 'I am struggling to focus my mind' 'I feel like I can't do it and everyone else can'

Some more examples of a 'next time try' statement might be:
Sometimes your guidance is better focused on something they can *do* to help themselves manage the situation better, rather than something they can say.

'Start by saying 'Next time try . . .'	'Taking five deep breaths and getting a drink of water and then try again' 'Going to the calm corner for a moment to clear your head' 'Asking whether you can see the therapy dog for five minutes to help you feel better' 'Doing some drawing to help you feel better'

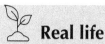 **Real life**

A group of children are playing outside in the playground and Tilly storms off and says, 'I am not playing with you! I am not your friend.'

She sits on the side upset and when you go over, she tells you that they are not listening to her ideas and they won't let her do her dance.

Instead of saying 'Girls, come on, play nicely together and listen to each other' you empower Tilly to manage the situation herself and say, 'That sounds really frustrating, it is hard when people don't listen to your ideas and now it is making you not want to play at all! You can sit here with me for a bit if you like to help you calm down. (Then, when she is calmer) Next time you could try saying, "I really want to play but I feel left out and nobody is listening to my ideas" or "I want to play but I feel left out, I am going to play something else for a bit".'

Putting it all together:

Name: Jack
Feeling: It sounds like you really wanted to score but felt left out, you got frustrated and overwhelmed
Behaviour: and so that you threw the ball over the fence
Encourage: (Jack is too dysregulated for an encourage response – save it for later)
Regulate: Let's go and get some water and calm down a bit and we can sort this out when we are all thinking more clearly
(has time to calm down)
Encourage: Jack, you are a really good football player and the boys love playing with you, remember that pass you did last week? You are a great defender!
Boundary: Let's go and get the ball and make amends with James, I know he will want to play with you again at lunchtime . . .
Teach: (after conversation or whilst getting the ball) You know, next time you could say 'Guys, nobody is passing me the ball and I am getting frustrated. I feel left out!'

Top tip: Avoid telling them to come to you!

Remember, 'next time try' statements are to help them navigate tricky situations by themselves. Try to avoid saying 'next time come and find me' or 'next time tell a teacher' because this can take the power away from the child and de-skill them. Of course, in some scenarios it is important for them to find an adult to help them, but don't allow this to become a crutch or blanket statement where it isn't needed. Focus your 'next time try' statements on specific things they can do or say, so that the next time they are in this situation and there is nobody to help them, they have a set of responses they can use.

Offering 'next time try' statements increases children's emotional intelligence skills and can be done from nursery age all the way through to teenagers and beyond. I used to do this all the time with nursery aged children. When I started my career, I was a TA in a 78-place nursery whilst I was finishing my training to be a play therapist and I spent most of my days using the therapeutic teaching responses, calming and regulating and using 'next time try' statements. The children were like sponges and would soak up the guidance, even when I used words like 'frustrated' or 'nervous.' I would give them specific sentences about what to say in different scenarios and within weeks I would hear them using and repeating these sentences in their own interactions and communications, especially within their friendship groups. Language went from 'I am not your friend' to 'I feel left out' It was wonderful to see and before I knew it, we had emotionally intelligent nursery aged children who were learning to navigate social interactions and challenges using therapeutic, connective responses and language.

'Next time try' statements are a brilliant part of your toolkit to help cultivate children's own strategies and skillsets. Children quickly find that people react better to their new responses and so that reinforces their use of them, helping to replace older strategies that were less effective. I have done this for years with my own children, and my daughter who is now 10 will come home from school and tell me a scenario and say 'Mum, what do you say when someone . . .' and I then give her different possible responses to that situation. I have been doing this with her since she was small and at every parents evening without fail, in every year of school, the teacher's first comment is 'she is so emotionally intelligent.' Starting young makes a difference!

Long term impact

The power of every teacher in every year responding to children therapeutically from nursery age means you can cultivate these skills in children from the age of 4 all the way to when they are 11 years old, contributing significantly to their most formative years. Embedding this approach throughout your school means that by the time your nursery children reach year 6, the levels of dysregulation, mental health problems and social skills will be significantly decreased and the levels of empathy, connection, problem solving, communication and regulation will have increased (amongst many other things). That is how we truly make a difference to children's mental health and wellbeing long term, each and every one of us can do that.

 Develop your practice:

As with your therapeutic responses, a good way to begin to embed this into your practice is to spend time creating a list of different possible 'next time try' statements you can use. This way, when you are with the children, it is easier to recall something that fits. Write down common scenarios that happen with the children and then write a list of possible 'next time try' statements to use and then go out there and practice!

Using the therapeutic teaching steps: Important things to be aware of

It takes no extra time

Although I have broken down the approach here into seven steps, the time it takes to respond in this way is the same (or less) as the time it takes to respond with your normal teacher responses. However, it can feel longer when you initially begin to embed the steps and this is purely because it is new! Whenever you are cultivating a new skill, at the start it can feel difficult and clunky (like when you first learn to drive a car). You are cognitively aware of yourself trying to remember what to do and what comes next, and it doesn't feel natural or easy. This is totally normal! It is important to push past this initial feeling and continue to practice your responses with the children. The more you do it, the more natural it will become. Be brave, put yourself out there and try things out! If you are confident, the children will feel that and sense you are in control and they will feel more at ease.

You have got this! Soon, you will find that the time it takes to respond therapeutically feels quick, easy and effective. You will also find that you feel far more in control and calm than you have before and you will be less likely to respond to situations with your own stress response, instead responding from the rational part of the brain with intention and consistency. The more you do this, the more you create a feeling of emotional safety for the child. The more emotionally safe the child feels, the faster they will respond to your approach and the less dysregulated they will be.

You don't need to use every step

It is really important to remember that this approach is designed to be used in whatever way suits the child and the scenario best. You might not always need to use every single step. Your job is to assess the level of need and become attuned to the child in the moment, this will help inform your response. I say this with caution though because this doesn't mean slipping back into old responses like sanctions, coaxing and rewards. Instead, I mean sensing when a boundary is needed and whether it can happen before or after regulation, and knowing the difference between redirecting a child because they are off track vs a dysregulated child. Knowing what to use and where will begin to feel more natural the more you practice but, in some scenarios, you might miss out steps depending on the situation, for example:

'You are feeling unsettled, let's get a drink of water'

(Feeling, Regulate)
'Sarah, you are so excited, you are bouncing about all over the place!'

(Name, Behaviour)
'The hall is so noisy, it is a bit overwhelming, you can do this though Connor!'

(Feeling, Encourage)
'Jack, remember we keep each other safe, put the pencil back for me'

(Name, Boundary)
'Everyone is feeling a bit tired this afternoon, let's do a five minute colouring activity to refocus us all'

(Feeling, Regulate)

These statements are all examples of therapeutic responses, they just don't need all seven steps. The more you ebb and flow like this, the more natural and frequent your therapeutic responses will become.

It might get worse before it gets better

When you begin implementing this approach, you will see changes very quickly and will find that levels of dysregulation will begin to decrease across the board. One of the schools on our online course saw a 50% decrease in SEMH needs across the school after training all staff as well as finding they had less CPOMS incidents recorded. However, when you begin to adapt your behaviour policy and swap sanctions for consequences, you may also find that some children seem to be 'bubbling' and it might feel like low-level incidents have increased or like more children are testing boundaries than usual. This can feel frustrating, especially when you know that the old point system or red card system would have nipped it in the bud. At this stage in the process, it is easy to begin to worry that the approach isn't working and to fall back on old strategies. But don't let yourself! What is happening here is twofold, firstly, the approach is new for you and therefore it can be hard to feel confident and comfortable in all situations and the children pick up on that 'unsure' vibe you give off. They then feel unsettled and begin to 'bubble' testing boundaries to see where they stand. The second is that the children are experiencing totally different responses to usual, and this doesn't fit with their expectations. They have ripped a book but instead of being shouted at and missing break, you are emotionally connecting and are asking them to tape it up. Instead of being reactive you are reflective and instead of being punished they are being helped. This can feel alien to a lot of children, especially those who struggle with their behaviour the most and who have the biggest emotional needs. They are used to predicting the outcomes of the adults around them and being able to do that brings them a level of comfort (even if the normal responses didn't actually help them). This new shift feels unsettling because it is unfamiliar, they are unsure about where the boundaries are and whether this is something they can rely on and trust. Their brains might interpret that feeling of unease as a possible sign of danger and as a result, you might see some children struggling or 'bubbling.' This is totally normal! They are just getting used to it, just like you. They need consistency so that they can experience your new response enough times for it to feel 'normal' and reliable. Being consistent allows the children and their brains to begin to trust and find security in your new responses.

Once it becomes embedded and part of your day-to-day interactions and culture, it will all begin to fall into place. I have seen this time and time again with children. The worst thing you can do, however, is to begin to fall back in to old patterns and responses because it feels more familiar to you and is easier to do. This will only create confusion and make it harder for children to trust you. Remember, children look up to us as if we have all the answers and know what we are doing! Changing the goal posts only creates a sense of unease.

Consistency is key

Consistency is the key here. When we are consistent, it means we are reliable, predictable and safe. Consistency quite literally equals trust. The more we can show children we mean what we say, we do what we say, and we respond similarly each time, the safer they will feel and a trusting relationship can develop. When an adult constantly tries new approaches, changes the goal post, uses different strategies each time and is inconsistent with their responses or boundaries, the child is left feeling overwhelmed and anxious. This adult is communicating that they have no idea what to do to help and that they are not in control. If the adult isn't in control, then the child will try to be, and the power dynamics will shift. Internally children will think, 'How can I trust you to keep me emotionally safe if you don't even know what to do when I am upset?' This is true of all children, but particularly true of those children who have been through childhood trauma and have had repeated examples of adults who cannot help.

Your goal is to help the children feel like you are reliable and trustworthy, even when they are struggling. You are the dependable, safe, calm adult who can help them calm down. So even if it feels easier to fall back into old patterns, remember this is damaging the overall goal. Try to be consistent with what you say and how you say it as well as with your body language and facial expressions, like we discussed at the beginning of this chapter. Saying the same phrases or words in your response, like 'you are feeling,' 'let's,' 'we' and 'next time try' begin to feel comforting to a child because they can predict them and that feels safe. So even if you are questioning yourself, keep going. Remember, the outcome isn't to stop the behaviour, it is to help the child feel emotionally safe and that takes time.

Remember, this is a whole school approach and being able to rely on your team for support, tag teaming things and providing the same level of nurture and therapeutic responses throughout the school team is key. It is also vital that you are looking after yourself and your own wellbeing too like we discussed at the beginning of this chapter. You cannot be emotionally available to the children, or respond with your rational thinking brain, if you are not in a good place yourself.

There is no quick fix

Supporting children with their emotions and behaviour is challenging at the best of times but with the increasing numbers of children struggling today, it can leave you feeling emotionally drained and exhausted. If behaviour is particularly challenging at your school and you feel like you are constantly 'putting out fires' it is easy to begin to feel deflated and stressed. That however, activates your own survival and fight flight freeze responses which can mean you become more reactive and less tolerant. It makes total sense to feel this way, working with children isn't easy, especially children who are struggling and it is easy to find yourself feeling desperate for a quick fix or a solution. Unfortunately, that doesn't exist. There is no magic strategy or response that stops children feeling emotionally dysregulated or unsafe. These are not children who choose to misbehave and can just stop choosing. Nor are they children who can be managed out of struggling with certain behaviour management strategies. Remember, for the most dysregulated children, who are frequently running out, climbing trees or jumping fences, their brains have literally been wired for survival. You are responding to a survival mechanism that is designed to protect this child, a survival mechanism that has been reinforced over and over again by the child's adverse experiences and relationships. In some cases, you don't just have the normal child development barriers to contend with, but you are also up against years of programming, abuse, hurt, pain and suffering. The only way to really help is to create meaningful, caring connections with the children that help them feel safe, loved and valued. You are not stopping behaviour. You are re-wiring the brain. With every interaction you are helping the brain to learn that some people can care, some adults protect, some people can be trusted. That takes time and isn't something it can believe straight away.

Using the therapeutic teaching approach does work, I have seen it time and time again, but it is a graduated, gentle journey that takes time. It doesn't mean that it will suddenly stop Adam from climbing trees or running away when he is overwhelmed. For those very vulnerable children, it might take a whole academic year or more before they feel safe enough to trust you. It might take months of repeatedly responding to dysregulated, sabotaging behaviours before they stop feeling the need to run. Every child is different. The best thing you can do, is not to place your focus on trying to stop the behaviour or on getting them to conform to the norm, but instead to take every scenario as it comes build on your relationship, be in the moment with the child, model that security and safety repeatedly and continue to be consistent. You might not see overnight changes in some children, but you will see changes, even if they are small ones. They might begin to calm down more quickly, recognise their own emotions and name them, manage challenges better and self-regulate more often. That small progress is actually life changing and will leave them with meaningful lessons that they can take into the future. As therapeutic teachers, we must realise that some children at school will not learn how to recite their times tables and do well in their SATS, in fact their outcomes might not be academic at all. But they might learn how to come to school and make friends and eat in the noisy dining hall. They might learn what anxiety feels like and learn that they are lovable. Their outcomes might be social and emotional outcomes and despite what the school system tells us, we have to be okay with that. Every child is different, and every journey is significant. Who knows, maybe supporting Jack through dysregulated behaviours now, means he will feel confident enough to come back into education and enrol in night school later. Children will learn when they feel emotionally able, that might not be just yet for some.

Focus on meeting their wider needs

Alongside supporting children in the moment, it is important to focus on their wider needs. If the root cause of behaviour is that they don't feel safe, then your goal is to help them feel safer. If they feel unseen then your goal is to help them feel worthy and noticed. Look at different ways you can meet these needs day to day. Can they be chosen for jobs around school, access a nurture group, access therapy or mentoring, be part of the school council etc. Meeting their emotional needs will help decrease the potential for dysregulation and ensure support is proactive and intentional and not reactive.

Next steps

So now we have looked at the therapeutic teaching approach, let's look at how that feeds into the therapeutic school approach and what else can you consider. We are now going to explore how you can adapt your behaviour policy and procedures to ensure that it mirrors this therapeutic, trauma-informed approach and then we will look at what you can do outside of your own responses with regard to the environment itself.

References

Goleman, D. (1998) *Working with Emotional Intelligence.* New York: Bantam Books.

Stump, S. (2022) 'Ophrah Winfrey recalls the final moments with her father before his death.' *Today*, 18 July. Available at: www.today.com/parents/parents/oprah-win frey-shares-eulogy-father-vernon-winfreys-funeral-rcna38715 (accessed 13 March 2024).

Winfrey, O. (2021) 'Oprah Winfrey discloses details of her abusive childhood in emotional interview.' Available at: www.youtube.com/watch?v=eiQbu5O_QFE (accessed 13 March 2024).

10
Creating a Connection and Regulation Policy

It is not our job to manage anyone's behaviour, it is our job to help them learn to manage their own behaviour

When we think about behaviour policies in school, they tend to be focussed on the conventional reward vs sanction model which we discussed in the redefining behaviour management chapter. In the therapeutic school approach, a 'behaviour management policy' is no longer an appropriate way to meet the emotional and mental health needs of children today. It is not trauma-informed or attachment-aware and neither is it inclusive. The concept of 'managing' someone else's behaviour is unrealistic and damaging and is not our role. We should instead be guiding and teaching children to manage their own behaviour and that is the focus of the connection and regulation policy. It does what it says on the tin, it is a document outlining how every adult in school can connect with a child who is struggling (not misbehaving) and help them to regulate and calm down (not stop the behaviour or make them behave). Whilst also allowing the brain to regain control and access their rational thinking capacity so that they can learn from the experience and develop emotional intelligence skills. However, creating a policy that captures all of this without falling back into the old narrative, language and processes can be tricky. In this chapter we are going to look at some key elements to consider when writing your policy, and what you can do instead of conventional behaviour management strategies.

If you are reading this thinking 'I am not in charge of the policy,' don't be fooled into thinking this then doesn't apply to you. Remember, you have so much more power than you think to influence change but learning and equipping yourself is the first step.

DOI: 10.4324/9781003410652-12

Before writing your policy

Who is the policy for?

Have a think about a conventional behaviour policy. Who has this been written for? The child or the adult? If we are honest with ourselves, it is probably more for the adults than the child or children. This isn't intentional of course and it makes sense that without an understanding of the science, we have created policies that try to 'manage' children and 'stop' 'difficult' behaviour. This frame of reference is focused on the adults need to get the child to behave so that they can continue to teach. In many cases, punitive measures can look as though they are working because for many children, they do indeed *stop* the behaviour but that doesn't mean they are teaching anything. We now know that conventional policies are damaging to children's emotional development and that although they might stop the behaviour, they don't stop the feelings, beliefs, thoughts and experience behind that behaviour. Instead of learning how to manage those, children are left feeling to blame and cannot learn socially, emotionally or academically. This failure to focus on the child's needs is often a huge contributing factor for why so many children struggle to come to school and cannot manage in mainstream schools. How can they manage if we are not teaching them how to?

When you write a policy, it should reflect both the best interest of the child who is struggling and the other children in the class. It is not in their interest to learn that when you struggle with your feelings, you are punished and told off. It is also not in their interest to feel rejected and shamed for not knowing how to manage their feelings or for being triggered into a survival or stress response. When you write a connection and regulation policy, it is important to ensure the child's voice and frame of reference is reflected throughout and that the focus is on meeting their needs.

What is the goal behind the policy?

The other thing to think about is what is your goal with this policy? Is it to stop children from misbehaving and to make sure everyone is following the school rules? Or is it more than that for you? Is it to help the children learn from their mistakes, teach them how to do things better next time? To give them insight into what is going on for them, to help them navigate tough situations and emotions, to build true real connections and relationships . . . the list goes on! Of course, most of the time when I sit down with Head Teachers, their intention *is* to help but the conventional behaviour policy does not reflect that intention and almost pulls them away from their own internal compass. Instead, a connection and regulation policy re-frames behaviour and aims to help guide and teach children, not punish, and reject.

Avoiding blame culture: 'good' vs 'bad'

It is also important to consider the messages a policy sends out to the children and school itself. If the policy is focused on telling children off, sending them away, sanctions and rewards we are silently communicating that there are 'good' and 'bad' behaviours, or worse, 'good' and 'bad' children, and although, yes, behaviour can be challenging, a reward and punishment culture assumes 'bad' behaviour is a cognitive choice rather than a response. This can create a comparison and judgemental culture in school where children are putting each other (and themselves) into a 'good' or 'bad' box. This isn't helped by some of the language we use such as 'good boy' or 'good girl' or by the parenting culture where phrases like, 'be a good boy today' are common. Remember, to be 'good' is often unachievable for some children, especially when they are constantly being hijacked into their survival responses. They are unable to make a cognitive, rational choice about their behaviour, but the outside world is telling them they should be able to. That can be really hard. It is also important to remember that our children are not animals to be trained: like dogs. They are humans with valid emotions, thoughts, beliefs and experiences that inform how they show up and behave. Our goal is not to 'train' them to be submissive and 'good' but instead to help them figure out how to navigate the tough stuff and thrive as individual human beings.

The culture we create in school informs the expectations of the children, parents and adults when it comes to punishment, and often a blame culture is created. When we 'reward' and 'punish' behaviour, we create an expectation that someone *should* be rewarded or punished. This black and white way of looking at behaviour isn't healthy and can negatively impact children's sense of self (remember when we talked about shame for those children who are struggling with trauma).

As you begin to make changes to your language and responses, you might worry about how parents will react to not having consequences like before. You might worry that they will demand a consequence after someone hurt their child for example. This can sometimes be tricky for both teachers and Head Teachers to navigate. However, it is important to remember two things here:

1. They only know what they know. Many of the parents themselves have grown up with punitive behaviour management methods both at home and in their own school lives. This is their expected norm and without an understanding of neuroscience, of course they will demand to see a consequence.
2. Schools reinforce the expectation. Until you begin to change your approaches, you too may have reinforced this 'good' and 'bad,' reward and sanction culture. This might have been through stickers and certificates and time out and warning cards for example. When you change that approach, parents and children will naturally feel unsure about it and will question things in search for the comfort of what they believe to be right.

However, just because it has always been done, does not mean you should continue to do it! Shifting culture and social norms is not easy, but when you know it is rooted in the best interest of every child, not only whilst they are at your school but for their trajectory of their lives, it is worth the battle.

A connection and regulation policy creates new cultural norms and a new set of expectations and it sends new messages to children and parents. The frame of reference is no longer, 'They misbehaved and so were punished.' Instead it is, 'They were struggling and so we helped' and this is true for all children across the whole school.

The culture is created not only through how the teachers speak to the children, policies and training but also through the assemblies you have, the conversations you have, and how you refer to incidents or children who are struggling. When a child is dysregulated, the other children are watching the way in which it is handled, they are learning from what the teacher says and their reactions. They learn a lot from how the teacher frames the situation to them. In a conventional behaviour policy, children who are struggling are given warnings, which their classmates see, they are then given consequences, which their classmates see, and this silently communicates the 'good' vs 'bad' punishment vs reward culture. Jack was bad so he was told off. Sarah was good so she was rewarded.

To come away from this, instead, highlight what is going on for the child who is struggling and also for the other children too! What you say makes all the difference. Too often a child is given warnings or consequences and then everyone is just expected to carry on with work. There is no explanation, guidance or insight given and the children make their own judgements based on the underlying messages. What is missing is that overarching therapeutic response that acknowledges the whole class. If a child is dysregulated, tips over some chairs and eventually is taken out of the room, we need to address what has happened with the other 29 children in the class. You might say, 'It is hard to see someone that upset' or 'James just needs a bit of time to calm down and then he will be back.' These responses normalise the fact that we all struggle with our feelings sometimes and offers a non-judgemental frame of reference that the children can model in their own thinking. The idea is that instead of seeing James being 'bad' and needing to be told off, they see James as struggling and needing help. Within this you would be using therapeutic responses to help the class feel more settled and validated, acknowledging that it isn't easy to see someone throwing over desks or pulling down displays.

'That was a bit tough to watch wasn't it, is everyone okay? Jack didn't mean to worry you; he is really unsettled and needs some help to calm down. We all get like that sometimes. Let's all have a drink of water and do some calm breathing before we carry on.'

Remember, it doesn't matter how 'good' some of these children are at school, they have all felt how Jack feels at some point and have also shown behaviours like this, probably at home over something silly like wanting to watch TV! It is important to remind them of this to avoid that 'bad boy' narrative. When Jack comes back to the room, again you address this and create a culture of understanding, 'Jack! I am so glad you are here, it's maths and you love maths!' or 'Jack, Sarah has missed you! She has been waiting for you to come back' thus helping the children to see that there is not a relationship disrepair or disconnection for Jack, which teaches them that 'bad' behaviour doesn't result in not being liked by you or being rejected. It also helps to reduce their own feelings of concern about being around Jack after he was so angry.

Outside of dysregulated behaviour, have conversations about emotions and feelings, help the children to see that 'naughty' is usually 'struggling' and help them to develop ways in which they can help each other when they are struggling. This approach not only builds emotional intelligence in every child, but it also reduces the child's expectation to see a consequence or punishment. Then instead of a child going home saying, 'Mum, Jack was naughty today, he pulled down a display and got a time out' they say, 'Mum, Jack was really struggling today, he pulled a display down because he was angry but we helped him feel better and he put it back up again!' I don't know about you, but I would much prefer my child to come home and say this to me. It is a sign of developing empathy and emotional intelligence. If you also use the 'show sorry' strategy they are more likely to say things like, 'Jack upset me today, but he made it up to me' rather than 'Jack upset me and the teacher didn't do anything.' You can use these same strategies with parents, through what you say and how you frame things, 'Jack got really overwhelmed today, the hall was a bit too chaotic, but we helped him calm down and talked it through' vs 'Jack didn't have a good day today, he pulled down the display and I had to put him on time out. I hope he has a better day tomorrow.' The parents' reaction will be different upon hearing these two different sentences. In the first, the parent is more likely to show some sort of empathy for their child's emotional state (not always however) and help them to process it. In the second, the parent is more likely to become angry or frustrated with their child and might give them a sanction at home. Language is everything!

Values vs Rules

Before you have any sort of policy, it is important to establish expectations with the children. Remember when we talked about reframing the rules from negative, buzz words to a set of connective values? Have a think about what your values are for the children and have them put up in every class-room in a nice frame for the children and teachers to see. Use these in your connection and regulation policy to centre the intention of your policy around developing the children themselves. Focusing it on what you do want to see (internal emotional intelligent skills) instead of what you don't want them to do (the external behaviours).

Replace rules:
    No swearing
    No phones

No fighting
No running

With values:
We listen to each other
We look after each other
We take care of our things
We support one another
We work as a team
We respect everyone's opinions

Then, use these values to communicate your expectation and boundaries to support your connection and regulation policy. So, 'Ben! Stop shouting out!' becomes, 'Ben, remember we listen to each other in this class, let me finish and then you can tell us your ideas.'

When writing your policy

Policy aims

The aims of a connection and regulation policy are very different to the aims of a behaviour policy. They should mirror the adults' intentions and shared goals and should be similar to these:

- To provide a framework that is trauma-informed and inclusive, ensuring that it is appropriate for all of the children at our school
- To create a therapeutic ethos in school whereby every member of staff responds to children's behaviour and emotions with insight and understanding based on neuroscience and trauma-informed techniques
- To create a nurturing, attuned environment where children are not punished for having big feelings but instead are guided through them
- To develop self-aware, empathetic and reflective thinkers whereby children are learning from their difficult feelings and behaviour and developing their emotional intelligence
- To support children through their difficult feelings and behaviour with the intention of teaching and guiding them through how to manage the same feelings/situation differently next time

- To respond to children with connection and understanding rather than disconnection and rejection with the awareness that this will help create an opportunity to learn and for behaviours to change
- For all children to feel safe in our care, especially when they are overwhelmed with their feelings
- To develop positive mental health and wellbeing through this approach

Responsibility of all staff

In a connection and regulation policy, it is essential that every member of staff acknowledges their own individual role in this process. Every single person in school is contributing to shaping the minds, perceptions, beliefs and relationships of the children as well as their sense of self. The connection and regulation policy holds everyone accountable to come together to support the children in a consistent, reliable way so that it doesn't matter if Mr Jackson in Year 1 or Mrs Smith in Year 4 is supporting them, the therapeutic responses are anchored in the same approach. A conventional behaviour policy assumes the child's behaviour is in the hands of the child. The connection and regulation policy realises it is in the hands of the adults. Without a caring, calm, nurturing adult helping the child through emotional challenges, they will never be able to learn to manage their own behaviours.

Tone of voice and language

In a connection and regulation policy, is important to consider the language used. The language you use, communicates your intention and perception of behaviour. There are some common praises we must reconsider and reframe to ensure the approach is reflected in the messaging. Here are some common phases schools use that need to be reframed.

Conventional policy excerpts	Why?
Children know that a negative action will result in a negative consequence	This assumes the children are choosing to misbehave and can control their responses and emotions. It also highlights the reward vs punishment, good vs bad narrative

(Continued)

199

(Continued)

Conventional policy excerpts	Why?
All children are aware of the behaviour promises, they are displayed in every class-room and regularly communicated	Behaviour promises assume children can promise to behave and then adhere to that promise despite feeling overwhelmed. Unfortunately, this doesn't consider neuroscience or childhood trauma responses and gives children a false sense of control they 'should' have. It also perpetuates a shame cycle when the child inevitably cannot uphold their promise
If a child is not following our behaviour policy, a warning is issued	The language used here feels clinical and operational 'warning is issued,' and suggests again that the child has made a cognitive, rational choice not to follow the policy and therefore needs a warning followed by a consequence
There will be consequences if they continue to behave in a way that is below the expected standard	Again, this is operational and clinical and doesn't sound child friendly or attuned to the child's needs. It also reinforces conditional relationships where a standard must be met in order to be accepted.
Children will be encouraged to make the right choices, and improve behaviours for next time	The word 'choices' implies the child is making a rational, cognitive decision about how they are going to respond to something difficult which isn't possible if the child is in their survival part of the brain.
We will strive to manage behaviour effectively	This falsely communicates that the adults should be able to 'manage' children's behaviour and stop it. This can often result in a feeling of disempowerment or failure for the teacher when they struggle. Instead of acknowledging they cannot control the child's behaviour but they can help and support them, which is far more achievable
We remind children to do the right thing	Using the phrase 'do the right thing' can be confusing for children who have experienced trauma in their lives. If at home, a child is running away when they are overwhelmed or scared and hiding under the bed to stay safe, then their brain believes that running away when they are overwhelmed or scared **is** the right thing. If their body is triggered to become overwhelmed and scared at school in a loud dinner hall, then running away and hiding in the toilets or up a tree is what their bodies and brains perceive to be 'right.' This has protected them from danger and kept them safe in the past. When we say 'do the right thing' we are expecting children to be able to use their rational thinking brain and reflect, problem solve and manage their emotions in the moment, but they can't. This terminology is confusing for both children and adults as it creates an expectation of control children just don't have.

A connection and regulation policy uses connective, therapeutic, trauma-informed language that helps the reader empathise and understand what is going on for the child as well as understanding what the process is to help them. Instead of 'Children are encouraged to make good choices' you would say, 'Staff are trained to help children calm down and regulate so they are able to reflect on the situation'; instead of 'We strive to manage behaviour effectively' you would say, 'We strive to support children emotionally.'

Words to reconsider:

- Poor choices
- Undesirable behaviour
- Good behaviour
- Negative behaviour
- Behaviour problems
- Misbehaviour
- Disobedience
- Negative consequences
- Sanctions

Words to consider:

- Support children
- Guide and teach
- Struggling with their behaviour
- Safe boundaries
- Dysregulated behaviour
- Survival responses
- Cognitive, rational responses
- Connection
- Connective language
- Help children
- Emotional safety

Therapeutic teaching steps replace the behaviour management steps

Trauma-informed, attachment-aware and therapeutic approaches avoid punishment, sanctions and rewards. This means not using outdated behaviour management strategies like time outs, sending children out, reward charts, tick charts, names on board, missing break time and so on. This is a really hard transition to make but in order to truly be therapeutic, the goal should be to remove these completely if you can. I am aware for some schools that isn't always possible, and for teachers reading this book, that might not be in your control, but the goal here is to try and be as trauma-informed as possible within the constraints that you may have.

In the 'behaviour management' chapter, we looked at what doesn't work for children struggling with insecure attachment and trauma and in the therapeutic teaching chapter we looked at how to enforce boundaries whilst still being connective and considering neuroscience and trauma. In a connection and regulation policy, you are coming away from the standard process of

- Verbal warning
- Sanction or consequence
- Sent to senior leader
- Parents informed/sent home/letter sent
- Exclusion

Instead the therapeutic teaching steps become the standard process, and you use the following steps:

- Initial therapeutic response: Name, feeling, behaviour, encourage
- Regulation time
- Boundary
- Teach

Warnings and chances

Warnings can often perpetuate a sense of anxiety, create disconnection and for some children, trigger their survival responses. Pairing this with a sanction like missing break can also perpetuate feelings of rejection. That said, you can still make a mental note of the number of times you have asked a child to do something and then follow that with a boundary, but this should be anchored in that particular situation rather than it being a series of steps in a policy. It should also be done in a natural, authentic way. So instead of saying 'Adam, that is your second warning' or 'Adam, I have given you three warnings, you now need to stay in at break' it could be 'Adam, I have reminded you a few times about shouting out, could we have a chat please before you go out to break.' This then stops being a punishment and becomes a natural consequence in the moment. The child doesn't miss their whole break, but they do miss part of it and you can then discuss the situation with the child in a calm way. Instead of the ethos being warnings and consequences it becomes reminders and making amends/discussions.

Connection vs rewards

Because this is a connective approach designed to raise emotional intelligence and help children to become self-aware and self-regulate, it isn't necessary to focus on reward systems and points-based systems that feed into the good vs bad, punishment and reward narrative. That will only continue to embed that culture and expectation in school. Rewards can sometimes be hard to let go of because they are deemed as positive, but the goal should not be to reinforce 'good behaviour' through reward, but to raise self-belief and self-concept through connection. This should be anchored in the relationships that are developed and not external things. The most effective and connective way to replace 'positive reinforcement' such as rewards in school is through what you say.

Verbal acknowledgement

When a child has done something well, tell them in the moment. I don't mean with praise like, 'good boy', for reasons we mentioned in the behaviour management chapter, but simple statements like 'That is so kind of you to help Tim with his coat' or 'You worked hard on that' 'you kept going, even though you felt anxious' or 'Sarah, you struggled with that, but you didn't give up' comments like this communicate that you have acknowledged their effort and noticed their personal qualities/feelings/actions/behaviours. This is far more valuable to a child than a sticker or promise of a reward and it removes all the connotations that come with *not* getting a sticker too! A sticker and certificate are short term reinforcements (like treats we give a dog) that have little meaning in the end and are fundamentally designed to 'train' children to behave. A connective statement or recognition forms their self-talk and self-perception and doesn't have to be hinged on whether they have 'been good enough' to get it. In truth, the connection with you is more important and valuable to any child than a sticker or certificate. It is the feeling of being seen, heard and validated that they need. Try to make your phrases simple and practical, focusing on what they did and what you noticed and avoid blanket statements and praise. Also avoid any promise or expectation for the future. 'If you keep this up you might get the Head Teacher's award this week.' Because you are suddenly creating conditional expectations and potential for future failure which will trigger attachment style responses from some children.

Raising emotional intelligence

Another way to replace 'positive reinforcement' strategies like stickers, rewards and points is to take the focus off the individual children all together and instead focus on cultivating the children's emotional intelligence skills as a team or group. The focus should instead be on their collective social and emotional skills, their ability to recognise each other's emotions, support one another, listen to one another, help one another and to care about each other. This is a different focus than rewarding 'good' behaviour. It also stops children who are not chosen for a reward from feeling unseen, left out or not recognised. The other twist here is that the children then take responsibility for recognising these skills in the group, and not the adults, removing that power dynamic that can also be difficult for many children. Here is an idea to help you do this:

The kind and caring jar
The kind and caring jar is a jar you keep in the classroom that is filled by the children with paper slips, detailing times that they have seen or experienced kind behaviours in the classroom or with their peers.

This helps to
- Encourage children to acknowledge feelings and emotions
- Promote intentional, meaningful examples of empathy and social skills
- Raises everyone's self-belief and self-concept

How it works

Each day the children can write comments on slips of paper to place in jar about things they have seen or experienced. For example:

'Naveed was kind to me today and let me play his game'
'Lucy listened to my ideas today'
'Charlotte sat next to Jack when he was feeling sad'
'Toby told Mr Ince I needed some help'

You then encourage the children to notice what is going on around them to cultivate those emotional intelligence skills, 'Oh look, Jack is helping Sarah with her coat, do you think that should go in the kind and caring jar?'

As the jar begins to get full, have a read through and add anything you think might have been missed. You can then read them to the class but with the focus being on recognising their collective efforts, avoiding anchoring it in praise. A top tip here would be to avoid reading out names, especially if you have a particularly high level of children who struggle with trauma or insecure attachment as it might trigger them if their name isn't in the pot (or sometimes if it is!) for this reason, it is best to read out the actions that have been documented without naming the children. 'I have read so many slips about people helping each other with their coats, sharing on the carpet and looking after someone when they get upset.' Or you could mix and match the reflections and blend some people's names with some more generic reflections that scoop up the other children and keep the focus on everyone, 'Sarah helped Jack with his coat. I have seen lots of you helping someone this week!' This keeps the focus on the whole class and makes it feel connective. However, that said, you could privately go over to children and say 'Someone put you in the kind and caring jar today for helping Sarah with her coat!'

Reflection time

With many schools moving toward relationship policies and restorative language, I often see behaviour policies referring to 'reflection time.' On the surface this looks positive. However, on reading the policy it is evident that the reflection time isn't focused on self-regulation and calming down, it is a 'time out' in disguise. Reflection time often happens after the incident and includes the child being taken to a specific room or missing their break time. Here they might be expected to have a conversation with an adult, think about what they have done or do a 'reflection sheet.' However, this expects them to be use their rational thinking brain to reflect, reason, have empathy and so on. But if reflection time comes quickly after the incident or later but it means they miss break, they are not likely to be feeling very calm. Instead, they are probably going to be feeling frustrated and unhappy. If we know that a child can only reflect on a something when they are calm but they are not given the opportunity to calm down, then we cannot use the word reflection. Instead, this is a consequence or a time out. It is confusing for the child to be told the space is for them to 'reflect' if they are not likely to be able to reflect properly because they are still upset. Similarly, they cannot be expected to 'reflect' rationally on what happened if they are frustrated that their break has been taken away and they are being made to sit inside. This is going to be perceived by the child as a punishment and will keep them in a state of survival and you are more likely to get a flight, fight freeze response. With some children, you will get them to go through the motions, but what are they really learning here?

In a connection and regulation policy, the 'regulation step' is where the child can calm down and regulate and the 'teach' step is where the child is able to reflect on what has happened. Reflection time is fine, as long as it comes after regulation time and isn't a form of punishment.

Missing break

Another common question I am asked is my stance on how to get children to make up lost learning time and many schools ask whether children should stay in at break. This is tricky and although I am aware that there are pressures to meet with regard to children completing learning and not being behind, we also have to consider what is realistic both for the teacher and the child. It can be really hard when a child has been dysregulated all afternoon and missed loads of learning, and it is only natural to want them to catch up with that learning so they are not behind. However, is this a realistic expectation long term? Especially for those children who are likely to be constantly missing learning because they are often overwhelmed and dysregulated. For children struggling like this, the focus can't be on whether they have done every lesson that week, but instead on their basic need to feel emotionally safe. A child who is constantly working from a place of survival isn't ready to learn and nonmatter how many times we put a book in front of them, their high stress levels will continue to hijack them and their learning will continue to be disrupted. Unfortunately, learning is not something they can cognitively do right now. This of course doesn't meet the demands and current expectations of school but unless that child feels emotionally safe, they are not going to learn anyway. The only goal here is to focus on their emotional need and mental health before any real learning can occur. That is not to say that you shouldn't help them recover their learning wherever possible, but this needs to be done in a calm, sensitive way when they are able to access their rational thinking brain, maybe in a small one-to-one session or a nurture group. If they have struggled with their emotions and behaviour, that shouldn't mean they deserve to lose their free time because this again will be perceived as a punishment and is working against the neuroscience not with it.

Keeping children inside to miss break or dinner either to catch up on lost learning time, or even as a 'loss of privileges,' is counterintuitive. Think about it like this: the child is overwhelmed and dysregulated, they need help calming down and regulating, they need connection time and time to organise their thoughts and feelings but then the consequence for struggling is that their free time is taken. This is when they can reconnect with friends, organise their thoughts, get fresh air and regulate. It doesn't make sense. Although, it is true that for some children, break and dinner time is triggering and sending them out into a big playground can make it worse, that doesn't mean that they should lose the option to have time to themselves. School is demanding in so many ways and the only time children get to play, socialise, get fresh air and have some control over the day is at break and dinner. This is a basic right for children and shouldn't be taken away as a punishment, sanction or consequence. Getting a break from learning isn't a 'privilege.' In fact, taking away their break perpetuates the demands and expectations of them and keeps them in a state of survival which is the opposite of what you are trying to do. It is far better to use playtime and dinner time to help children to regulate, play and calm down. The cognitive break is a brilliant way to help children re-set. Now, we have to recognise also that not all children benefit from running about outside (we will look at this in the next chapter) but if a child has been struggling, then break should be used to allow them some time to play quietly with Lego, go for a walk, get on a bike, go to the sensory room or whatever else you can think of to bring those stress levels down. Taking that time away doesn't help the child or you in any situation and often leaves them more frustrated, angry and upset than they were before!

Internal and external exclusion

If your focus is to help children regulate and connect with the adults around them, then traditional exclusion both internal and external doesn't fit the ethos. The decision to exclude is often one of the hardest things Head Teachers have to do, it can be emotionally difficult and can come with feelings of guilt. This is especially true when you know you are sending a child back into a home environment that might be harmful for that child. School is a refuge for so many vulnerable children and having to send them home can be heartbreaking, but when faced with unhappy staff, parents and children who have been physically hurt repeatedly, sometimes it feels like the only option. The policy doesn't help! Once it is written down, there is an expectation and you are bound to follow the process laid out in writing.

However, maybe there is another way. Now, as always, I am questioning norms and encouraging you to be brave enough to move away from common culture. That said, I am also aware that this might not fit every organisation and I know this isn't always possible given individual constraints or roles, but ideally you would remove external exclusion from the policy for all intents and purposes unless it is a final unavoidable resort.

How?

The first thing to change is the word 'exclusion' because that doesn't fit with a trauma-informed approach. Exclusion does exactly what it says on the tin, and it perpetuates a feeling of rejection and shame by sending children away when they are struggling. They are being 'excluded' from the school community, classroom and others as a form of punishment for their behaviour. This isn't helpful when it is the most complex, vulnerable children who reach exclusion level and those who need connection the most! These children are constantly being hijacked by their survival responses and are often the children who are already more likely to believe adults cannot be trusted, will let them down, abandon them and reject them based on their experiences so far. Their behaviour is often a sign of these beliefs as they push adults away and sabotage for fear of getting too close and then being let down. Sadly, we then do the very thing they are fearful of and confirm their core beliefs through exclusion. We confirm, yes, we will reject you when you are at your most vulnerable and need us the most. Yes, adults cannot be trusted. Yes, adults cannot meet your needs. It is heartbreaking!

The second thing to consider is not sending the child home at all, and instead having some sort of emergency, internal support available to children when things get this bad. Something that is focused on nurture and regulation. When children are struggling so much that they are at exclusion level, they are usually repeatedly being triggered into high levels of fight, flight freeze responses throughout the day, you'll see them lashing out, trashing rooms, spitting, scratching, fighting, harming others, running away and possibly hurting themselves. As a trauma informed, attachment aware therapeutic teacher, you can recognise that this is a dysregulated child who is overwhelmed and scared and who has no healthy coping mechanisms to fall back on. This behaviour is a huge red flag and a sign they need help and support, and their core need here is to feel emotionally safe. This is not a child who is choosing to harm people and is making a cognitive choice. This is a child in real distress who needs help. However, the behaviour may be so challenging that you need to do something to keep the child themselves safe, and the other children too.

Instead of exclusion, which rejects their need for help and sometimes forces them back into an even more threatening environment at home, consider how you can meet these emotional needs as a matter of urgency. Like a rescue pack or first response at the scene of an emergency. A paramedic responding to an emergency doesn't look at the person in crisis and say 'sorry, you need to go away from me until you have healed yourself' no, they get out their medical tool kit and they get to work, responding to the emergency and supporting the person through it. A child in this acute level of distress needs the same sort of response.

If their basic need here is to feel emotionally safe, then the question is, how can you meet that need? Sometimes, the right thing to do is strip back perceived expectations and social norms and put the child at the core of the decision. I know this might not feel like a school's job, but truthfully, if you don't do it, who will? You might be thinking, 'If the child is that bad, then mainstream school isn't for them' but with the increasing numbers of children struggling like this, maybe it's time to start thinking about why. Maybe it isn't the child that is the problem, but school itself. Maybe the system itself is getting it wrong and we need to be brave enough to listen to what children need from us and make some changes. Change starts with you!

If you could take everything away and focus only on what this child needs right now, what would that be? To create a sense of emotional safety. An alternative idea to exclusion could be to provide some respite from the world and all its stressors, a place they can go for a period of time, instead of being sent home. It might be a small room with fairy lights blankets, books and teddies. Somewhere that isn't too big and too overwhelming. They could have their breakfast, lunch drinks and snacks here and have somewhere where all of life's pressures, stressors and traumas are taken away for a while. This will give their brain time to reduce some stress hormones and their body can begin to regulate. For some children, it will have been years since they had this space and sense of calm, if ever. Whilst the child is in this respite room, you could focus on filling developmental gaps through reading to the child, listening to audio books, watching films under a blanket, and letting them have naps. Encourage play with playdough, drawing and painting and revisit earlier types of play. Focus on helping the child feel seen, heard and validated. Somewhere with structure, routine and connection and where they can experience what it is like to be taken care of with no expectation or demand.

When the child is ready, slowly reintroduce small challenges into the day until they were able to feel emotionally safe enough to navigate the school day. I would also recommend looking at other ways to help meet this child's emotional needs after this period, such as one-to-one time each week, play therapy, calm time or reading time with a safe adult every day.

Although this takes more resources and time, this sort of response is more likely to make an impactful difference to the child. It will meet the emotional need, focus on the internal problems behind the behaviour and is likely to have a better outcome than excluding them. Remember that whatever you do, it won't stop the child from struggling and 'fix' their behaviour. Excluding them won't do that either. It will, however, show this child that there is compassion, love, connection and kindness in the world, and it might even begin to re-wire the brain connections they have. If this is 'connection time' or 'respite time' replaces an exclusion and sits alongside wider whole school approaches like consistent therapeutic responses from teachers, a wellbeing curriculum, therapeutic environments and a whole school trauma-informed approach, you are more likely to help the children feel increasingly safer in your school and bit by bit may reduce dysregulated behaviour.

Important note: On reading this you might be thinking: if I do that then won't that just make them behave badly to get in to 'respite time.' My answer would be this: children can't make themselves dysregulated on purpose, and if it seems like their behaviour is escalating more quickly to reach crisis and therefore get respite time, then that is because they are desperately in need of it. Their brain has found a new, healthier coping mechanism that helps, and they are seeking it out. This is a good thing because through repetition, you will reinforce safety and emotional stability. Remember, we are working with the science here and so when a child feels emotionally safer, the stress levels will naturally decrease, and they will be able to access their rational thinking brain more often. You will see this shift because they will have more control over their responses, concentrate for longer, manage their emotions better and verbalise their needs more. They will naturally no longer reach those high levels of distress because chemically and hormonally the levels in their body have decreased. This is when those distressing behaviours will decrease or stop. The child will no longer reach acute levels of distress to get respite time, but they might still ask for it and we still need to be listening. Connection, empathy and true relationships will always have a bigger impact than disconnection, rejection and punishment.

When you have written your policy

Letting the children know what is new

It is important to prepare the children for any changes you will be making so that they are aware of new expectations and focuses. If you are coming away from sanctions, punishment and rewards and focusing on feelings, emotions and emotional intelligence then they need to know! This helps avoid confusion and helps them to settle into the new expectations more quickly. It doesn't mean they won't test you to try them out, but it will feel safer than just suddenly experiencing changes and feeling unsettled by them.

211

A good idea would be to sit down with the children – either in their classrooms, assembly or both – and talk about the new values and focuses for your school. You might explain a bit about the brain and flight fight and freeze and then say something like: 'From now on we are going to try to think about our feelings a bit more. I want you think about how your feeling, how your friends might be feeling and how we can help each other.' You might follow this with a circle time or discussion 'Sometimes we have very big feelings . . . can anyone name some?' and then end by letting the children know what the new rules and incentives are and why you are doing them. Of course, you don't need to go through every step and stage with them but pulling out some key highlights will help, especially when it comes to why you are no longer using stickers or ticks by names for example.

You could also kick start your new approach by creating a whole school super learning week or focused lessons where each teacher shares resources, videos, delivers circle times or reads books that are all rooted in feelings, emotions, behaviours and the brain!

Letting the parents know

Parents will also need to be aware of the changes you are making and although this might be met with questions and potential push back, it is important to see this as an opportunity to re-educate them too! You could do this by sending home letters, flyers or information packs. You could even create a short video using pupil voice to share the new ethos and approach. You could also put together a little coffee morning or parent assembly and get them involved in the new narrative. Get discussions going where you ask them how *they* felt at school and what their experiences were like, did they get sent out? Did they get detention? How did it make them feel? Did they have a favourite teacher – why? Help them feel part of the culture and ethos and help them connect with their own stories. Be brave! Some of this will be a totally new concept for many parents but once they understand it and can connect to it, they are far more likely to be on board and see the benefit for their child and everyone else's.

Part of the journey with this approach is to create a culture that runs right through the school, this is made up of the relationships between children and staff, the therapeutic teaching approach, policies and procedures and also the environment itself. Let's move on to the next chapter and explore what that means.

11

Therapeutic Environments and Therapeutic Classrooms

Currently, in the society and culture we live in, it is expected that children attend school for the majority of their childhood and for the duration of their teenage years. Fulltime education is compulsory for all children aged 5–16 years. That is 14 years in education. 14 years, spending six hours (or more if they go to afterschool club and breakfast club) in an environment that isn't their home and with adults who are not their parents. Although this is the cultural norm, it is a huge ask for children (and teachers) when you consider that these are the most fundamental years for their development. Their brain is developing, creating neural connections formed by their daily experiences which constantly evolve into their adolescence. They are developing social and emotional skills, figuring out how to navigate the world, going through puberty and so much more. These are the most important years we have as humans, and they inform the rest of our lives. When a child comes through the doors in the morning for their first day of nursery, every adult interacting with that child from that point on is contributing to their development. Every peer they meet, interaction they have, experience they have, challenge they have, it all counts. Children are in the care of the adults at school often longer than they are at home, so although the world tells us that our focus should be on academic outcomes, it is impossible and unrealistic to focus only on that when we are quite literally having a direct hand in raising these children.

As a therapeutic school, it is essential that a child's social, emotional and mental development is just as important (if not more important) than their academic learning which is why our relationships, interactions, behaviour policies and PHSE curriculum count so much, because they form the 'second parenting' role that school inevitably fills.

DOI: 10.4324/9781003410652-13

Now, we know that the circumstances children experience at home differ hugely, some children have loving nurturing parents who spend loads of time with them, some have busy working parents who are tired and stressed, some have blended families who are chaotic and loud. Some live with siblings, some have no siblings, some speak dual languages, some live with extended family, some have lots of money, others have little money. Some spend time outdoors, others stay indoors. Some are living through adversity and trauma. The list goes on! You cannot control the external environment a child lives in at home, but you *can* control the environment you create for them at school, and we have already established that for many children, school is their refuge so the environment you create matters.

The environment is made up of two key things: first the parental figures that are there to take care of them i.e., the teachers and the relationships they cultivate, values they instil and lesson they teach (which go beyond academically); and, second, the physical environment itself. So far in this book, we have talked about what you can do to create emotionally safe relationships with the children. Now we are going to talk about how you can create emotionally safe environments.

Just as relationships, environments impact children's mental health and wellbeing in a very significant way. Waking up in a warm home with a cosy bed, surrounded by teddies and soft carpets is very different to waking up on a mattress on the floor, with one dirty sheet, hard floors and no heating. Considering that again, we cannot control the environments children experience at home, it is vital we begin to reassess the environments we are creating in school.

The school environment is made up of the indoor spaces and the outdoor space and both need some consideration. As always with the therapeutic school approach, I am going to challenge your perception of what our environments look like and also how we use them, but it is important to remember that everything I am going to discuss here uses the neuroscience, childhood trauma theory and attachment theory we have looked at in this book as the underpinning knowledge and the 'why' for the rationale. As always, every single child's mental health and wellbeing is considered in this approach with particular attention to those more vulnerable children who are struggling with trauma and adversity. My initial explorations around how trauma, technology and social media are contributing to increased stress levels and poor mental health are also just as relevant in this chapter as in previous chapters. We now know our primary goal should be to calm the stress hormones down and help the children feel emotionally safe before anything else. This is not only something we can do through our interactions with the children but also through the environment we create and I believe our conventional school environments do not meet the mental health and wellbeing needs of our children.

The conventional classroom

Let's first begin by looking at the conventional classroom. The average UK classroom hasn't changed much in the last 50 years+ and that is particularly true of the furniture that is used. In fact, that the plastic school chair in your classroom today is modelled on a post war chair! They were introduced in the 1970s, replacing wooden chairs, and were made of a polypropylene plastic that was considered contemporary and revolutionary at that time. These chairs were light, cheap to produce, and tougher than previous materials and were ideal for budget furniture that met the needs of schools. The very same chairs, paired with conventional classroom tables have been a staple in every classroom for decades and they are what we have come to expect as standard. Classrooms today don't differ much from the classrooms I was taught in at school and probably not from the one you were taught in either. This is a problem. Post war classrooms were designed to meet the needs of post war children, not the children of today and if we really step back and look at our classrooms, it isn't difficult to see that they might actually be contributing to the problem.

What isn't working and why

As part of my therapeutic classroom approach, I identified a number of elements in a conventional classroom that I felt were not working. I then asked over 500 children up and down the country to give me their own organic thoughts and feedback about their classrooms (this was done through questionnaires or face to face). The children were unaware of my own thoughts but unsurprisingly, their comments and reflections were aligned with mine. Here are some of the key issues:

Chairs and tables

Plastic classroom chairs are first and foremost uncomfortable. Children do not like sitting on them and are forced to move around, sit on their knees or fidget, to try and find 'a good spot.' Children have told me that they do everything they can to make themselves more comfortable, including sitting on their hands and putting their jumpers on the seat. We all know how horrible it can be to sit on a plastic chair, either from our own memories of school or from sitting on them in a staff meeting! The plastic is hard, it sticks to the back of your legs and it digs into your back, but tragically even though we know this, we still make children sit on them all day and then we tell them off when they are fidgeting! The other issue with plastic chairs is that they are often too small for the children, especially in Years 5 and 6. Jill Wright, a Head Teacher in Liverpool told me that many of her Year 5 and 6 children didn't physically fit the furniture and were squashed on their seats. She also described how the children then didn't fit under the tables properly which was causing them to be even more uncomfortable. Interestingly, a group of Year 6 children in a school in Salford told me the exact same thing, 'The chairs are too small, and the tables are too low' they said.

It is hard enough to expect the most enthusiastic learner to sit on a plastic chair but for children who are already struggling with high stress levels, it is torture. Imagine constantly living in a state where you are uncomfortable internally and where everything feels like a challenge and then being forced to sit on an uncomfortable chair that mirrors your internal state all day! Expecting children who are constantly navigating difficulties to sit on a chair that reinforces that internal feeling of endurance is unfair and is, of course, not trauma-informed or attachment-aware. It is also not inclusive! I remember speaking to a Year 5 boy who had autism, he told me all about his problem with the plastic chairs, saying 'If you are wearing your shorts, or uniform without this on (points to his top) it just feels very uncomfortable, and I am always trying to find a good spot, and when you get off your chair and have playtime and you come back in and you sit down on your chair, it's just freezing cold.' This was endearing and made others smile but essentially what he was saying was that the feel and sensory experience of the plastic chair didn't meet his needs.

These comments are not unique, hundreds of children from Years 3–6 have told me the chairs are uncomfortable. Here are some of their comments:

'It's uncomfortable when you are writing and I can't settle and I can't concentrate and this bit is always sticking into your back, so it is hurting you while you are writing'

'The chairs are very uncomfortable, there is this bit on it (points to the back) and when you are try to work it just always kind of digs into your back and when you sit on it, it isn't as comfortable as you want it to be when you are writing'

'The chairs are not comfortable. Also, I feel cramped on my table and bang my elbow on the table next to me'

'I feel trapped, and the chairs numb my butt!'

Aside from being uncomfortable, sitting in one chair for most of the day can also impact learning and turn off children's thinking brain because the body is inactive (Harvey and Kenyon, 2013).

Along with the chairs, standard classroom tables are also an issue. Children are often too big to sit comfortably underneath the table and so will push their chairs out to make more space to write, unfortunately this then means that their chair is in the way of people walking by and they are constantly asked to push themselves under their table. Children tell me they get sore elbows, sore knees and feel squashed up against another person. Consider what it is like for a child with insecure attachment needs or adverse childhood experiences, to be expected to sit closely next to someone else all day (often touching elbows or fighting for space) whilst attempting to do work. It is challenging and triggering for so many children because they feel trapped physically and emotionally. It is uncomfortable for them to allow people to be so close and causes them to respond with fight, flight or freeze behaviours. Unfortunately, this is a huge barrier to learning before they even attempt to do any work and it switches off the rational thinking part of the brain. No wonder then that they find excuses to leave the table.

The tables also cause a problem with space, too. Due to their design and shape, they often take up a large proportion of the floor, making it difficult for teachers to organise their classrooms in a way that free's up floor space to ensure there is enough room. Tables are often put together in random shapes and configurations to fit 30 children around them but that leaves the room feeling small and cluttered. This is again a problem when considering inclusivity as it means there is not enough space for children with mobility needs or wheelchair users. It limits the accessibility of the classroom for them, and I have been told by a few Head Teachers it has left children stuck on the outskirts of the room near the door, causing them to feel physically excluded from the classroom which has affected their wellbeing and sense of happiness at school. The conventional classroom set up of chairs and tables is outdated and no longer meets children's individual learning styles which is causing them to become distracted and disengaged.

The colours, surroundings and displays

Another common cultural practice we need to reconsider is the colours we use in the classrooms, especially in primary schools. Somewhere along the line we have come to believe that bright colours should be in classrooms, and this has resulted in every educational supplier producing everything in bright colours. From rugs to backing paper and pull-out draws, there are different colours everywhere. This can feel overwhelming and chaotic for many children and is often triggering for those with sensory needs as well as those with high levels of stress or trauma. Imagine living in a world where everything is chaotic and life feels as though it is bombarding you wherever you turn, and then you walk into your classroom which is plastered with bright coloured boards, washing lines, posters, chairs and tables. The room itself becomes a visual representation of your internal state and can trigger survival responses. This is not only true for our more vulnerable children but of every child! It is hard to concentrate in a space that is bright and loud and where every wall is full to the brim with 'stuff.'

It isn't just the colours that present a problem, it is the vast array of washing lines, displays, laminated posters, work and resources that create a sense of chaos. I say this with the utmost respect for teachers, and I fully recognise that you work so hard to create your classrooms with the intention to provide welcoming, vibrant places to learn, but you can only work with what you have. As a collective group of professionals, we must stop to question whether it is working. With the numbers of children struggling with concentration and wanting to leave the room, isn't it time we consider that the problem could be the environment and not the children?

The other thing to think about is the use of displays and the number of displays in every classroom. I write this half closing my eyes because this is where I get the most push back, but stay with me! Classroom displays have been a staple expectation of the standard classroom for decades, but they pose several challenges for both children and staff. My question is, who are they for, and do we really need them? The first issue is how the display is created, rather than what is displayed. They are often backed in clashing bright colours, maybe with red backing paper, blue and green borders and then yellow double backed work. I get it, sometimes that is all that is left in the stock cupboard! But again, this perpetuates that sense of chaos and overwhelm and can be difficult for children to process, especially when there are five different boards around the room surrounding them. When we consider those more vulnerable children, with high levels of stress, the bright, chaotic walls can cause them to feel trapped, increase stress hormone and turn off the rational thinking part of the brain. In fact, studies have shown that displays can affect children's ability to maintain focused attention and learn (Fisher, Godwin and Seltman, 2014) and particularly affect the attention of children with autism (Hanley et al., 2023)

Display boards have different functions, some of the boards in a classroom are there to display working prompts or reminders to help the children which is great but often children tell me that they can't see them from their seat. They also explain that the colours and 'stuff' makes them feel confused rather than helped, one girl in Year 5 said:

> 'There is so much stuff around, like stuff for Geography, Maths, English, it can sometimes help me, but sometimes when I am trying to concentrate on one thing, all the other things round the room mess with my head.'

Other boards are used to showcase topics and children's work, but who are we doing this for? Is it for the children, or parents, visitors and Ofsted? The idea of displaying children's work is difficult when you consider trauma-informed and attachment-aware approaches and they can feed into that 'good' vs 'bad' culture we talked about. Having work up on the board might:

- Cause children to compare themselves to their peers which takes away from the great work *they* have done
- Be triggered into a cycle where they suddenly self-sabotage because of the expectations it brings
- Perpetuate the 'good' and 'bad' culture because to them, having your work chosen means it was good, not having it up means it was bad. This could lead to feelings of shame or a conclusion that they themselves are therefore not good enough

Lots of children love seeing their work on the board, but in a trauma-informed setting, my advice would be to avoid the potential to trigger children by championing children's work in a different way. This will not only improve attention and learning outcomes for children but remove that compare culture. You could do this by telling children directly what was good about their work, or showing parents privately which is more empowering for children on an individual basis.

The last thing to consider with displays is the time and effort they take to produce. Teachers spend hours creating, changing and repairing displays which impacts their own wellbeing and mental health. Imagine, instead, a world where you didn't have to salvage backing paper from a storeroom, double back work and cut out headings and where you could use your time more productively for other things. This is one of the reflections teachers make after teaching in one of my therapeutic classrooms!

Maybe it is time to reconsider the value of a display board in a classroom. Maybe we need to question whether they are needed and look at alternative ideas that still help children but in a different way. However, there is no judgment here! Ultimately it is your decision whether you keep display boards or let them go and if you decide to keep them, there are still lots of things you can do to make them more trauma-informed and inclusive. I will share some more tips later in this chapter.

The lighting

Most lighting found in schools is overhead fluorescent lighting which is often bright and clinical and can leave children feeling hypersensitive and over stimulated. This is an obvious problem for children who struggle with ADHD, autism and who have sensory processing needs. In fact, people with autism report fluorescent lighting triggers their sensory stress (Autism speaks, 2024) Studies have also shown fluorescent lighting can contribute to headaches and increase eye irritations as well as decreasing productivity and alertness. They can also increase physical and mental fatigue, dizziness and low mood. Interestingly, some studies have even shown that they link to increased feelings of anxiety and sleep problems. Aside from the studies, the affect the lighting has on children and staff is evident in practice. You can see children rubbing their eyes, and teachers complaining of headaches. I myself used to get eye irritations and headaches when I was in classrooms with fluorescent lighting.

Lighting is a really important part of the classroom, but it sometimes stops children from learning rather than helps them and that needs rethinking.

Learning styles

Every child that comes into school is an individual with different learning preferences and needs. Conventional classrooms and classroom culture doesn't account for this when the usual expectation is that the child should sit on a chair and in the same place all day. We all learn differently and what feels comfortable for one child is not the same for another. When I used to teach classes, I would let them lie on the floor, lean on the wall, sit on the tables and even sit under them. I never asked them to sit up straight and cross their legs, it didn't matter to me where they chose to learn, as long as they were engaged and learning! The result was a class that was more connected to one another, me and the lesson. Our goal should be to ensure every child feels physically comfortable enough to engage their rational thinking brains and be interested in the lesson. Forcing a child to sit on a plastic chair in the same spot, next to the same person, or on the carpet with their legs crossed isn't going to do that. Where we learn is important.

 Self-reflection

If I asked you right now to go and write me an essay. Would you choose your classroom? Is that where you would produce your best work and feel inspired and comfortable? I have asked teachers this question up and down the country and the answer is always no. As I write this sentence, I am sat on my sofa under a blanket with my laptop and a hot water bottle on my knee, the window is open and the rain outside is pouring, I have soft calm music playing in the background and dim lighting around the room. I feel comfortable and engaged in my writing. This is where I know I will write my best work. Sitting at a table on a chair in an office just wouldn't work for me. What about you? What would you do? Would you choose to be in an office, bedroom or on the sofa? Would you choose to sit at a cosy café on a stool or on your dining table? Do you need to be around noise or do you need quiet? Wherever you choose, it is very unlikely to be in a classroom and there lies the problem.

If we wouldn't choose to work in a classroom, why do we expect the children to?

When we think about creating trauma informed, inclusive classrooms we must consider all styles of learning. We must cater for the child who prefers lying on their tummy because the pressure helps them feel grounded, the child who prefers to sit with a small group instead of a big one and the child who learns best sat on the floor instead of at the table. Our classrooms should be designed around the needs of the children, rather than expecting them all to conform to one standardised set of rules.

Expecting children to conform to one way of learning sends confusing messages that can make children believe they are not suited to school or learning itself. This isn't true, it is the classroom that needs to change not the child. Sending children out into the world thinking they are not good learners is a failure on our part when a simple shift will make all the difference.

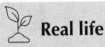 **Real life**

When I first started the therapeutic school approach, I worked with a brilliant Head Teacher, Kyrstie Stubbs, who led a large school in Yorkshire. She was a naturally inclusive thinker and hers was the first to roll out my therapeutic teaching course to all the staff. As a result, some of the teachers began introducing flexible options in their classrooms. One day, one of them came running over to me excitedly. She told me about how she had started 'Flexible Fridays' which was where the children could choose where they wanted to learn. She said one boy, who would often refuse to engage and couldn't sit down for longer than 15 minutes, had done a lesson of maths! She said he chose to sit under the table with no shoes on and was completely engaged in his learning. He had never worked as long before and she couldn't believe it! Over time, she saw his attention and concentration was significantly better on a Friday compared to any other time in the week.

Providing flexible options for seating in a classroom could be the key to unlocking children's enthusiasm for learning and help to turn on their rational, thinking brains. Now, of course there needs to be places where children can practice their handwriting and sitting on the floor might not be an option for every task, but making an option available is the key here!

The feeling it evokes

When you stand in a conventional classroom, how does it make you feel? For many children the rooms make them feel anxious, uncomfortable, overwhelmed, over stimulated and for some, even trapped. This is a problem. The environments we surround ourselves with have a direct impact on our sense of wellbeing and can affect our mood and productivity. The atmosphere and feeling of being in a classroom space, is just as important as the items we put in it! If our goal is to support children's mental health and wellbeing and be trauma informed, attachment aware and inclusive, then classrooms should help us to do that. Creating a feeling of calm and emotional safety is a fundamental part of that offer. These two feelings will help reduce those stress levels in the body, reduce the survival responses and increase the likelihood of children being able to use their rational brain. Our classrooms should work with us not against us!

The therapeutic school approach includes looking at classrooms more closely and being brave enough to make changes that ensure the rooms have children's mental health and wellbeing at their core. This can be done in small and big ways depending on your role in school and of course budget. My therapeutic teaching course has taught schools how to do this for years and teachers always report a significant impact on the children's attention, noise levels and overall happiness. The course focuses mainly on the small changes you can make and we will talk about some of these suggestions later in this chapter. Now, although it is wonderful hearing the positive outcomes of the smaller changes happening up and down the country, the concept of a therapeutic classroom has the potential to go beyond that. We have just discussed the multitude of barriers conventional classrooms have and I have always felt there is another version of a classroom that could exist in the world.

That is where the therapeutic classroom was born!

Therapeutic classrooms

The journey

In 2021, just after the schools open again following covid, I sat down with one of the Head Teachers from a school in Wigan, Andy Houghton. He had signed up to the Therapeutic School Award and was in the process of rolling out the modules to the teachers. Andy was a forward thinking, innovative Head Teacher who already had beautiful environments in his school. I remember visiting and being so excited to finally see a school with break out spaces in the corridors and a warm cosy library with an armchair. It was exciting talking to someone who had just as much passion as I did and who was already thinking out of the box in so many ways, Andy had a school radio station, a school café and was in the process of creating a school spa! He was totally aligned with my vision, but his classrooms were still like every other classroom in the UK (albeit not so bright!). Andy and I were sat discussing how children were struggling with their mental health more than ever and reflecting on how suddenly very single child in school had an adverse life experience due to covid. At this time, across the UK staggering numbers of children were refusing to go into school and when they did, things like anxiety were daily battles. It was during this conversation I asked him a question that took the concept of a therapeutic classroom out of my head and into the real world. I asked whether he would be brave enough for me to totally transform one of his classrooms which included removing all standard classroom tables and chairs. It was a big ask but he said yes, and we got to work! The budget was £2,500 and the impact was huge!

We filmed the process and put it on YouTube and I documented our story in the national *Head Teachers' Update* Magazine. Before I knew it, I had more schools asking me to transform their spaces too. It has been an evolving journey, and I have spent the last two years transforming settings across the UK in every school demographic you can think of. I have transformed environments in prep schools, mainstream primary schools, SEMH schools and special schools and have worked with big schools, small schools, leafy green suburban schools, and schools in areas of deprivation. Every time the outcome is always the same. The impact of these spaces is astonishing and often overnight, but, before I talk you through the impact. Let me tell you what a therapeutic classroom is.

What is a therapeutic classroom?

A therapeutic classroom is designed to meet the needs of the children first and foremost, acknowledging that without the right conditions, many children will struggle to learn. These are not just good-looking spaces, they are not a fad or a trend, they are, what I believe should be the new standard of classroom in every school.

Figure 11.1A Shevington Vale, Year 3 classroom before area 1
Copyright: TPC Therapy Ltd.

Figure 11.1B Shevington Vale, Year 3 classroom after area 2
Copyright: TPC Therapy Ltd.

Figure 11.2A Shevington Vale, Year 3 classroom before area 1
Copyright: TPC Therapy Ltd.

Figure 11.2B Shevington Vale, Year 3 classroom after area 2
Copyright: TPC Therapy Ltd.

Every classroom should be:
   Trauma informed
   Attachment aware
   Inclusive
   Neurodivergent sensitive
And also:
   Be calm, safe and welcoming
   Be comfortable and purposeful
   Help children feel emotionally safe
   Help children self-regulate
   Aid concentration
   Reflect different learning preferences/needs
   Meet their emotional and mental health needs!
   Feel like home

Figure 11.3 Example of a Therapeutic Classroom: Cookridge Primary
Copyright: TPC Therapy Ltd.

Figure 11.4 Example of a Therapeutic Classroom: Eton End Prep School
Copyright: TPC Therapy Ltd.

Essentially every classroom should be an environment where every child can thrive. A place that is designed with the child at the centre so that we can come away from trying to adapt current classroom standards to meet the needs of children and instead, raise the standard itself. We shouldn't be adapting the room for a child with autism, anxiety or wheelchair user, the room should already have been designed with them in mind!

There are specific elements that make up one of my therapeutic classrooms, each contributing to the overall goal and each carefully and purposely considered to ensure they are meeting the criteria above. Every therapeutic classroom I create has the following elements:

Comfortable seating

As a basic standard, children should have something comfortable to sit on all day. In my therapeutic classrooms I always source soft, upholstered chairs and the children love them! Using soft chairs is not only comfortable but supports a trauma-informed space.

Why?
- Soft comfortable seats help reduce stress levels in the body
- If a child is comfortable, they will concentrate for longer
- They help children self-soothe by running their fingers over the chairs as they learn
- The more comfortable children are, the more likely their brains will associate learning with happiness, and will feel more productive and ready to learn

Neutral colours

A therapeutic classroom is decorated with home in mind and in colours that will support a sense of calm and peace. The room considers that everyone is affected by colour differently and so avoids overuse of colour to ensure it is as inclusive as possible. The colours aim to aid learning, rather than distracts from it so uses colour minimally. Walls are painted in a light grey or stone or an off white, which evoke a sense of calm and comfort whist also keeping the space light and airy. I avoid anything with a yellow tone that will continue to yellow over time like cream. A therapeutic classroom then has neutral colours like wicker, wood, white and grey around the room which might be in the form of baskets, pillows, blankets or pencil pots. Sometimes I add one accent colour to the space, like blue which I often do when a classroom has a blue carpet! Finally, the rooms have pops of green in the form of plants.

Why?
- Colours can impact task performances and emotional responses like feeling calm or stressed (Sevic, 2014)
- Neutral colours calm the mind and help reduce stress levels
- Neutral colours increase concentration and productivity
- When a room is decorated purposefully the room feels more welcoming and children want to be in it
- Green and blue are connected to safety and calmness
- Studies have found neutral earth tones are relaxing because they remind people of nature (Eiseman, 2006)

Soft lighting

Floor lamps, warm LED lamps and fairy lights are used in a therapeutic classroom, enhancing the room's feeling of safety and calm. The main fluorescent lighting is turned off as much as possible and the classroom makes use of natural light from the windows and warm lamps instead. Many of the schools on the therapeutic school course or award have seen a dramatic improvement in noise levels and concentration just by simply turning off the main light and adding fairy lights to the room. This simple tweak makes a big difference and can help children feel more engaged in the room. I acknowledge that there will be times when the main light and bright lighting is required, it is important to highlight that the addition of soft lighting does not dismiss the importance of a well-lit room for learning, however adding soft lighting gives teachers the option to change the mood of the room depending on the nature of the lesson and needs of the children. Thus, making it an inclusive, flexible working space. If children are struggling with attention and noise, simply turning off the lights and turning on the lamps will help.

Why?
- Calm lighting helps reduce stress levels and calms the body and mind
- Calm lighting reduces noise levels for our children
- Sensory stimulation with warm lights helps emotional regulation (Golden, 2005)

Calm areas

Every therapeutic classroom includes a calm area within the space. This is often a sofa with a coffee table and rug, or arm chairs and includes soft furnishings such as soft lighting, blankets, and pillows. The beauty of a therapeutic classroom is that once you change the classroom furniture, there is more space! I have transformed huge rooms and tiny rooms and can usually fit in a sofa! The calm area is a functional learning space for the children, rather than a separate area. They can work from here, listen to learning input and do group work. It also helps children who need some one-to-one time or some alone time to self-regulate and calm down. If a child is feeling unsettled, knowing they can sit on the sofa under a blanket to do their maths helps reduce their sense of stress and helps them continue to learn. They can have independent autonomy over where they will work best based on their needs in that moment. Some children will take a few moments out to calm down and then come back to the space, others might 'opt out' and not want to learn. Having a calm area within the classroom reduces children's need to escape the room when they are becoming unsettled. The room is designed to help them manage their emotional state and then return to learning when they are ready without it being a big issue. It is really hard to come back into the classroom after being dysregulated and walking out, it is much easier to join back in from the sofa or quietly pick up your workbook again.

Why?
- Calm areas aid self-regulation
- Calm areas provide flexible seating
- Calm spaces support emotional and mental wellbeing (Yan et al., 2024)
- Calm spaces reduce barriers to learning
- Calm spaces help children feel safe

Plants

Plants are used in every therapeutic classroom on tables, desks, bookcases and storage to promote wellbeing and a sense of connection to nature. These can be fake or real depending on the preference of the teacher and both have the similar benefits. The green colour of the plants contributes to a feeling of peace and calm and gives the room a little, gentle pop of colour and the plants themselves improve wellbeing and mental health. Plants are a cost-effective addition to any classroom.

Why?
- Plants enhance a person's quality of life
- Plants reduce anxiety, stress and depression (Beukeboom et al., 2012).
- Plants improve attention and visual response (Hall and Dickson, 2011)
- Plants improve memory retention
- Plants increase feelings of emotional wellbeing and happiness

No displays

A therapeutic classroom has limited or no display boards, instead the walls are used to hang shelves (which can be used for storage, lighting and books) or for pictures of the children. The walls are used to create a sense of home and adding a photo wall of the children is one of my favourite ways to do that. Printing out a picture of every child and hanging it on the wall promotes a sense of connectiveness, togetherness and belonging. The classrooms belong to the children and representing them in this way helps them to feel that the space is theirs.

I also remove any unnecessary posters, prompts and washing lines but without taking away from the intention of those resources. Instead, I ask schools to think about creative ways to make learning aids available to the children in a practical, productive way. Can prompts be put in books that children can go and select when they need the support, can they be put on laminated sheets on the table in a caddy, or on their laptops if they use them. We do not want to reduce children's access to visual support, but we do want to enhance it and ensure that it is purposeful.

In rooms where display boards are kept, I recommend using one neutral colour as backing paper (wallpaper is also a brilliant option), keeping information minimal and purposeful and ensuring they are calm by adding fairy lights and ivy around them.

Why?
- Our physical space impacts wellbeing, cognitive performance and behaviour (Djimantoro, 2018)
- Calm rooms improve concentration and attention
- Calm rooms reduce stress and anxiety
- Removing classroom décor and displays increases learning gains and concentration (Fisher et al., 2014)
- Removing visual displays improve attention for all children especially those with ASD (Hanley et al., 2017)

Soft furnishings

It is essential that every therapeutic classroom has soft furnishings available to the children. Although these help a room look and feel welcoming and cosy, their purpose is more physiological. Soft rugs, blankets, pillows and teddies help children to regulate and self-sooth and are a brilliant, non-intrusive way for children to learn to manage their own emotional states whilst in the classroom. Allowing children to pull a blanket over their knee or round their shoulders can increase feelings of safety and reduce anxiety and stress without disrupting learning. Blankets are also a brilliant tactile sensory tool for children with sensory needs and weighted teddies or blankets are good additions for children with autism, ADHD and anxiety (Baric et al., 2023). Again, this challenges perceptions about what is normal, or allowed in a classroom but if a child is learning productively with a blanket around them, that is a far better outcome than them becoming dysregulated and leaving the room. Soft, clean blankets are affordable yet easy additions to a classroom and improve children's overall sense of wellbeing and aid mental health. I also replace bright, colourful rugs with neutral soft rugs. These often go in front of the board and under the sofa. Sitting on a soft rug helps children feel comfortable and allows them to self-soothe by running their fingers or toes through it. My schools have found the inclusion of a soft rug reduces fidgeting with shoes and distracting others.

Why?
- Soft touch objects like pillows or weighted blankets can feel comfortable and enhance feelings of wellbeing (Vinson et al., 2020)
- Weighted blankets improve emotional regulation (Lönn et al., 2023)
- Soft furnishings reduce stress levels and anxiety
- Soft furnishings help children self-sooth and regulate (Yan et al., 2024)
- They help create a sense of peace and calm
- Cuddling a teddy can reduce the feeling of social exclusion and increases prosocial behaviour (Kenneth et al., 2011)
- Teddies can reduce trauma and stress responses in children (Sadeh et al., 2008)

Flexible seating

A fundamental element of a therapeutic classroom is replacing traditional classroom furniture with flexible seating options to reflect different learning needs and to create a more productive learning experience. My classrooms include:

- Low floor seating paired with floor cushions
- Free standing desks
- High bar style tables with comfortable highchairs
- Calm areas with sofas and armchairs
- Collaborative large tables
- Smaller tables

There are also different shaped tables such as small square tables, rectangle tables and round tables, All providing different benefits and zones. I might also include beanbags within the space and a tent too. The room is designed to be creative, inspiring and purposeful and children can choose where they sit. This encourages them to identify their own learning preferences depending on their emotional state or need that day or session. If a child is having a tricky morning because the weekend was hard, they might choose to sit up on a high table with just one other peer positioned near a window. A child who needs connection might choose a larger rectangle table that seats eight children. They can choose seats each lesson to reflect their needs and move around the space if appropriate. For example, for a taught session some children might sit on the floor with blankets and others on the sofa, they then might be sent off to do an activity and some might choose the floor table whilst others choose the high table. The option for flexible seating meets individual learning needs, improves concentration and independence, and cultivates a sense of connection to learning.

The relationship between teacher and child is also enhanced because teachers can sit alongside children in their preferred space which feels more connective and relational compared to them bending down beside a chair or table.

The beauty of flexible seating is that it can evolve depending on the needs of the children, for example in my course I recommend using plastic washing baskets with pillows in to help children with ADHD or sensory processing needs. One of my schools did this and found that one child worked longer and harder when sat in the basket compared to other forms of seating. It also became her safe space in the room! Where children sit and how they sit, should no longer be in the hands of the adults or confined to plastic chairs in rows. The room should mirror the evolving world outside. More adults are opting to work in a cafe or on their sofa rather than at a desk in an office, and large corporations are harnessing this by creating flexible workspaces for their employees. If we truly want to prepare our children for the world then our classrooms should feel innovative and be fluid workspaces that cultivate the imagination and interest of the learners.

Another important reason for changing the furniture is to create more space in the classroom. Flexible seating removes the barrier traditional furniture creates and allows for more fluid, natural movement around the room, which is essential for every child and teacher, especially children with mobility issues.

Why?

- Flexible seating stops children feeling trapped and creates a sense of freedom
- It reduces stress hormones and fight, flight, freeze responses
- Being comfortable in a learning environment improves attention and meaningful learning experiences
- It promotes inclusivity
- A flexible classroom encourages interaction and connection between the teacher and children and between peers (Rands and Gansemer-Topf, 2017)
- Flexible seating encourages movement in the classroom which improves engagement and attention (Harvey and Kenyon, 2013)
- Flexible seating can encourage positive behaviour and reduce disruptive behaviour (Havig, 2017)

Organisation and storage

A therapeutic classroom is clutter free and organised. Clutter can contribute to feelings of stress and sensory overload, especially for children with autism or sensory processing needs. Decluttering can make all the difference and is an important first step. Throw away anything old or unused, organise storage cupboards and utilise the space you have. Pair this with purposeful clever storage but without the colourful plastic trays and boxes! In a therapeutic classroom, resources are stored in wicker baskets in cupboards or on shelves and storage is available in clever ways like inside a footstool or on shelves and in purposeful storage units that match the room décor. Seeing lots of resources around you can lead to feelings of overwhelm and anxiety. If your environment is disorganised, your mind could be too! A trauma-informed classroom acknowledges that if a child is coming into school feeling internally chaotic, the classroom should help them feel calm, this is especially true for children struggling with ACES.

Why?

- Organisation helps improve concentration, quality of thought and learning
- It will promote a sense of calm and order internally
- It will contribute to increased productivity
- It will reduce a child's fight, flight freeze response

What does this mean for teaching and how do you use the classroom?

Teaching in a therapeutic classroom doesn't change what you teach but enhances how you teach. It asks you to change your perception of what children can do in the room and how the room is used for example, children go from sitting on the same chair every day to being able to choose. This can sometimes be a worry at first, for fear of children arguing, but feedback suggests that children are great at sharing the space and will naturally flow throughout the day, meaning they all get a chance to sit on their preferred furniture at some point. The ability to share the room and use it collaboratively promotes emotional intelligence and social skills which in turn will benefit the children's overall learning. Ultimately though, the teacher decides how to organise this depending on the needs of the children and the circumstances. You might choose to have children in the same spots for certain lessons or allow flexible choice at certain times.

The other change is for you to be comfortable with children working in different zones of the room at different levels all at the same time, you might have some on the sofa, on the floor and on high tables. Moving around these spaces and meeting children wherever they choose to sit is a new way of working, but one you soon get used to. Teachers tell me they prefer this more and have far less bumps and bruises from navigating around small furniture and table corners! Many have also said they now have less backache because they can sit next to the children or stand alongside them rather than crouching down. When you replace the furniture or add different zones it changes the way the room is used for both teachers and children, but the change feels natural and more aligned with a connective way of teaching. However, how far this goes is up to you. The way the room works will reflect how comfortable you are to adapt your expectations of the space and the children. How does letting children sit on the sofa during a lesson feel? Or allowing children to use blankets? It will only go, as far as you let it but remember, change is good, we just have to be brave enough to do it!

Early years/foundation stage

When I talk about classrooms it is important to recognise that the Nursery and Reception classes are included in this. The early years rooms shouldn't be forgotten when you are transforming your spaces, they are a vital part of school and the first rooms children will experience with you. What you do in this part of the school sets the expectation and tone for what 'school' is for the children. Feeling calm and safe in foundation stage is fundamental for all of the reasons we have discussed but also because this might be the first time they are leaving their parents full time.

The early years environments traditionally mimic many of the issues I have discussed above especially the bright colours and displays. However, lots of settings are now championing natural wooden furniture and neural tones instead, this fits in beautifully with the therapeutic school approach. A therapeutic early year's setting would include many of the elements of a normal therapeutic classroom especially with things like soft lighting, plants, calm areas, no display boards, soft furnishings and flexible seating however special considerations would be as follows:

- Add more than one low table option for children to play at, with pillows on the floor
- Create separate zones using carpets and furniture to make the room feel cosier and smaller which will help those children who feel overwhelmed
- Add cushions and rugs to different zones to encourage floor play
- Add cushions, pillows and blankets in front of the board
- Limit conventional boards and add positive quotes where possible
- Hang large photographs of the children playing together in frames around the room
- Use low lighting as much as you can, fairy lights and floor lamps are brilliant in foundation stage
- Introduce 'closed' spaces like a wooden playhouse or tent which include soft furnishings like a soft rug or duvet, pillows, and fairy lights to give children safe spaces to retreat to and play in
- Use wooden or wicker baskets as storage or resource boxes
- Choose wooden toys/tents/resources over plastic ones
- Add small and free-standing fake plants to the room paired with fake ivy around displays or windows
- Create a calm area using a sofa you would find at home, pair this with a rug and teddies, this is a brilliant place to do story time

Chairs

At the moment, in the evolution of a therapeutic classroom, there are not upholstered chairs available for early years children due to their size, but it is something I will be closely monitoring as it develops. However, because the children move around the space so much more, wooden tables and chairs are an appropriate option as long as the children also have access to plenty of floor and low seating, a calm area and enclosed safe spaces within the room.

Dinner halls

Part of the therapeutic school approach is to look at every environment and cultivate a more trauma-informed offer. Dinner hall environments can cause a plethora of problems and can be where many of the dysregulated behaviours begin. Dinner halls can be noisy, overwhelming, and chaotic and trigger survival responses. Decisions like, choosing where to sit and choosing their dinner can be difficult, especially for the more vulnerable children, so creating a calmer more connective experience of dinner time can make all the difference. This is the time of day where children should be able to re-focus, connect with friends, rest and nurture themselves through food. Finding ways to meet their needs so that they can get the best from this time of day will make a big difference.

Re-design the space

This might not be possible for everyone, but ideally, we need to consider re-imagining the lunchtime experience. When I transform a dining room, I create a space that feels more like a café or restaurant than a dining hall. Moving away from cattle like lines and rows of seating and instead investing in round tables and individual seats and adding plants and soft lighting to make the space feel safer. Of course, this needs some logistical planning if the hall has different purposes, but changing the environment in which children eat their dinner helps the space feel more inviting and less overwhelming.

Other ways to calm the space would be to play relaxing music to help lower the noise of the space and calm internal states. If you can, consider offering outdoor seating too so that those children who struggle with large spaces and lots of people have somewhere to escape to.

If this isn't an option for you, could you create a mini dining room for those children who need it? Somewhere they can eat that feels more nurturing and quieter, and that isn't overwhelming? Again, it might take more resources to set this up, but in truth, the conventional dinner hall isn't trauma-informed and it is unfair to expect some children to cope in that environment when their survival instincts won't allow it. In every school there are children who prefer to eat in the classroom or nurture room with their teachers, maybe we need to lean into this and set up a purposeful space where they can go. Some children just need a different experience to help them get what they need from their dinner time.

Reimagine the process

The way in which we serve lunch could also be reimagined. The idea of lining up to be served can cause children to feel anxious, with many worrying about what is left or struggling to pick. They might also be worried about who to play with and where to sit. They find it hard to make decisions and to think rationally because their survival brain is trying to process all of the unknown factors that dinner time brings. Instead, remove the anxiety for them and introduce some reliability and routine. You could try a system where children choose their meals at the beginning of the day and are then served at their tables. Creating a more nurturing, connective lunchtime. The meals could be served by lunchtime organisers or even the children themselves. You could start a life skills program where some children set the table and others clear it away. This way they are learning through responsibilities like getting water for the table or putting out everyone's knives and forks and then clearing away the plates. This not only provides structure and routine but harnesses another opportunity to teach and cultivates skills they will use in the future.

Impact, outcomes and case studies

Although we are still in the process of gathering data, the feedback and data we do have is significant. Head Teachers have seen their school refusers suddenly come into school every day! Children with autism and ADHD are more engaged and can concentrate for longer in the classroom. Behaviour has improved, social skills have improved, eye contact has increased, and children are reporting feeling calm and safe in their environments. Yes, they use the word 'safe'! I have stayed in close contact with many of the schools who have been brave enough to roll out this approach and together, we have looked at impact over time. We have found that after transforming a classroom:

- Children are more engaged
- Noise levels are lower
- Children concentrate for longer
- Children with ADHD and Autism are accessing learning
- There is less dysregulation
- There has been an increase in eye contact, communication skills, social and emotional skills
- School refusal numbers decrease
- Children on half day time tables are now back in class
- Children feel safe
- Teachers feel happier

And so much more! Here are what some of the Head Teachers have said:

> 'We have seen the benefits of this room in such a short space of time. Children who were previously reluctant to come in, are now here on time, ready to learn. Children with additional needs are able to self-regulate. I would never have imagined it having such a positive effect on our children, but it does – it works!'
> Helen Smart
> Head Teacher at Worsley Mesnes Primary

> 'The impact is really hard to put into words. We have happy children who love coming to school and who want to learn. We have children who are no longer attacking staff, kicking walls and trashing rooms!'
> Graham Carter
> Personalised Learning Pathways Manager
> Great Oaks School
> 'I know that there is a huge impact on wellbeing, just for the fact they are in the classrooms! Parents gave feedback on the children's transitions recently and they are saying the kids can't wait to come to school! Before, they were not accessing any learning, but they are all

sat around the table doing phonics, we are all excited! I can't thank you enough! It has been incredible. I have no before and after evidence, but I do have a huge amount of experience in the field and have opened other provisions before, even with small classrooms and it hasn't been like this! It has been such a privilege to do this with you. They are all going full-time – these kids have not done a full day in years, but they are all saying I can't wait to come back!'

Dan Tresman
Founder and Head Teacher
Light Years School

'The school has seen an increase in attendance levels across the school since the classrooms were modified and the few instances we had of emotionally based school avoidance, have ceased. Our children want to be in those spaces and the autonomy they have about where and how they learn gives them ownership and buy-in. We have also noticed a decrease in the number of incidents of 'unkind' behaviour amongst our children since we adopted the therapeutic approach to teaching and supporting behaviour, I have no doubt that these approaches combined with the classrooms has been the driving force in this reduction. Our children are already more in tune with their emotions and reactions than they were twelve months ago.'

Rachael Cox
Headmistress Eton End Prep

"Children on heath and care plans have never ever been more settled, they have accessed the curriculum and have for the first time ever scored above average. The children in the first classrooms we transformed have had their assessments and have made additional progress, above what we expected"

Claire Holloway
Head Teacher St Olves Prep School

One of our Head Teachers recently spoke to me about the increase in safeguarding disclosures the school has seen since the classroom changes. They felt that children were able to disclose because were in an emotionally secure environment, sitting under a blanket on a sofa having a conversation.

Regardless of whether the school is a mainstream primary, SEMH or prep school, big or small, wealthy or deprived, the outcomes and impact are the same across the board all over the country, and children themselves love their rooms. They have said things like:

'I like this classroom because it feels like home, I feel safer'

'A normal classroom is bright and stuff and this is calm and peaceful and not like, "oh look there is a bunch of displays there!" It is more peaceful'

'When I first sat on the chairs, I loved it! They are soft and very comfortable'

'I like this room because it is more comfy and I hated them wobbly blue chairs, they just annoyed me! I like the tables how they are circled, they're just the best shape, you have more space to put your stuff!'

'It looks more comfier, more cosier and you don't have to gather up too much information at once, so your brain doesn't explode (from the boards)'

'I feel stressed at school, this room would make me wanna get up and wanna do more stuff in school . . . without getting mad or sad!'

'When I sat on the chair. You could actually sit back and write, instead of leaning forward to write. It doesn't hurt your back when you try and move'

If those comments are not worth changing classrooms for, I don't know what is!

What Ofsted thinks

The big question! Several of our schools have been inspected since they transformed their rooms and despite some fear over the reaction they might receive, every inspector has commented positively on the spaces! Some have even mentioned them in their reports as strengths of the school. I recently had an email from a Head Teacher, he told me his inspector said there is no official preferred way of working with a learning environment. He was very positive about how the therapeutic classroom approach was calming and positively impacted children's wellbeing. He was also enthusiastic about how the reduction of cognitive overload and displays had the potential to improve memory and retrieval.

Sometimes there is a perceived belief about what you 'have to do' as a teacher or school to meet the requirements of Ofsted. I have found some of this to be based more on common cultural practices that have evolved over time, rather than actual expectations and mandatory rules. The thing is, we are always going to expect the expected, it is only when that begins to shift that expectations can be raised. That is what we are doing here!

Sourcing furniture

As with any new approach, sourcing furniture for classrooms was an evolving process. At the beginning of my journey, there wasn't anything out there designed for children, so Andy and I transformed his Year 3 classroom with items from the high street and online stores. The focus at that time was to prove concept in a cost-effective way. Due to the demand for therapeutic classrooms, I followed this model for a little while with other pilot schools but quickly realised that the furniture, although much preferred by staff and children, was not durable enough for a classroom long term and my focus shifted. I had proven concept, but now I needed to focus on durability. It is important to ensure that the rooms will not only significantly improve wellbeing and mental health but also that they will last. Now, not much can outlive a plastic chair, and there isn't an alternative just yet, but the goal here isn't to be on par with a basic plastic chair, it is to create a new standard of furniture all together. I soon began speaking to suppliers who could make durable and hardwearing furniture for my rooms and to my specification. My goal is to find furniture that will replace the current 'go to' options and this is evolving all of the time. When the time is right, I plan to open a therapeutic classroom furniture store so that schools have another option! The children and teachers love their spaces and are constantly providing feedback that helps me continuously improve standards. I have assembled a team of Head Teachers who form a Therapeutic Classroom Advisory Board and together we are evaluating, trialling and tweaking things to evolve the approach. With the continued help of amazing, inspiring Head Teachers who are brave enough to transform their spaces, I am on an exciting journey toward figuring out what a new era of classroom furniture looks like!

If you are inspired by this chapter and my therapeutic classroom approach and want to go out there and create your own spaces, please be mindful of the furniture you choose. Sourcing good quality, durable furniture is essential for this approach to have longevity and hopefully become the new normal. There is a long way to go, but getting there is part of the story!

Smaller changes you can make

You might be reading this chapter with excitement and enthusiasm but be unable to transform the whole classroom environment in this way. Don't worry! There are so many elements of this that you can do to any standard classroom and still see a significant impact on the children. My top tips would be:

- De-clutter
- Decide on a colour theme
  For example, neutral display boards with ivy and fairy lights round the borders or hessian with black borders
- Remove some or all of the display boards
- Replace work on display boards with positive quotes and add fairy lights round them.
  This will increase self-belief and positive self-talk and could be messages of hope, encouragement or connection
- Add a photo wall and frames filled with positive affirmations
- Add plants
- Add lamps and fairy lights
- Add blankets, pillows and soft rugs
- Add a calm relaxing corner
  You can get second hand sofa's online
- Consider adding some flexible seating options
  This might be bean bags, floor seating, one high bar table or free-standing desk

Small changes can make a huge impact! Head Teacher of Green Lanes Primary, Michele Johnson, rolled out the therapeutic teaching course in her school and along with embedding the therapeutic teaching approach, they also made many of these smaller changes to their environments. Michele contacted me the following year and said, 'Last year we signed up for the whole staff TPC online training. Our whole school SEMH has dropped by 50%. The classrooms are calmer and so are staff. We have also seen a drop in behaviour incidents.' She later shared that all of her ESBA children now attended school and less incidents were being recorded on CPOMS.

Whatever you decide to take from this book, you really can make a significant difference to the children you teach. Don't let your role or money become a limitation or barrier. There is no such thing as can't!

Other ways to cultivate a therapeutic school environment

Remember, the classrooms are just one element of the whole school environment. These changes should also be made to corridors, staffrooms, intervention rooms, one-to-one rooms and dining rooms to see a real impact across the school. There are also other things to consider about the environment and other ways to enhance them.

The power of music

Using music around school is another significant part of the therapeutic school approach. Music has the power to alter our emotions and hormones and is a brilliant tool to help calm the minds of our children. Using music takes very little effort from you but can significantly improve noise levels in your classroom and help elicit a feeling of peace in the classroom. One of the most powerful ways to utilise music is to play it before the children come into the classroom, both in the morning and also after break and dinner. My favourite way is to play a calming relaxation video on YouTube that has soft repetitive music paired with a relaxing image like trees or water. This then becomes a sensory experience of both sound and sight for children which feels soothing. Pop it on the whiteboard as the children come into the classroom and create a routine whereby they come in, sit down and sit quietly for a few moments just listening and watching. They could choose to do some calm breathing or even some calm colouring too. This only needs to be for five minutes and might just be whilst you do the register but it allows the children to transition from the outside world, into the safe classroom space you have created. Doing this each day not only offers the children a consistent, reliable routine that will help them feel emotionally safer throughout the day, but will also calm stress hormones and bring them back into the present moment. This small tweak will help shift the brain from a state of stress into a state of calm and help children feel ready to learn and is great for children who have had a tricky morning at home or a chaotic break time.

You can also use music as a tool when you sense the children are getting unsettled in the classroom during learning. Playing some calming music is a great way to reset the children and refocus their minds. Or, alternatively, you could have a dance party! My daughter's Year 5 teacher, Miss Blomfield, has a jar in her classroom. Each week the children add their favourite songs to the jar and every now and then, when she thinks the children need it, she stops the class, chooses a song and they have a dance party together. This blast of connective togetherness is a lovely example of how we can support children's mental health and wellbeing. It communicates to the children that you are in-tune with their internal and emotional needs and it raises their emotional intelligence and models a tool they can use in the future. My daughter thinks it is the most amazing thing in the world and it contributes to her love of school!

Daily practices

Part of the therapeutic school approach is giving the children the life skills they need to understand and manage their own wellbeing and mental health. This is essential for every child, especially in the busy world we live in today. There is very little time for developing self-reflection skills and mindful moments, but these are tools that children can apply throughout their lives. An easy way to normalise self-reflection and mindfulness is to introduce them into the day to day running of your classroom. This can just be 10 minutes of your day each day. Here are some ideas (you can do one of these regularly or mix and match throughout the year):

Journalling

Writing down how we feel is a powerful way to express our feelings. Giving the children a blank workbook or journal can be a great way to help children to do this. You could do journaling together as a class or just allow them to use the books when they need them. You could:

- Ask them to write down three things they are grateful for this week
- A positive statement or affirmation like, 'I can do anything I put my mind to.'
- A memory that makes them smile
- A poem that expresses how they feel
- Words that describe their best qualities

However you use the journals, remember that these are not pieces of work to be marked. They are just a tool for self-expression.

Mindful colouring

Colouring is calming and relaxing and is great for the mind. It is also a simple effective tool to have on hand in the classroom. You can use colouring as a method to calm the class, 'Let's do five minutes of colouring' or to start or end your day. You could also include colouring when listening to relaxing music after break or dinner to get them ready to learn. It can also be used as a regulation tool if someone is bubbling. Keep colouring pages and pots of pencils ready to pull out when you need them.

Drawing

Drawing is also very healing and can help children explore how they feel and express their frame of reference. Allow the children to express themselves through drawing outside on the playground, in wet break and whenever else you can find time. You can also include drawing in one-to-one sessions or if you are supporting a child who struggles in the classroom. The trick is to let them draw whatever they want and then comment on what you see in a therapeutic way, without praise or judgement, 'He looks sad,' 'It looks dark in that house,' this can open up conversation and opportunities for the child to talk about what they are struggling with. You could also be more direct and use drawing to help children express how they feel, 'Can you draw how you feel right now?'

Meditation

Meditation and mindfulness are brilliant tools for the classroom, not only can they calm the class and reduce stress hormones, but they are a powerful way for children to take control of their thoughts and minds. You can do meditations before the school day and at the end of the day, during wet break or in the middle of a lesson (if things are getting a bit unsettled and high energy). Some meditations are done with just calming breathing, but I find the best ones for children are where they are being guided to think of something. There are loads of guided meditations for children online, just pre-listen to them before hand to ensure they are appropriate.

Mindset work

Lots of children struggle with their beliefs about themselves and intrusive thoughts. You can help raise children's self-belief and frame of reference through small mindset strategies in the classroom. Here are some ideas:

- Have a mirror in the room with positive affirmations around it, 'I am amazing' 'I can do anything' 'I believe in myself' encourage the children to stand in front of the mirror or write their own affirmations
- Have a positive board or jar where you and the children write down good things that have happened that day
- Ask the children to answer the register with a positive statement about themselves
- Frame affirmation statements and put them on your walls for the children to read subconsciously throughout the day

This will help reframe their thinking and perceptions and can improve mindset and wellbeing. Remember, however, this isn't about teaching them to avoid difficult feelings – if a child is upset, they still need to acknowledge and process their feelings.

Dinner, break time and outdoor spaces

It is easy to assume that running around to play at break should be fun, but dinner and break time can be a really difficult time for children and is often a source of anxiety or stress. Especially for children who are struggling with adverse experiences, have additional needs or operate at a high stress level already. Sending a child away from the adults to navigate social interactions, eat, play and have 'free time' by themselves is a big ask! It expects children to be able to use the rational thinking part of the brain and their emotional intelligence skills to figure out how to manage it all. This is hard enough for most children, but it can be impossible for some. If stress levels are already very high, being left alone to deal with the chaos of break or dinner is likely to trigger a child into their survival responses very quickly. Suddenly there are minimal adults, more children, more noise, and less structure. There is also an increased feeling of the unknown and more potential for 'danger' socially. Children might worry about who they will play with, what they will eat, where they will sit, whether they will score at football or if they will be left out. They might have a multitude of thoughts running through their minds like, 'Will Jack sit with me?' 'What if there is no pasta left?' 'Where will I sit?' 'What if there are no spaces on the table?' 'Has dad packed me crisps?' 'What if I don't like the dinner?' 'What will I play?' 'Will I have enough time to play?' 'What if they don't want to play my game again?' 'What if I don't get out quick enough for football?' 'It is too noisy!' 'Everyone is running so quickly!' 'Where is Elliot?' 'I can't see my friends!'

Break demands that children fend for themselves socially, deal with challenge or conflict and manage differing opinions. These are all important lessons but are hard for vulnerable children, especially when left to figure it out alone. This pressure can then be heightened by the adult expectation for them to have a 'good' break. The truth is, there are so many things that trigger children to feel emotionally unsafe, threatened or attacked during this part of the day and it is no wonder that this is where we find the most arguments and incidents occurring.

 Real life

When I was a therapist, I remember working with a girl in Year 6. She would be sent out to play but by the time I counted to ten on my fingers, she was back in swearing, kicking the walls and shouting at the teachers. For her, just being sent outside and trying to play with people presented her with so many triggering moments that she just couldn't do it. She had moved from another country with her family, leaving extended family back home whom she missed very much. Her mum had always struggled with depression and now had suddenly been diagnosed with cancer, and her dad was trying his best to hold it together. This girl was processing so much, and her stress levels were already so high so the smallest thing could happen and her fight mode was triggered. To others she looked like a rude girl who was misbehaving at school. To me, she looked like a scared child who was terrified her mum would die.

Considering what children need from their break and dinner time is a significant part of the therapeutic school approach, especially because of how important breaks are in a child's school day. They provide the 'down time' children so desperately need after being in the classroom, and they also help the brain process and organise what they have learnt so far. Breaks help develop their social skills, provide exercise, fresh air and so much more. However, not all children need or want to run around and play. Some need to escape, find solitude, have quiet and regroup. Others need time to refocus their minds and some just want to chat with friends. Think about yourself for a moment, what do you like to do when you have a break? Maybe you chat to your friends, have a drink and want to sit down. Other people might read a book, and some might go for a walk. As adults, we recognise our needs are different and we have the autonomy to choose for ourselves how best to use our time. The children need the same autonomy over theirs! Just like in the classroom, we should be providing opportunities for children to take ownership of their own needs and have the options available to them to meet those needs.

A therapeutic, trauma-informed approach

Break and dinner time should include two things

1. Opportunities to play
2. Opportunities to regulate

These should both be on offer at the same time and children should be able to choose from a variety of options within each category. A therapeutic school approach to break time is one where staff and children take out resources each day that allow for different styles of play and regulation. Some of these might stay outside, others will come in and out. A good idea is to have monitors who are in charge of setting up different areas and gathering them up again. Just like in the classroom, the playground should be split into zones, offering different things to the children.

Play

Play should be an essential offer throughout year groups, regardless of their age. This means year five and six should have access to sand and toys just like nursery do, but unfortunately this isn't the norm. It is so easy to assume that older children no longer need to play, but the opposite is true. They need it more! Remember, children are in a play deficit these days, with many opting to play on technology for most of their free time, instead of going outside. It now falls to school to fill those developmental gaps and help children continue to play as long into their childhood as possible. Play is the super food of childhood and one we must harness in education to help improve social, emotional and academic outcomes.

I began my career specialising in play – I ran play schemes and after school club sessions and I nannied groups of children during the summers, filling their days with different play opportunities. I then later became a play therapist and used play to help vulnerable and often traumatised children heal. I have seen firsthand how transformative play can be in children's lives and I am always disappointed when I see Year 5 and 6 children wandering about the playground with limited resources like one football and some skipping ropes. It breaks my heart that older children are led to believe they don't need to (or can't) play anymore, especially when deep down, they still want too! Children have an innate natural drive to play, which has always been present in childhood throughout history and our job is to let them! Giving children time and space to play is invaluable as it has developmental and healing qualities that cannot be as easily replicated in any other way. In fact, children learn faster through play than any other medium and it helps build cognitive, physical and social and emotional skills. Play helps:

- Shape brain development
- Develop social skills and communication skills
- Reduce depression, anxiety a sense of helplessness in childhood (Gray 2011)
- Improve physical, social and emotional wellbeing
- Explore and organise difficult thoughts, emotions and life experiences

- Build resilience, self-esteem and confidence
- Problem-solve and cope with challenging situations
- Build independence
- Children learn how to make decisions, solve problems, exert self-control and follow rules (Gray 2011)
- Make friends and socialise
- Children learn how to express themselves

These are skills every child needs to develop, and play is the easiest way to do it. All it takes from adults is to set up play opportunities and children will do the rest! Play is also essential for good mental health and wellbeing and is especially important for children who are struggling with adversity and trauma, as it helps them work through their feelings and emotions in an age appropriate, symbolic way without having to use words. By enhancing your outdoor provision, you are providing children with ways to solve their own problems and help themselves develop and grow. This is essential for a therapeutic, trauma informed, attachment aware setting.

One of the most exciting things about visiting schools for me is seeing their outdoor provision. I can tell a lot about a school's investment into children's wellbeing and mental health through what is available to the children, and I have seen so many wonderful examples of good practice that I want to share with you here. These are some easy ways to provide both play and regulation time at dinner and break.

Self-regulation opportunities

We know from reading this book that children need to learn to self-regulate. Setting up different ways children can do that during their break will help them manage their emotional state and come back into the classroom ready to learn. These calm quiet ideas will help reduce stress hormones, organise thoughts and calm the minds of the children (some of them are weather dependant).

Safe spaces

Add playhouses to the playground and pair them with soft, interlocking foam flooring, books and teddies to give the children somewhere calm and enclosed to spend their breaktime. These safe spaces will help reduce the noise of the playground and offer retreat to children who struggle with the chaos of children running around. You could also add movable tents for a more cost-effective solution. Remember though to choose the items wisely being aware of your use of colour. Neutral is always best!

Calming activities

Buy some foam flooring and fill some baskets that have handles with books, construction toys, pencil crayons and colouring and set up some quiet calm zones in the playground. Lots of children prefer sitting down to do something instead of running about and this is a great way to help them focus their minds and 'switch off' from school for a bit. This is a perfect idea for any unused areas of your grounds or playground and setting the zones up takes less than five minutes. The foam flooring makes the floor comfier for children to sit on and marks out a 'zone' and you could have one or two of these out with different activities on. Before you do this, create some rules about resources staying on mats and choose some calm zone monitors who set these areas up and put them away at the end of dinner.

Music

Utilise the power of music and help children regulate outside with music on portable speakers in the calm area or playhouses. If you are lucky enough to have a sensory garden or quieter space then playing calm music in the background whilst children relax will make a huge difference to how they feel.

Sensory garden

Create a sensory garden in an unused area of your playground where children can take out bean bags and calm activities in caddies. Your garden could include different tactile elements things like floor textures, artificial grass and wooden bark pathways and have nice smelling plants like lavender or jasmine. You could play soft music in this area too or include outdoor sounds with wind chimes for example.

Hammocks

Hang hammocks from your trees to provide comfortable places to relax during break. The ability to swing on a hammock promotes self-soothing and rocking would regulate children. Again, there would need to be rules around this but I know schools who have done this successfully.

Co-regulation opportunities

Meditation

Break and playtime doesn't always have to be outside. Can you set up some meditation sessions at breaktime or dinnertime inside with an adult? Giving children the opportunity to regulate before the afternoon. This doesn't need to be for the whole break, but maybe 15 minutes before coming inside or before they eat. In these sessions the adult could read out a calming meditation or story for the children to visualise, or they could play one on YouTube. I have some free meditations on my website and course platforms you could use.

Reading

Could you have members of staff outside with books who could read to the children? Reading to children has so many benefits and can help increase a sense of connection as well as calm children down. It is also a brilliant way to focus the attention of children who might struggle on the playground. You could have some blankets in a basket and some books and the children could listen to a story and then read to themselves or each other. This is a lovely idea for summer and is especially nice when you have mixed ages on the play-ground because you'll find the bigger children reading to the younger ones which is a brilliant way to develop emotional intelligence skills and self-worth.

Drawing

Could some members of staff draw with the children at break or dinner? I love the idea of drawing benches with drawing pages and pencil crayons avail-able, but you could also have colouring sheets on clip boards put out on a blanket on the grass too. Drawing with an adult is again a connective, focused activity that will help children feel emotionally safe at break and dinner.

> **Top tip:** to say true to the therapeutic, trauma-informed approach, avoid praising children's drawings and making it about how 'good' their pictures are. Instead comment on the image by pointing things

out 'he looks so happy' or 'it is so colourful' rather than 'that is so good.' This will reduce the children's need for praise and the need to ask staff if they like their drawing. You want to avoid the activity becoming about 'good' drawings because this distracts from the act of drawing itself which should be the focus. Drawing isn't about the product, it's about the process!

Play opportunities

Offering different resources and 'set ups' on the playground will help focus children's attention and make break time meaningful and purposeful. The idea is that you set up different zones that children can play in. For example, you might have a calm zone, a building zone and a game zone.

Bikes and scooters zone

Yep, no more leaving them in the bike shed! I saw this in practice at a wonderful school in Northumberland. The Head Teacher, Alison Hawkins, encouraged children to bring their own bikes or scooters on to the playground. She also had spares for those who didn't have one. During break she allowed them to whizz about the playground freely. The children knew where the designated area of the playground were to do this, and it allowed them to release internal energy and get a sense of freedom whilst outside. It is also a wonderful way to help children learn to ride a bike or scoot if they don't have access to on at home!

Invest in a sandpit and embrace water play

The addition of a large sand pit complete with tractors, cars, buckets and spades, that is accessible for every year group is invaluable. Allowing them to dig, mould and build will contribute to feelings of mastery and control and is a great way to fill developmental gaps, especially for children who feel as though they have very little control in their lives. In fact, providing opportunities to have control through play like this can actually reduce the number of power struggles you see children displaying elsewhere. You could also introduce water play if you are brave enough and put out buckets and old guttering so that they can build streams and channels. Don't be afraid to embrace the rain during wet dinner times either and instead send the children outside in waterproofs and wellies to get wet (yes, Years 5 and 6 included!)

Playing with toys

Allowing the children to become someone else can help them process experiences, thoughts and feelings and experiment with different roles. You can easily encourage this by allowing children to take out resources such as dressing up clothes or props. You could have an outdoor mud kitchen or playhouse. Don't be afraid to do this for older children too. After doing my Therapeutic Teaching Course, Sarah Pollard, a Head Teacher from a school in Grimsby put baby dolls and prams on the junior playground for the children to use at break and dinner time. She found that the children began role playing together and that some children found comfort in carrying the dolls around. I went to visit the school once and saw this in action, and when I spoke to them, the Year 5 and 6 children told me their breaks were so much better now there were things to play with!

Harnessing relationships through play

Another important consideration on the playground is how you use the adults. Jill Wright, Head Teacher of Whitefield Primary School in Liverpool, has a wonderful outdoor ethos and told me that all of her staff are trained to play with the children. They don't walk around watching but instead get involved with games, set up games and play! This is a powerful way to make connections and relationships and also reduce behaviour incidents and fall outs! Lots of children don't have adults in their lives who play with them, so this could be transformative in itself!

Although I haven't mentioned them, alongside these ideas you would still have your play equipment, skipping ropes and footballs. There are so many ideas for break and dinner, do some research and get creative! Whatever you decide to do with breaks and dinners, be brave enough to do things differently! If it involves a bit more tidying and a re-think with regard to logistics then so be it! Supporting children's wellbeing and mental health is worth it!

Closing thoughts

Well, there it is, my first ever book. I hope you close this book feeling renewed and inspired and I hope that you have taken away lots of golden nuggets that will bring you closer to supporting children's mental health and wellbeing. I know there is a lot here and much of what I have written questions the norm and champions change. I also know I might have challenged your perceptions and beliefs about what school or teaching should be. But I hope, that, after reading this book, you feel excited and empowered to go out there and make a real difference.

Although the education world is talking about trauma-informed practices and improving children's mental health, it isn't there just yet. As more of us become trauma informed, as more of us question the norm, as we change practice, raise standards and embed a new culture, the more likely it is that we will make a real, lasting impact on the lives of children. Whatever your role, whatever your budget, whatever your circumstances, we all have the capacity to truly have an impact on the children around us and literally change children's lives. I hope that you put down this book knowing that you have the power to cultivate new thinking, change brain pathways, improve relationships, empower self-belief and have a direct hand in changing children's outcomes. It isn't easy, it isn't the norm, but it is the way forward. If enough adults can begin to lead with therapeutic, trauma-informed ways of working and increase children's awareness and emotional intelligence, we might just contribute to a happier generation of children who believe that they are loved, worthy and enough. That to me is worth the work.

Embedding trauma-informed therapeutic approaches is an ever-evolving journey. If you decide to embed my therapeutic teaching approach into your practice that is an amazing step in the journey. But don't let that be where it ends. It is important to constantly improve your skillset, learn and evolve. There will always be more you can do and more you can learn, with new science and amazing approaches developing all the time. We owe it to the children to be the very best teachers we can be, so never stop wanting to evolve and grow.

References

'Autism speaks' (2024) *Sensory Issues*. Available at: www.autismspeaks.org/senso-ry-issues#:~:text=Many%20autistic%20people%20experience%20hypersensi-tivity,people%20can%20easily%20tune%20out (accessed 13 March 2024).

Baric, B.V., Skuthalla, S., Pettersson, M., Gustafsson, A.P., and Kjellberg, A. (2023) 'The effectiveness of weighted blankets on sleep and everyday activities: A retrospect follow-up study of children and adults with attention deficit hyperactivity disorder and/or autism spectrum disorder.' *Scandinavian Journal of Occupational Therapy*, 30(8), 1357–1367.

Beukeboom, C.J., Langeveld, D., and Tanja-Dijkstra, K. (2012) 'Stress reducing effects of real and artificial nature in a hospital waiting room.' *J Altern Complement Med*, 1(4), 329–333.

Djimantoro, M.I. (2018) 'Multisensory experience for mental health in higher education classroom design.' *IOP Conference Series: Earth and Environmental Science*, 195(1), 1–8.

Eiseman, L. (2006) *Color: Messages and Meanings. A Pantone Color Resource.* Gloucester, MA: Hand Books Press Distributed by North Light Books.

Fisher, V.A., Godwin, E.K., and Seltman, H. (2014) 'Visual environment, attention allocation, and learning in young children: When too much of a good thing may be bad.' *Psychological Science*, 25(7), 1.

Golden, R.N., Gaynes, B.N., Ekstrom, R.D., Hamer, R.M., Jacobsen, F.M., Suppes, T., Wisner, K.L., and Nemeroff, C.B. (2005) 'The efficacy of light therapy in the treatment of mood disorders: A review and meta-analysis of the evidence.' *Am J Psychiatry*, 162(4), 656–662.

Hall, C., and Dickson, M. (2011) 'Economic, environmental, and health/well-being benefits associated with green industry products and services: A review.' *Journal of Environmental Horticulture*, 29(2), 96–103.

Hanley, M., Khairat, M., Taylor, K., Wilson, R., and Riby, D.M. (2017) 'Classroom displays: Attraction or distraction? Evidence of impact on attention and learning from children with and without autism.' *Developmental Psychology*, 53(7), 1265–1275.

Harvey, E.J., and Kenyon, M.C. (2013) 'Classroom seating considerations for 21st century students and faculty.' *Journal of Learning Spaces*, 2(1), 1–13.

Havig, J.S. (2017) 'Advantages and disadvantages of flexible seating,' *Minot State University ProQuest Dissertations Publishing.* Available at: www.proquest.com/openview/acb159485a636303e2b8f4e1b2f54474/1?pq-origsite=gscholar&cbl=18750 (accessed 13 March 2024).

Kurt, S., and Osueke, K.K. (2014) 'The effects of color on the moods of college students.' *Sage Journals*, 4(1).

Lönn, M., Aili, K., Svedberg, P., Nygren, J., Jarbin, H., and Larsson, I. (2023) 'Experiences of using weighed blankets among children with ADHD and sleeping difficulties.' *Occupational Therapy International*, 2023(1–12). Available at: https://downloads.hindawi.com/journals/oti/2023/1945290.pdf (accessed 13 March 2024).

Rands, M.L., and Gansemer-Topf, A.M. (2017) 'The room itself is active: How classroom design impacts student engagement.' *Journal of Learning Spaces*, 6(1), 26–33.

Sadeh, A., Hen-Gal, S., and Ticotzy, L. (2008) 'Young children's reactions to war-related stress: A survey and assessment of an innovative intervention.' *Paediatrics,* 121(1), 46–53.

Tai, K., Zheng, X., and Narayanan, J. (2011) 'Touching a teddy bear mitigates negative effects of social exclusion to increase prosocial behavior.' *Social Psychological and Personality Science,* 2(6), 618–626.

Vinson, J., Powers, J., and Mosesso, K. (2020) 'Weighted blankets: Anxiety reduction in adult patients receiving chemotherapy.' *Clinical Journal of Oncology Nursing,* 24(4), 360–368.

Yan, S., Azmi, A., Mansor, N., and Wang, Z. (2024) 'Healing spaces as a design approach to optimize emotional regulation for patients with mood disorders.' *Buildings MDPI,* 14(2), 472.

Index

Note: Locators in *italic* refer to figures, and **bold** refer to tables, respectively.

Index

Pollard, S. 256

prefrontal cortex 38, 42–44, 52
psychotherapy 109

rational/thinking response 42–44
reading 155, 158, 254
reflection time 120, 205–206
refusals of children 33
regulation in therapeutic teaching 150–161; giving space 159–160; helping children regulates 154–155; mindful of language 159; real life example 153; therapeutic teaching steps 155–159; time 160; tips 160–161; see also co-regulation opportunities
relationship management 119
relationship struggles 33
repetitive trauma 111
responsibility boundary 173–175
restorative conversation approach 180
rewards 82–84, 186, 194, 201, 204, 211; charts 83; connection vs. 92, 177, 186, 187, 194, 201, 203; as method of behaviour management 92; pathways 30
Roadblocks 27
rules: as boundary 161–164; values vs. 197–198

safe spaces 252–253
sanctions 92, 177, 186, 187, 194, 201, 211
school: childhood trauma and technology impact on children at 32–34; culture xii–xiii, 72, 102, 107; system 70–72, 92
second parenting 213
secure attachment 56–58, 65, 90, 95, 104, 163. see also insecure attachment
self-awareness 12, **118**, 118, 134, 151; development 106; lack of 33, 53

self-harming 20, 21, 93
self-management 118–119
self-reflection 34, 41, 101, 103, 112, 115, 131–132, 160, 221, 246
self-regulation 118–119, 152; lack of 33; opportunities 252
self-sabotaging 10–11, 82
sensory garden 92, 253
sexual abuse 11, 62, 111
shame 79–80
shouting/showing anger 87; modeling 90–91; shutting down brain 89
skillset and development of children 105–106
sleep 15, 16, 18, 30, 45, 49–51, 72, 116, 131
Smart, H. 240
smart phones 30
social awareness **118**, 119
'Social Dilemma, The' documentary 29
social media 26–31
sourcing furniture for classrooms 243–244
staffrooms 105
stress xii, 15, 36–37, 44–47; contribution to problem of 94–95; hormones 45, 116
Stubbs, K. 222
survival brain 38–42, 123–124, 126–127
survival/emotional response 38–42, 51–52
sympathy 119–121

teacher(s)/teaching xiii, 178; conversation 179–180; long term impact 184–185; 'next time try' response 180–184; role in classroom 33; skillset and development 103–104; in therapeutic classrooms 236–237; using therapeutic teaching steps 185–191
Teaching Positive Connections (TPC) 3
team work 73–74

264

triggers 48–52
Tufte, E. 29
Twitter 29

unconditional love, children
    experiencing 68
Update Magazine 224

values 161–164, 197–198
verbal acknowledgement 203–204
voice, tone of **199–200**, 199–201

wellbeing 3–4, 15, 20, 100, 256;
    brain's impact on 37, 91; in
    classroom 18–19; emotional 12,
    105, 107; feelings and 134; key

factors at play for 21–24; life skills
for 246; role of school system
in 92, 102, 246; taking care 16;
therapeutic classroom and 218, 231,
232; therapeutic school approach
223
whole school approach xii 100, 102,
    104, 105, 189, 210
Winfrey, O. 111
withdrawal 33
work 72–73
working with children 13, 67, 111, 115,
    189
Wright, J. 216, 256

YouTube 27, 29, 224, 245, 254

Printed in the United States
by Baker & Taylor Publisher Services